Cecilia Norman was born in Chelsea, London and studied domestic science. After marriage and raising her two daughters, she returned to teaching as a home economics teacher in secondary and further education. At Croydon College and the Polytechnic of North London she is currently lecturing in Recipe Development and the Preparation of Food for Photography for third year diploma students. She is an expert on microwave cooking and opened Britain's first Microwave School in September 1980. She takes an active interest in the Association of Home Economists, of which she is a member, and the British Standards Institution. She has written many books, among which *Pancakes and Pizzas* and her *Microwave Cookery Course* are also available in Granada Paperbacks.

D1375475

By the same author

Microwave Cookery for the Housewife
The Heartwatcher's Cook Book
The Colour Book of Microwave Cooking
Freezer to Microwave Cookery
The Crepe and Pancake Cookbook (re-titled *Pancakes and Pizzas* for paperback)
Microwave Cooking
The Sociable Slimmer's Cookbook
Microwave with Magimix
Cecilia Norman's Microwave Cookery Course

CECILIA NORMAN

The Pie and Pastry Cookbook

GRANADA
London Toronto Sydney New York

Published by Granada Publishing Limited in 1983

ISBN 0 583 13705 9

A Granada Paperback Original
Copyright © Cecilia Norman 1983

Granada Publishing Limited
Frogmore, St Albans, Herts AL2 2NF
and
36 Golden Square, London W1R 4AH
515 Madison Avenue, New York, NY 10022, USA
117 York Street, Sydney, NSW 2000, Australia
60 International Blvd, Rexdale, Ontario, R9W 6J2, Canada
61 Beach Road, Auckland, New Zealand

Reproduced, printed and bound in Great Britain by
Hazell Watson & Viney Ltd, Aylesbury, Bucks
Set in Times

Contents

Preface

'Rub in until the mixture resembles breadcrumbs,' my teacher said to me at my first pastry lesson and suddenly I was up to the wrists in sticky gunge.

When I grew up, to everyone's surprise, I took up Domestic Science (the predecessor of today's Home Economics). There is much more to this training than cookery and the course was made more interesting because we were taught the *science* aspects too. The reasons for various techniques and processes in cookery were explained, so that pastry-making became simple. But why didn't that teacher tell me my hands were too hot?

Unless you take a serious cookery course no one tells you why you mustn't forget the salt, what the lemon juice does, why any old flour and fat won't do and how you can avoid producing tough, tooth-clamping pastry. Explanations in technical books can often only be understood by experts but there is no doubt that better results are obtained if somebody explains basic principles in simple terms and that is what I hope to do here. I have learnt so much in my research that I am quite proud of my pastry making and have mastered no less than thirty-seven different types – and in fact there are many more. Most of them are simple to make and can be an improvement on the two old stand-bys, shortcrust and puff. What is rubbing in anyway?

All About Pastry Making

Pastry has been used all over the world since man has used fire for cooking. While simply pounded grain and water can be made into a dough, the resulting pastry is very dry indeed. The only way we now use this technique is to make a gluten paste for sealing the pie crust to the dish, rather like cement. Pastry as we know it is a blend of flour and liquid, enriched by the inclusion of some sort of fat. While gifted cooks may guess at quantities when making cakes, they rarely attempt this in pastry making which is really a science. Proportions and choice of ingredients are vital. To ensure success you must understand the whys and wherefores and whether, just because you've got hot hands, you must count yourself a failure. The truth is that some pastries actually *like* warm conditions, and those needing to be kept cool *can* be made with an electric mixer or processor if necessary. Even if you can't afford one of these, a curved and bladed pastry mixer can be bought quite cheaply at most hardware counters.

Pastry crops up somewhere in every menu and on every table in every type of cuisine and in all courses. It comes in many different guises from the basic shortcrust to the complicated strudel. It is used over fillings, under fillings, rolled around fillings as a kind of sandwich in double crust pies, cut into attractive shapes for croûtes or garnishing as biscuits, in gâteaux, baked, fried, steamed, from the modest Cornish pastie to the outrageously luxurious croquembouche. From jam tarts for tea, to honey and nut-laden baklava as an exquisite pâtisserie. The list is endless. Although the mixes and frozen pastries are very good they only come in the two most commonly used forms: shortcrust and puff.

In this section of the book I hope to show, why because its rules are so precise, pastry making isn't an art at all. The art part comes in re-shaping, finishing and decorating, in knocking up the edges and getting the thickness even, in putting on the glaze, choosing the most suitable fillings and judging the appearance of correctly baked items. Once you have got the hang of the scientific part, all this will become miraculously clear. Each type of fat and flour produces its own particular results, as does the quantity and temperature of the water and the addition of lemon juice, salt, baking powder or egg and to get the best results, you must use the ingredients recommended for each type of pastry. For example, most rubbed-in mixtures use very little water and have to be short, while pastries, where the flour and fat are layered, require more water to give a flaky effect. Then there are others, some of which employ melted butter, some where a strong flour high in gluten enables the dough to be stretched and some which use boiling water.

RUBBING IN

Let's go back to the beginning. As I said in the preface, what is rubbing in anyway? Rubbing in is when the fat has to be mixed into the flour and broken down into tiny fragments. At the same time, it is important to keep these nodules firm and incorporate as much air as possible to keep the texture light and airy. To do this, put the lump of fat in the mixing bowl with the flour and cut it up into sugar lump sized chunks. The knife used should always be like a round-bladed table knife, rather than a sharp pointed kitchen knife and must be stainless steel so there is no chance of the pastry becoming discoloured. Now with fingers slightly spread apart, press and rub the coated butter lumps between the fingertips of both hands, at the same time lifting the mixture in a cloud about 8 cm (3 in) above the bowl and allowing the mixture to fall. Repeat this until the entire contents resemble freshly made bread-crumbs. From time to time shake the bowl so that the mixture bounces up and down and lo! there on the top any outsize lumps will appear. Now you should have a light mix of identical nodules.

Any other dry ingredients are added at this stage, and then the liquid is poured in. This is how the shortness of the finished pastry is determined.

Almost every particle of flour is now wearing its fat vest and needs to put on an overcoat of liquid. When the mixture is lightly gathered together (by something that isn't hot, such as the clammy hand which would oil out the fat), all the particles are standing side by side, but not so close that all the air is squeezed out, since there are still some grains of flour left that are not coated with fat.

LIGHTNESS

The lightness of the pastry depends on the cold air incorporated during making. Cold air expands on heating and fills out all the tiny spaces throughout the pastry. The more fat or the less liquid that is used, the shorter, or to use the technical term – friable – the pastry will be. However, if no liquids were added, the result would be shortbread and difficult to roll out.

SHORT

This word 'short' is often bandied about but rarely defined. This is because it is a feeling of texture and sound rather than a visual determination. Short is when the pastry can easily be broken down without crumbling, but has some slight resistance. The texture should at the same time be soft yet crisp, but the crust should not adhere to the roof of the mouth.

A piece of baked pastry should be feather-light and the crumb, that is the texture of the inside, must be an even minute honeycomb of solids and air pockets. A good short pastry will never be hard, chewy, or over-brittle, nor will it be clinging or crumbly.

FLAKY PASTRIES

In rough puff, flaky and puff pastry there is very little rubbing in and it doesn't matter if you are heavy-handed. A considerably greater quantity of water is added and the air is incorporated in thin layers during the folding and rolling processes. The water and flour, and in some cases a small amount of fat, form an elastic dough which encloses the remaining fat. During the folding and rolling process, which I explain later, the fat and water-laden dough layers are separated by trapped air. When the pastry is baked in a hot oven, the air bubbles expand, the water turns to steam, bursting all the starch cells simultaneously, so that they can absorb the fat. When the pastry is cooked, it will have risen considerably and set in flaky layers. These pastries cannot be described as short. They are crisp and flaky when freshly cooked, but become tough when cold.

FLOUR

There are of course speciality flours, made by certain manufacturers, but usually the easily obtainable self-raising or plain flours are used in pastry-making, and the self-raising variety is usually plain flour with an added raising agent. It is very difficult to tell the difference between self-raising and plain flour if you have them in similar canisters, so please remember to mark each one clearly. You can however tell the difference between a strong plain flour and a plain flour, because the strong one will absorb more water.

Wholemeal or whole wheat flours are 100% extraction, with none of the husk and bran taken away. These flours, much favoured by health food devotees, are of course full of roughage (fibre) but they tend to produce a tough, hard pastry. You may prefer to sieve them first and fold in the separated bran afterwards. Wheatmeal flour is less dense, because not all of the roughage has been returned to it, but when a wholemeal flour is called for the best results are obtained by using a mixture of wholemeal and plain white flours in a ratio of three parts wholemeal to one part plain flour.

Unfortunately flour is not an international commodity, so it is difficult to produce exactly the same pastry results using flour bought for example in France, America or the United Kingdom. However, the differences in results are far more noticeable in bread and cakes than in pastry. You will get consistent results if you always use the same make of flour.

Choice of flour is, as you can see, important in successful pastry making. Although pre-sifted flours are now easily obtainable, flour should always be sieved for added aeration and it is better to sieve it together with the other fine, dry ingredients to ensure even distribution. Self-raising flour, because of its added raising agent, will make the pastry puff up slightly, producing a spongy texture. It is therefore a good choice for suet pastry which may be either steamed or baked. It is not generally used for rich pastries, where the proportion of fat to flour is high, but if you prefer to lighten these mixtures, use self-raising flour or add baking powder to plain flour. Up to one level teaspoon of baking powder when mixed with 250g (8 oz) plain flour will help to puff up and raise pastry where the amount of fat is less than half the weight of the flour. If the flour plus raising agent is used, there will be less need to let the pastry stand before using.

Plain flour is versatile because not only can you add a raising agent, but it is also rough enough to produce the elastic dough needed for the flaky-type pastries, and it's also the favourite choice for the rubbed-in mixtures.

In certain recipes, where I recommend strong plain flour, this does not mean that plain flour cannot be used. However for best results use the strong plain which has a higher gluten content, especially for the flaky types. The higher gluten content produces a more elastic dough. This can be stretched to form a surface resistant to the penetration of cold fat. Strong plain flour should be used for all the quick flaky methods as resting periods may be almost omitted. However provided the pastry is chilled between folds and rolls a good result can be achieved using plain flour.

GLUTEN

Gluten is a substance in the flour which, when moistened, becomes sticky and tenacious. In short pastry the gluten is broken up, because the water is added after the fat has been rubbed in. In the flakier types the gluten forms long strands, which when heated, balloon up and set firmly. Strong plain flour has more gluten than ordinary plain and so forms an elastic dough when mixed with water that can be stretched, so that it will withstand all that rolling and folding.

WATER

Some flours absorb more liquid than others, so that it would be impossible to advise on exact quantities. The correct amount of water is, however, essential. If the pastry is too dry, it will be difficult to handle, will crack during rolling out, crumble after baking and be too dry to eat. If too much water is added, the pastry will shrink and lose its shape during baking and be hard and tough to chew. In most cases at least two-thirds of the given quantity of water must be added to the dry ingredients before mixing. In the case of rubbed-in mixtures, the water should be evenly sprinkled over the surface. This will avoid overworking the gluten and produce a firmer and smoother dough. Take particular care to add nearly all the water when mixing the foundation dough for puff pastry.

When cold water is recommended it should be freshly drawn or ice cold, to keep everything cool.

FATS

The right fat for the job is another must. Don't just open the fridge and use up all the bits that you have left. Butter gives a very good flavour because of its fatty acids. It produces a crisp, fairly short pastry and is very pleasant when used in pastry that is likely to be eaten cold.

Margarine is cheaper than butter and comes in different degrees of softness. Be sure to use a cheap hard type for shortcrust and a slightly softer, though still block, margarine for the flakies. Margarine is not such a pure fat as butter and contains a high percentage of water. It is also less waxy than butter. In pastry making, particularly the rubbed-in kind, the fat must be waxy or plastic, so that it can wrap around the flour grains without oiling out. Soft margarine, while being entirely acceptable, has a different effect altogether, giving a crispy flaky result. Since it has a slightly bitter flavour the pastry is much improved if mixed with milk rather than water.

Oil is easy to mix in and very little water is required, but it doesn't disperse so efficiently through the flour particles. The resulting dough is very short, very soft but somewhat dense and is more suitable for tarts than covered pie crust.

Lard is possibly the best single fat but used alone gives a slightly meaty flavour so I only recommend it for use in savoury dishes. When mixing equal quantities with butter, you get the best mixture of all – the lovely butter flavour and the shortness of the lard, which is 100% fat with no water content. Lard has a very low melting point, so the slightest warmth will cause it to oil out and this should be noted by hot-handed cooks or by anyone working in a warm kitchen.

Use solid vegetable cooking fat for crisp very short results, but don't expect much in the way of flavour; make sure the fillings are well spiced and seasoned. The soft white cooking fats are aerated in manufacture, which makes it possible to mix without any rubbing in at all. The pastry is popular since not only is it easy to make, but it is also soft and easy to cut.

Suet, though mostly used in meat puddings and pies, can also be used with fruit and these puddings are either steamed or baked. Suet is a dense, heavy fat and must be finely grated so that it will melt properly and it is available in this grated form.

In the same way that different flours affect the amount of added liquid, fat also has an effect on the amount of liquid required. The choice of fat must also be suitable for its pastry type. With the exception of suet, any of the fats mentioned could be used for shortcrust pastry. The flaky types must include a firm fat, so that oil and soft fats would be excluded. Never use fats that come directly from the freezer. They must be firm but not too hard to shape.

LEMON JUICE AND SALT

Having chosen the right flour, the right fat, the right liquid at the right temperature, there are one or two other points worth mentioning. A small quantity of lemon juice makes the dough softer and more elastic and helps rising, and also counteracts the richness of high fat ratio pastries. Do not be tempted to add more than is stated or the pastry will flop and taste strongly of acid. Salt adds flavour, hastens browning and strengthens the gluten. Never forget to include it, no matter how little the recipe calls for.

HANDLING THE DOUGH

Except when making yeast dough or the doughs with the high water content such as puff, knead with the fingers only. Use a pressing and squashing motion and do not use the knuckles. To knead a yeast dough pull part of the pastry towards you between the flattened fingers and the heel of the palm in a grasping motion. Lift up the dough and punch it back into the dough ball. For puff and flaky pastries in the initial kneading process, press the dough into a flattened sphere, then lift up and tuck all the edges into the middle and rock the dough gently on the work surface so that all the seams disappear.

Remember the more you knead the tougher the pastry gets, but to some extent this can be countered by leaving the dough to rest before baking, preferably in a freezer, but in any case chilled. This allows the elasticity to reduce again. Pastry made by electric mixer is frequently over-kneaded, but I have never found harm has come to it by following these methods. Provided the pastry goes into a pre-heated oven, there is little difference from hand-prepared doughs. Food processors may produce a denser dough as no air is beaten in, but this can be overcome by giving only the minimum mixing time.

When a ball of dough is being rested it should not be frozen unless adequate time is allowed for it to completely thaw before rolling. Sometimes dough balls are chilled or rested for only a few minutes. In this case wrap them in foil or cling-film to prevent a crust forming.

ROLLING

When the dough is ready for rolling do so on a smooth floured surface. Marble used to be the favourite because it remained cold, but I doubt if many wash-stands are left to be broken up for marble tops. You can buy a piece of marble for pastry making, but there is always the bother of finding storage space and it is very heavy. Nowadays people use their laminated tops. If the kitchen is cool there should be no problem. This does not apply to melted butter pastry.

Choose a heavy rolling pin (preferably without elongated handles), and make sure it is dry and undented. Give the pin a mere dusting of the same type of flour that was used in the pastry recipe. Don't use excessive flour when rolling out, as the pastry may pick up too much during shaping and then the proportions could be upset, resulting in tough finished products. For similar reasons, always scrape the board to remove flour lumps before starting on a new piece of dough.

Rolling out seems to cause quite a few problems, but if the dough has been properly made in the first place it should be nice and smooth. Press the rolling pin down on the ball of dough a few times to flatten lightly. Now you are ready to roll, starting at the edge close to you. Place the palms at the base of the fingers along the top of the pin, so that the hands are just clear of the sides of the pastry. As the size of the pastry increases, move the hands further apart. It is essential that equal and even pressure is applied when rolling and if the hands are not correctly placed, one side will be thinner than the other. One of my reasons for disliking rolling pins with handles is that if you press down too hard on one side, because it is closer to the pastry, you are likely to roll out an uneven thickness. Milk bottles can cause the same problem because of the shape of the neck.

To get a nice even result without undue pressure and without bending the fingers, push and roll the pin, using a forwards rather than a forwards and backwards movement, lifting the pin after each action. This should only flatten the first inch or so. Now repeat the process starting a little further towards the middle of the pastry. While all this is happening you will find the pastry starts to go out of shape and before you know it, it will look like a jagged map of Great Britain, especially if you are rolling a large piece. To avoid this turn the pastry after every two or three rolls and pat the edges inwards with the sides of the hand.

To loosen the pastry from the board, slide the flat side of a long-bladed palette knife underneath the pastry. You should have enough flour on the work surface to prevent adhesion, but in the event of a real stick-up, you may be able to fold the pastry upwards and then flour the exposed surface gently. The palette knife encourages the flour to slip underneath. But turn the pastry as seldom as possible to avoid incorporating extra flour and to give the fair side a smoother look. It is quite acceptable to dust the top of the pastry, caressing it over with the hand.

When pastry has to be folded and rolled, whisk the surplus flour away with a pastry brush. Leave the pastry to rest for a few minutes longer in hot weather. It will help it to regain its composure after all that pummelling. Trim to roughly the finished outline but a little bigger than the finished shape.

Pastry is rolled out to differing thicknesses according to how it is to be used. On each pastry I have given an indication of the yield likely from the amounts of ingredients in the recipes. Left-over pieces should be baked up separately and sprinkled over other goodies or given to your dog, who won't mind that they're left-overs at all.

LINING THE DISHES

Fold delicate pastry into quarters, like a handkerchief, and place the point into the centre of the flan rings or 2.5 cm (1 in) deep dishes, then unfold gently. For top crusts or lining shallow dishes roll up the pin loosely in the pastry. Lift the pin only as high as is necessary to transfer to the dish, balancing the flap of the pastry on top. Lower the pastry on to the pie, releasing the flap so that it just covers the edge, then unroll over the remaining pastry. To transfer easily crackable, very short pastry, loosen from the work surface with a palette knife, slide both hands palms uppermost underneath, spreading the fingers slightly and lift unhurriedly.

Cut the pastry for flan rings or tins approximately 2.5 cm (1 in) bigger in diameter than the ring itself. This is to allow enough pastry to fit around the sides. You can measure more exactly if you place the ring on the pastry and tip it sideways, so that you can mark the edge at three or four places before cutting. Probably the pastry won't fit comfortably into the corners. Encourage it to fit in loosely by easing in from the edges. Make a ball from the pastry trimmings and dab it into the base, corners and sides.

If you are fitting the pastry into an open flan ring, first set the empty ring on a baking tray. You may have read elsewhere that the baking tray should be upturned, so that the flan can be easily removed using fish slices. However should a crack develop and the filling ooze, the sides of the baking tray will prevent mess in the oven, so I am not in favour of the upturned baking tray method. If you are frequently unsuccessful with flans baked this way, you could try placing the ring on a bigger piece of foil and then fold it up and around the ring. If the pastry is soft enough, you can quite easily patch it, first damping the pieces. Firmer pastry will adhere better if moistened with egg white. Egg white is also useful to brush the inside of uncooked pastry cases which when put in the oven, will provide a seal to prevent wet fillings seeping in. The best chefs do this as a matter of course.

When fitting pastry into patty tins, cut the pastry circles about 1 cm (½ in) bigger in diameter, so that they will fully reach up to the rim. Patty tins will not need trimming since a cutter will have been used to ensure a smooth edge.

TRIMMING

Pastry-lined flan rings, tins or pie dishes will have to be trimmed. Balance the dish or baking tray comfortably on the palm of one hand and using a sharp knife held vertically, point uppermost, cut away surplus pastry with a firm slicing action. But be careful because it is such a disaster if a whole baking tin, pastry and all, tip on to the floor. Another system is to roll the rolling pin over the edges when the trimmings should drop off, but I would not use this method on fluted flan rings where there is an outer solid collar. The surplus pastry nestles in the cracks and is fiddly to dislodge even when baked.

Shrinking will occur if the pastry is not left to stand before baking, especially when plain flour has been used. It is so disappointing, having carefully fitted pastry into a flan ring or covered and knocked up the edges of a pie, to find that after baking, the pastry has shrivelled, leaving the sides looking like a little boy with his socks crumpled around his ankles. To ensure that it doesn't shrink during baking, with the ball of the thumb held sideways, press up the pastry around the sides of the flan rings about 5 mm (¼ in) below the rim until it protrudes a similar amount above.

FINISHING, SEALING AND DECORATING

Top-crust pies should have a thicker edge to work on. For a neat finish, trim with a vertical knife in the same fashion as before. Reverse the trimmings so that the evenly cut side is outermost and, using water to dampen both the edge of the dish and the surface of the cut trimmings, tuck a border of the surplus pastry underneath the pie crust to make the edges double thick. Knock up the edges: that is, attack them horizontally with a sharp knife until thin flakes or steps are formed. To make a pretty shell put a finger on the pastry and press the rim outwards. At the same time make a vertical dent with the side of a spoon handle at regular intervals.

To seal the edge of a double-crust pie, dampen the edges of the lower crust, cover with the lid and knock up as described above or pinch the top and bottom edges together, to form a stand-up rim, which can then be evenly fluted with the forefinger and thumb. It is in fact easier to do this with the forefinger on the inside of the rim, so a natural twist will occur. Trim these edges before finishing, using kitchen scissors. The top layer of pastry on top-crust or double-crust pies should be pierced in at least one place to allow steam to escape.

For plate pies, cut the top-crust pastry about 2.5 cm (1 in) wider in diameter than the sides of the plate and fold it over, then under the dampened edge of the underside of the pastry, like making a bed. Press the pastry on to the edges of the plate with the prongs of a fork. Pastry trimmings can be cut and shaped in several different ways to make pies and tarts more attractive. Here are a few suggestions:

Rope

Press the pastry vertically between the thumb and forefinger, pushing the thumb, knuckle inwards.

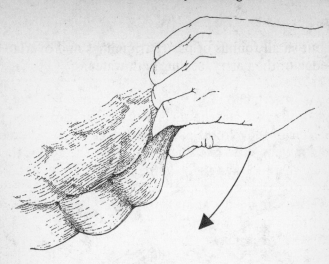

Flute

With one finger inside and one outside the pastry edge, push towards one another.

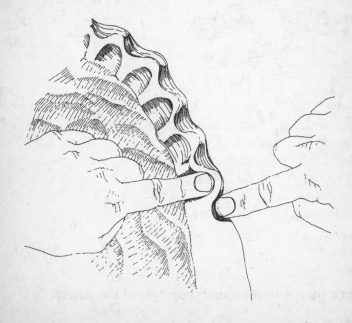

Coins

Cut out small rounds of pastry trimmings and overlap on the edge of the pastry, sealing with water.

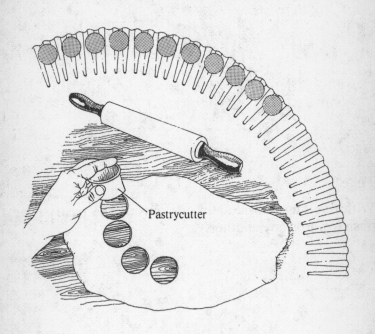

Pastrycutter

Spikes

Run a pastry wheel round the edges of the pastry.

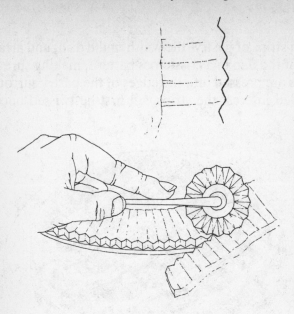

Track

Press all round with the prongs of a fork.

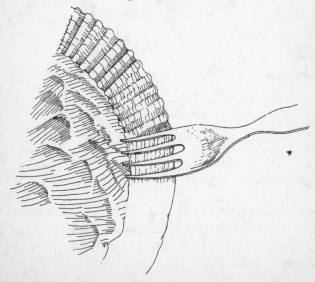

Lattice

Cut thin strips of pastry, the width of the dish, and arrange on top of the flan in a criss-cross pattern, making sure that the ends are pressed into the edges of the pastry surround. For added interest the strips can first be twisted once or twice.

Leaves

Roll out a thin strip of pastry 1–2 cm (½–¾ in wide) and cut into diamond shapes. Mark veins with the back of a knife. Aspic cutters can be used to cut out other decorative shapes.

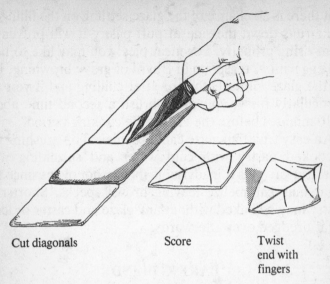

Cut diagonals   Score   Twist
                                end with
                                fingers

GLAZES

Unless you are baking open undecorated tarts or flans or
you prefer a matt look, you will want to use some form of
glaze to give a shine and enhance the colour of the finished
dish. Brush away any stray flour particles from the pastry
surface, then skim with any of the following:

Beaten whole egg
Beaten egg white mixed with a pinch of sugar or salt
Beaten egg yolk mixed with a teaspoon or so of milk or
  water
Beaten egg yolk and single cream which will give the
  brownest finish

Don't use undiluted yolk or you will find globules of
yellow solids settling on the pastry. Take particular care
not to let beaten yolk run down the sides of the pastry, as
it will set against both the sides of the pie and the baking
sheet, leaving a yellow stain. It may be better to brush
pastry strips for a lattice before placing them on the pie, so

that there is no chance of the glaze settling on the filling. If glaze runs down the side of puff pastry it will prevent it from rising properly. For meat pies, you may like to beat the egg with ¼ teaspoon of Bovril or gravy browning. Put on the glaze either before or after chilling and if you are particularly fussy, you could brush a second time about 5–10 minutes before the end of the cooking period.

An easy fruit flan glaze can be achieved by brushing the uncooked pastry with cold water and sprinkling with caster sugar. This is inadvisable in very hot ovens since the sugar may caramelize leaving brown specks. Shortcrust pastry may be baked without any glaze and caster or icing sugar dredged over afterwards.

BAKING BLIND

In many of the recipes instructions are given for baking blind. In some pastries thorough pricking, which allows the hot air to pass through, is sufficient. However, in most cases pricking is less effective and more drastic measures must be taken to prevent the pastry bases from rising and the sides from caving in. To bake blind, tear a piece of greaseproof paper, or better still non-stick paper, larger than the width and depth of the tin, but not so big that the sides flap about in the oven, because heat could cause them to ignite. Use butter or margarine wrappers for small flans. Put the paper over the uncooked pastry case and pour in as many dry beans, lentils or similar hard pellets that it will take to weight the paper down, smoothing them into the sides and corners. Bake in a hot oven until the pastry is set (about three-quarters of baking time). Lift off the greaseproof paper making sure that none of the beans falls into the pastry and return the pastry to the oven to either finish cooking or dry out according to the recipe. If you have a suitable container these pellets can be used time and time again. Mine are five years old. If you do a lot of pastry baking you can buy ceramic beans in specialist kitchen shops.

For small tartlets or if you have no beans in the larder use the crumpled foil method. First prick the pastry thoroughly, then put a large piece of foil into the pastry case, smooth the base and sides, then fold over all the surplus edges of the foil to crumple into the empty shells. Use this method only in pastry which has a high fat content as if there is not enough fat in the pastry the top layer will stick to the foil. You can bake tartlets or patties blind without beans if they are to be filled without further baking. Reverse the patty tins on to a baking sheet and press the cut-out pastry circles over the upturned moulds previously lightly floured. When baking blind be careful not to overbrown if the pastry is then going to be baked with the filling.

BAKING TINS AND DISHES

Your choice of baking dish depends on the pie or tart that you are making and such pans as you have in your cupboard. Darkened or dull, well-used tins are best because they conduct the heat. Pastry tends to slide back down the sides of new tins unless they are non-stick. Tins should be heavy so that they transmit the heat to brown and crisp the pastry underneath as well as on the top. The bases of both the tins and the baking sheet must be even and unbuckled and if you are going to bake in lightweight dishes or aluminium foil containers because they are shiny and reflect the heat, put them directly on to a baking sheet.

Use flan rings for unmoulded tarts when you have become proficient at rolling out and lining without cracks. Fluted rings are traditionally used for sweet fillings and straight-sided rings for savoury dishes. Loose-bottomed flan dishes, as long as they are not distorted, give more protection and the sides may be removed, leaving the pastry to finish browning and be served on the base. Pastry cases baked blind in one-piece dishes must be removed carefully, but if baking is continued after filling, the pastry will have to be served from the dish. Sandwich cake tins are not recommended when baking blind as the sides are generally higher than flan dishes and the walls of the pastry may droop.

The white French-type dishes are ideal if you require a softer finish and Pyrex-type dishes whether placed directly on to the wire rack in the oven or on a baking sheet, give excellent brown and crisp results. You can tell when pastry cooking in glass is ready, not only because you can see through the bottom of the dish, but also because the pastry shrinks away from the sides, making it very easy to remove. Greasing of baking tins and dishes is only required if there is a very low proportion of fat in the pastry recipe.

Top-crust pies are usually baked in lipped ovenproof dishes. The edge of the dish can be dampened and a thin strip of pastry placed between the rim and the pastry lid, making it easier to achieve a perfect finish. Use ovenproof plates or shallow tins for double-crust pies and bun or patty tins for little tarts with sloping sides. Specialist kitchen shops stock all shapes and sizes of baking tins, and mundane recipes will appear more appetizing when baked in exciting shapes.

Use edged baking trays for all pastry, but particularly for pastry with a high fat content, such as puff. This is just in case the fat oozes. Flat baking sheets can be used for less rich recipes.

Make sure that there is ample space between the baking tray and the sides of the oven so that the hot air can circulate freely. Don't bake short pastry in the oven alongside the Sunday joint or open casseroles as the moisture created will spoil the pastry.

Non-stick baking tins are usually rustproof but others

must be carefully dried before putting away. Put them in the oven while there is residual heat after you have finished baking.

FREEZING PIES AND PASTRIES

Pastry may be frozen before baking or after baking. To freeze unbaked pastry, chill in the freezer until firm, then wrap in double-duty plastic film or freezer foil, making sure that the package is airtight. Baked pastry must be cooled quickly before wrapping for the freezer, otherwise condensation will form inside the plastic bag, dropping back onto the pastry as ice particles, and when the pastry is thawed, this water will seep into the pastry crust. Unbaked frozen pastry cases need not be thawed before baking. Make sure that the oven is very hot when they go in. Baked filled pies should be unwrapped and left to stand at room temperature for at least half an hour, then put into a moderate oven, 180°C/350°F/Gas 4, until heated through.

Take special care with meat fillings, as bacteria multiply in a warm atmosphere and meat fillings must be thoroughly hot. With the exception of custard and cream, which may separate, or meringue tops which tend to toughen and shrink away from the edges of the pastry, most fillings freeze well. Baked pastry will keep longer in the freezer than unbaked pastry.

If you regularly use the same dish or tin, roll out pastry and cut out circles about 5 cm (2 in) larger than the diameter of the tin. Stack, separating each pastry piece with wax paper or freezer film. Place the stack on a flat plate and open freeze for an hour or two. Remove the plate, then wrap the pastry and seal in the usual way. Rolled-out pastry will thaw more quickly than when frozen in a lump – the flaky pastry types are best defrosted standing in the refrigerator, so that the consistency is the same throughout. Since pastry freezes so well, always make up the full quantity, storing any that you are not using immediately.

OVEN TEMPERATURES

Ovens must be pre-heated as the immediate heat sets the pastry in its correct shape and makes cooking time easier to predict. Since ovens vary considerably in temperature, you will have to use your own judgement as to what is hot and what is a very hot oven. Both the gas and electricity people employ Home Economists who will carry out tests (they have a special cake recipe for this) on your oven if it is cooking unevenly. Throughout the book the temperatures are given in Celsius, Fahrenheit and gas, indicating the level of temperature required.

A cool oven is 160°C/325°F/Gas 3,
a moderate oven is 180°C/350°F/Gas 4,
a fairly hot oven is 190°–200°C/375°–400°F/Gas 5–6,
a hot oven is 220°C/425°F/Gas 7,
a very hot oven is 230°–240°C/450°–475°F/Gas 8–9.

Bake in the centre or just above, reducing the temperature according to the filling or if you are cooking other dishes at the same time. Unless it is a convection oven the temperature on the lower shelves will be cooler, so that you may find that you can cook puff pastry in the upper section and shortcrust in the lower.

If the edges of the pastry brown before the filling is cooked, cover with a strip of foil, shiny side outwards.

Bake the pastry according to its type and recipe. Many of the fillings are interchangeable, but you must check the pastry quantities carefully. Unsweetened pastry, except when containing unsuitable herbs, can be used for savoury or sweet dishes, but pastry containing sugar can only be used for the latter. Hot water crust pastry and rich raised pastry are interchangeable. Choux and suet crust should be used only with the fillings recommended. Only puff pastry is suitable for the high risers such as vol-au-vents.

WEIGHTS AND MEASURES

The quantities of pastry and dish sizes where applicable are mentioned in the recipes. The weight of the pastry will be more than the weight of the flour. If elsewhere you see, for example, 250g (8 oz) pastry mentioned, this means 250g (8 oz) flour plus the other ingredients. Because there is a wide variety of pastries in this book it is not possible to lay down hard and fast rules of how much pastry is required for any particular size dish. These too are indicated in the recipes. The thickness of the pastry not only depends upon the ingredients but also on the nature of the fillings.

METRICATION

In making pastry the proportions are more important than the actual weight and these may not tally throughout the book. Where the weights, particularly those of the fillings, are less critical, the measurements have been calculated to fit in with dual weighing scales. Pan and dish sizes cannot be given exact equivalents, so that although the weight of the completed dough may not be the same as when weighed in imperial measures, metric quantities should fit into metric-sized dishes. The main maxim is never to try and measure some things in metric and some things in imperial. Use either one or the other.

Remember that the old 'half pound' block of fat is 8 oz no longer, but measured in metric is 250 g and in imperial, just under 9 oz, so that a simple division of eight will no longer produce 1 oz sections.

A level spoonful means that the contents fill the spoon only to the rim. To measure exactly draw a knife across the surface. A rounded spoon means that there should be the same curve to the ingredients above the rim as there is in the bowl of the spoon. A heaped spoon is as much as can be balanced on the spoon without anything falling off. A generous spoon is as-it-comes without removing any surplus, e.g. with golden syrup where there will also be a coat on the underside of the spoon. An as-it-comes spoon means just that; it doesn't matter how much you dollop on. Where fractions of a spoon are indicated, this means fractions of a level spoon.

American Pie Pastry

Nearly everywhere in the USA you can eat apple pie, pecan pie or blueberry pie and the pastry melts in the mouth and is very short. The American all-purpose (plain) flour is milled from hard wheat and absorbs a lot of liquid. Consequently a higher proportion of fat is required to produce a tender crumb. The flour in the UK is quite different making it impossible to achieve the same results. However I find American Pie Pastry particularly good for use in all types of pie and have had considerable success using a firm margarine such as Krona which has a buttery flavour, although traditionally this pastry is made with lard or solid vegetable cooking fat. Margarine produces a flakier pastry and lard a shorter one. This quantity is enough to cover an 18 cm (7 in) diameter pie dish or to line a 23 cm (9 in) flan dish, as for this the pastry will be rolled out more thinly.

Ingredients for Basic Recipe

125 g (5 oz) plain flour
½ teaspoon salt
70 g (2¾ oz) firm margarine *or* lard *or* solid vegetable cooking fat at room temperature
1½–2 tablespoons ice-cold water

Sieve the flour and salt into a mixing bowl, then add the margarine, chopping with a round-bladed knife until the crumbs are the size of small peas. Still using the knife, add only as much water as it takes to hold the dough together. Knead lightly. Roll out and use as required. Bake in a hot oven, 220°C/425°F/Gas 7, until the pastry is a light golden brown, then reduce the heat to 180°C/350°F/Gas 4 until the filling is cooked.

PECAN PIE

Pecans in the shell look quite different from walnuts, but when shelled the shape of the kernel is remarkably similar. Pecans are shiny and dark in appearance and are richer and softer in taste than walnuts. They are not always easy to find in the shops so substitute walnuts if necessary. The pie has a sweet sticky filling and it hardens as it cools so do not overbake. Serve hot, warm or cold with tablespoons of whipped cream.

> One recipe (125 g (5 oz) flour etc.) American pie pastry
> (p. 35) (made with margarine *or* solid vegetable cook-
> ing fat)
> 50 g (2 oz) granulated sugar
> 85 ml (3 fl oz) golden syrup
> ½ level teaspoon salt
> 40 g (1½ oz) butter
> 1 size-2 whole egg ⎫ beaten together
> 1 size-2 egg yolk ⎭
> 25 g (1 oz) fresh brown breadcrumbs
> 75 g (3 oz) shelled pecans *or* walnuts, chopped

Roll out the pastry and use to line an 18 cm (7 in) fluted flan ring. Chill while preparing the filling. Slowly heat the sugar and syrup together until the mixture comes to the boil. Remove from the heat and stir in the salt and butter. Allow to cool down slightly before adding the egg, breadcrumbs and nuts. Stir thoroughly, and pour into the prepared pastry case. Bake in a hot oven, 220°C/425°F/Gas 7, for 10 minutes, then reduce the temperature to 180°C/350°F/Gas 4 for 20–25 minutes until the pastry is golden brown and the filling has set. Serves four to five.

PORK PATTIES

Meat pies are often made with the flaky, buttery pastries. American pie pastry is less rich and the pork filling goes well with it. Serve hot.

Double recipe (250 g (10 oz) flour etc.) American pie
  pastry (p. 35)
15–25 g (½–1 oz) lard
350 g (12 oz) belly pork, diced
1 medium onion, chopped
1 level tablespoon flour
396 g (14 oz) can tomatoes
Few drops tabasco pepper sauce
Salt
Pepper

Heat the lard in a large pan and fry the pork, a few pieces at a time, stirring briskly until white on all sides. Don't add too much to the pan at one time as this immediately reduces the temperature of the fat, causing the meat juices to ooze out. As soon as all the meat is sealed, add the onion and an extra knob of lard if required. Fry until the meat and onions are light brown. Stir in the flour, tomatoes and their juice and season sparingly with tabasco, and salt and pepper. Bring to the boil, stirring all the time, then cover with a well-fitting lid and simmer over a low heat for 20 minutes. Inspect at least once to make sure the sauce does not dry up. Cool rapidly. One way to do this is to transfer the mixture to a pre-chilled shallow dish. Divide the pastry into four and roll out about two-thirds of each piece to line individual oval deep dishes. For extra accuracy measure from edge to edge round the deepest part of the dish. Roll the remaining pastry to form lids. Dampen the inside rims of the pastry and press together firmly to seal. Decorate, finish and glaze as you please. Put the pies on a baking tray and bake in a hot oven, 220°C/425°F/Gas 7, for 20 minutes, then reduce to 160°C/325°F/Gas 3 for 15–20 minutes to be sure the meat is thoroughly reheated. Serves four.

VEAL AND KIDNEY DEEP DISH PIE

Since this is a large pie you should use a pie funnel or some support in the centre, otherwise you may find the pastry will sink in the middle and become very soggy. This is an ideal dish for a cold winter's day. Serve piping hot.

Double recipe (250 g (10 oz) flour etc.) American pie
  pastry (p. 35)
2 tablespoons vegetable oil
1 large onion, chopped
450 g (1 lb) stewing veal
450 g (1 lb) lamb's kidneys
2 rounded tablespoons flour
600 ml (1 pint) beef *or* chicken stock
650 g (1½ lb) carrots, scraped and thinly sliced
1 level tablespoon fresh rosemary leaves
2 tablespoons Worcestershire sauce
Salt
Pepper
Beaten egg to glaze

Cut the veal into 4 cm (1½ in) cubes making sure to trim away any fat or gristle. Remove the suet and membrane surrounding the kidneys. Cut out the core. Roughly divide each kidney into six. Heat the oil in a heavy-based saucepan, add the onion and cook slowly until transparent. Then raise the heat and add the meat, a few pieces at a time, sealing it on all sides. Stir in the flour, cook for 1 minute, then gradually add the stock. Bring to the boil, stirring all the time until the sauce thickens. Add the carrots, rosemary, Worcestershire sauce and season to taste. Cover and simmer for 30 minutes, stirring occasionally until the meat is knife tender. Put the stew into a 1.7 litre (3 pint) pie dish. Cool rapidly. Roll out the pastry and use to cover the pie dish. Any trimmings can be used to decorate the top. Brush the top with beaten egg and bake in a hot oven, 220°C/425°F/Gas 7, for 15–20 minutes until the pastry is a light golden brown, then reduce the temperature to 180°C/350°F/Gas 4 for 30 minutes to thoroughly reheat the meat. Serves eight to ten.

American Self-Raising Pie Crust

American pie pastry can also be made with self-raising flour, when the crumb will be short and tender yet easy to manage and it doesn't crack too much when rolling. It is ideal for small tarts and patties. To keep the pastry soft do not put in any salt at all. The quantity given is enough for nine to twelve tartlets.

Ingredients for Basic Recipe

100 g (4 oz) self-raising flour
60 g (2½ oz) soft white cooking fat
1–1½ tablespoons ice-cold water

Sieve the flour into a mixing bowl, add the fat and most of the water at the same time. Mix to a soft dough with a round-bladed knife. Form into a ball and chill for 30 minutes before rolling out thinly on a generously floured surface. Bake in a fairly hot oven, 200°C/400°F/ Gas 6, reducing the heat as soon as the pastry is pale gold and then continue cooking depending on the fillings.

Pastries made with self-raising flour puff up more and so usually need to be weighted down where they are being baked blind. Alternatively cut out circles 1 cm (½ in) wider than the tops of the pattie tins. Turn the tins upside down and mould the pastry firmly over the upturned shapes, then prick the tops thoroughly. This method is only suitable where pastry is to be baked completely and filled afterwards.

APRICOT AND PINEAPPLE TARTLETS

These fruit tartlets are topped with a pineapple meringue.

One recipe (100 g (4 oz) flour etc.) American self-raising pie crust (p. 40)
1 × 410 g (14½ oz) can apricots, drained
1 × 198 g (7 oz) can pineapple pieces, drained
1 egg white
50 g (2 oz) caster sugar

Roll out the pastry and line nine to twelve patty tins. Bake them blind in a fairly hot oven, 200°C/400°F/Gas 6, for 10 minutes. Remove the weights. Meanwhile finely chop the fruit and prepare the meringue topping. To do this, whisk the egg white until thick, then whisk in just under half the sugar, beating until the mixture is stiff again. Fold in the remaining sugar with a metal spoon. Divide the fruit filling between the pastry cases and top with the meringue, spreading it to reach the edges of the pastry. Bake for 10–15 minutes until the tops are brown and crisp. Remove from the tins with the help of a grapefruit knife.

CORNED BEEF PASTIES

This is a variation on the corned beef pasty theme. Roll the pastry thinly, bearing in mind that American self-raising pie crust rises during cooking. Use up left-over potato for this dish. Serve hot or cold.

One recipe (100 g (4 oz) flour etc.) American self-raising pie crust (p. 40)
100 g (4 oz) corned beef
1 small onion, finely chopped
100 g (4 oz) cold mashed potato
Salt
Pepper
Beaten egg to glaze

Roll out the pastry and cut out three 15–18 cm (6–7 in) circles. Mash the corned beef and mix in the onion and potato. Season with salt and pepper. Divide the mixture between the pastry circles, leaving a 1 cm (½ in) border. Moisten the edges of the pastry and lift the sides, pressing the edges together across the top to form an upstanding frill. Brush the pastry with beaten egg and bake in a fairly hot oven, 200°C/400°F/Gas 6, for 25–30 minutes until the pastry is golden.

TIPSY CHERRY TARTS

These are memorable patisseries that should be made with luscious fresh ripe black cherries, but the recipe will also work with frozen or well-drained canned fruit.

> One recipe (100 g (4 oz) flour etc.) American self-raising pie crust (p. 40)
> ½ kg (1 lb) black cherries
> 150 ml (¼ pint) sweet red wine
> 1 level tablespoon cornflour
> 150 ml (¼ pint) milk
> 50 g (2 oz) sugar
> 2 size-4 egg yolks
> 2 tablespoons single cream
> 4 tablespoons redcurrant jelly

Stone the cherries and soak in the wine for at least 3 hours, stirring occasionally so that all are equally flavoured. Roll out the pastry and cut out nine to twelve 8 cm (3 in) circles. Fit into patty tins using the head of a rolling pin to ease the pastry in evenly. Prick thoroughly and bake blind in a fairly hot oven, 200°C/400°F/Gas 6, for 10 minutes. Remove the weights and continue baking for 5 minutes or until golden and crisp. Remove from the tins and cool on a wire rack. To make the filling blend the cornflour with a little of the milk, then add the remainder.

Heat gently until thick, stirring continuously. Mix in the sugar. Cool slightly, then beat in the egg yolks and lastly the cream. Divide the filling between the pastry cases and cover with well-drained cherries. Melt the jelly over low heat and brush over the cherries to make them shine.

Banana Pastry

Banana pastry is easy to mix and roll out. It holds its shape well so is ideal for use in flan rings. When cooked the pastry is a pleasing fawn colour and its keeping qualities are good. Use firm but not green bananas for this pastry – they must be mashable but not mushable. While there is no reason why banana pastry should not be used for savoury dishes, I normally combine it with sweet fillings. Banana pastry is useful in low sodium diets, since bananas are low in sodium and unsalted butter is used. Of course you would have to make sure the filling was also acceptable. Adequate for a 20–23 cm (8–9 in) flan ring.

Ingredients for Basic Recipe

150 g (6 oz) plain flour
Pinch of salt *or* salt substitute
75 g (3 oz) unsalted butter, firm
50 g (2 oz) peeled banana
1 tablespoon cold water

Sieve the flour and salt into a mixing bowl and rub in the butter. Mash the banana with water, stir into the mixture, then knead as little as possible. Only add more water if the mixture is very stiff. Roll out the pastry, then shape and leave it to rest for 15 minutes, but do not chill as this could cause discoloration. Bake in a fairly hot oven, 200°C/400°F/Gas 6, reducing the temperature if the fillings so require.

ALL-WEATHER FLAN

Soft pulpy dried fruit on a custard base covered in a glossy apricot sauce. Add more sugar if you have a sweet tooth but I think it detracts from the natural flavour of the fruit.

One recipe (150 g (6 oz) flour etc.) Banana pastry (p. 44)
225 g (8 oz) mixed dried apricots, pears, peaches and apples
150 ml (¼ pint) fresh orange juice
200 ml (7 fl oz) water
25 g (1 oz) demerara sugar
1 size-2 egg
150 ml (¼ pint) soured cream
1 generous tablespoon apricot jam

Clean the fruit and soak in the orange juice and water overnight. Add the sugar and cook very slowly until the fruit is soft. Drain, reserving the liquid. While the fruit is cooking, make the pastry. Roll out and fit into a 20 cm (8 in) flan ring. Bake blind in a fairly hot oven, 200°C/400°F/Gas 6, for 15 minutes. Remove the weights and then reduce the temperature to 160°C/325°F/Gas 3 for a further 10 minutes until the pastry is just fawn and dry. Pour in the egg and cream, beaten together, and bake for a further 10 minutes or until the custard has thickened. Remove from the oven and leave to cool. Spread the fruit over the custard without any pressure. Heat 3 tablespoons of the reserved juice with the jam, bring to the boil and pour evenly over the fruit. Serves four to six.

BUTTERSCOTCH TART

A rich soft dessert interspersed with crispy nuts. For easy slicing plunge the nuts briefly into boiling water before slicing, otherwise slice in a food processor. Serve warm or cold.

One recipe (150 g (6 oz) flour etc.) Banana pastry
  (p. 44)
75 g (3 oz) unsalted butter
100 g (4 oz) dark brown sugar
½ teaspoon vanilla essence
50 g (2 oz) cornflour, sieved
150 ml (¼ pint) single cream
3 size-3 eggs, separated
50 g (2 oz) Brazil nuts, thinly sliced and toasted
100 g (4 oz) caster sugar

Roll out the pastry and use to line a 23 cm (9 in) greased flan ring. Bake blind in a fairly hot oven, 200°C/400°F/Gas 6, for 15 minutes, then remove the weights and reduce the temperature to 190°C/375°F/Gas 5 for a further 5–10 minutes or until the pastry is an even fawn colour and cooked through. While the pastry is baking, make the filling. Melt the butter in the top of a double saucepan or in a bowl over a pan of simmering water, add the sugar and vanilla essence, stirring until the sugar has dissolved. Blend the cornflour with the cream and egg yolks. Pour into the melted mixture and stir until thick and creamy, making sure that the water does not at any time touch the bottom of the bowl. Stir in the nuts. Remove from the heat. Working well away from the steamy atmosphere whisk the egg whites until stiff. Whisk in less than half the sugar and when the mixture regains its stiffness, fold in the remainder. Pour the custard filling into the pastry, cover with the meringue spread right to the edges and return the pastry to the oven and bake at 190°C/375°F/Gas 5 for 10–15 minutes until the meringue is light brown. Serves four to six.

LOW SODIUM SAFFRON PIE

Salt (sodium chloride) is not permissible for the blood pressure brigade – the substitute is usually potassium chloride and is obtainable under various brand names. Healthy salt addicts may do as they like but even they would benefit from using a little less. All these ingredients have been chosen because of their low sodium content. Serve warm.

One recipe (150 g (6 oz) flour etc.) Banana pastry (p. 44)
1 small onion, diced
25 g (1 oz) unsalted butter
2 teaspoons rosemary leaves *or* ½ teaspoon dried rosemary
200 ml (7 fl oz) water
Few strands saffron
25 g (1 oz) split peas, previously soaked for 2 hours
50 g (2 oz) diced carrots
50 g (2 oz) cooked French beans, cut into thin strips
Salt substitute
Black pepper
225 g (8 oz) cod fillet, skinned and cut into 2.5 cm (1 in) cubes
Lettuce hearts and tomatoes

Roll out the pastry into a 25 cm (10 in) circle. Dab a 1 cm (½ in) border and curl the pastry edges to form a rim. Place on a greased baking sheet and wrap a collar of four-folded foil around the sides. Prick thoroughly and bake blind in a fairly hot oven, 200°C/400°F/Gas 6, for 15 minutes. Remove the weighting, reduce the temperature to 180°C/350°F/Gas 4 for a further 15 minutes to completely cook the pastry. Meanwhile sauté the onion in the butter, adding the rosemary as soon as the onion is soft. Stir in the water, saffron, drained split peas, carrots and beans. Season with salt substitute and pepper. Bring to the boil, then add the fish. Cover and cook over a low heat for 20–30 minutes until the split peas are cooked and the mixture is thick. Pour into the pastry case. Serve with a lettuce and tomato salad. Serves three.

TARTE AU CITRON

This sweet 'n' sour tart filled with smooth ground almonds isn't much to look at but it tastes super. Use the surplus lemon juice in other recipes or freeze in the sections of plastic egg boxes.

One recipe (150 g (6 oz) flour etc.) Banana pastry (p. 44)
2 lemons
3 size-4 eggs
150 g (5 oz) caster sugar
100 g (4 oz) ground almonds
150 g (5 oz) butter, melted

Roll out the pastry and use to line a 23 cm (9 in) greased flan ring. Refrigerate while preparing the filling. Prepare a fairly hot oven, 200°C/400°F/Gas 6. Grate the lemon rind finely and squeeze the juice from half a lemon. Beat the eggs and sugar until thick, then stir in the lemon rind and juice, ground almonds and butter. Taste and add more lemon juice to suit your palate. Turn into the pastry case and bake in the pre-heated oven for 25–30 minutes until the pastry is a deep fawn colour. The filling may still be soft but will become quite sticky when cold. Serves four to six.

Biscuit Crust

The original French recipe for biscuit crust used no fat at all and was as a result a hard and crisp pastry of iron-like resistance to seepage or weighty fillings. Nowadays sophisticated tastes would find this pastry less than perfect. In this recipe I have used hard margarine in a smaller proportion than the other pastry recipes. Suitable only for sweet dishes, the recipe contains a large proportion of sugar and it is this that causes the rapid browning. Granulated sugar adds a sparkle but the more you put in, the more likely it is that the pastry will burn, so do not bake at a higher temperature than 180°C/350°F/Gas 4. Biscuit crust is delicate and although a certain amount of kneading is necessary, take care that it does not become too warm during handling. This quantity is sufficient for a 23 cm (9 in) tart or fifteen individual small tartlets.

Ingredients for Basic Recipe

225 g (8 oz) plain flour
Pinch of salt
60–70 g (2–2½ oz) granulated sugar
100 g (3½ oz) hard margarine at room temperature, cut into small pieces
1 size-3 egg, beaten
1 tablespoon cold water
¼ teaspoon vanilla essence

Sieve the flour, salt and sugar into a mixing bowl. Make a well in the centre and add the other ingredients. Using the fingers of one hand first mix the margarine with the liquid, then gradually draw in the flour from the sides of the bowl. As you work you will find it harder to mix and more pressure may be required. Knead the dough until smooth, then cover and chill for 30 minutes. Use in tartlets and baked blind for flan cases. The pastry should be chilled after shaping to prevent it from shrinking down the sides of the flan case.

APPLE TART

Cut apples blacken on contact with the air. It is best to slice immediately before use but if you have to keep them for a short time, immerse the slices in cold salted water. Rinse before use. The Grand Marnier will foam and the alcohol evaporate if added while the jam is boiling. Serve apple tart cold with dollops of whipped unsweetened cream.

One recipe (225 g (8 oz) flour etc.) Biscuit crust (p. 49)
½ kg (1 lb) cooking apples
2 teaspoons lemon juice
2–3 tablespoons caster sugar
4 as-they-come tablespoons apricot jam
1 tablespoon Grand Marnier

Roll out the pastry and use to line a 23 cm (9 in) flan dish. Bake blind in a moderate oven, 180°C/350°F/Gas 4, for 15 minutes. Remove the weights. Peel, core and slice the apples thinly, immediately arranging them over the pastry in overlapping circles. Sprinkle with the lemon juice and the sugar in an even layer and bake for a further 15 minutes or until the pastry is pale brown and the apples just tender. Spoon any juice that has accumulated in the flan into the apricot jam and heat, stirring until just boiling. Remove from the heat, leave for a few minutes and add the Grand Marnier. Strain over the apples so that all are coated and leave to cool. Serves four to six.

CASSÉ TARTLETTES

The miniature tarts have a predominant cherry flavour and the cherries show through the surface of the sponge. The icing is the most complicated part and properly made, produces a crisp brittle finish. Remember to take care and use oven gloves when making syrups.

One recipe (225 g (8 oz) flour etc.) Biscuit crust (p. 49)
75 g (3 oz) soft margarine
75 g (3 oz) caster sugar
1 size-3 egg, beaten
40 g (1½ oz) ground almonds
40 g (1½ oz) self-raising flour, sieved
2 tablespoons sherry
75 g (3 oz) glacé cherries, chopped
150 g (6 oz) cube sugar
7 tablespoons water

Roll out the pastry to a thickness of 5 mm (¼ in). Cut out circles with an 8 cm (3 in) fluted cutter and use to line fourteen to sixteen deep greased patty tins. Cream the margarine and sugar until fluffy, then gradually beat in the egg. Fold in the ground almonds and flour, then add the sherry and cherries. Divide between the pastry cases, spreading the mixture evenly. Bake in a moderate oven, 180°C/350°F/Gas 4, for 25–30 minutes or until golden brown and firm to the touch. Cool on a wire rack. When the cakes are quite cold make the icing. Combine the cube sugar and water in a heavy-based pan over low heat and stir until dissolved. Without further stirring, boil the syrup to 138°C/280°F when a spoonful dropped into cold water forms brittle strands. With extreme caution immediately remove from the heat and plunge the base of the pan into warm water to prevent additional cooking. Using tongs, quickly dip the cakes into the syrup, then stand them on non-stick paper. The icing should set crisply.

COFFEE AND PEAR FLAN

Gently poached pears in a coffee-flavoured mousse. Serve cold.

One recipe (225 g (8 oz) flour etc.) Biscuit crust (p. 49)
    using 50 g (2 oz) sugar
3 large firm pears, peeled, halved and cored
2 rounded tablespoons brown sugar
6–8 cloves
2 rounded tablespoons caster sugar
2 size-3 egg yolks
150 ml (¼ pint) double cream
2–3 teaspoons coffee essence (or to taste)
40 g (1½ oz) butter
40 g (1½ oz) flour
300 ml (½ pint) milk
1½ level teaspoons arrowroot
Angelica for decoration

Roll out the pastry and use to line a 23 cm (9 in) greased fluted flan ring placed on a lightly greased baking tray. Bake blind in a moderate oven, 180°C/350°F/Gas 4, for 20 minutes. Remove the weights and the metal ring and bake for a further 10 minutes until crisp and dry. Allow to cool. Put the pears, brown sugar, cloves and 150 ml (¼ pint) water in a saucepan and poach, basting frequently until the pears are tender but still holding their shape. Reserve the syrup and drain the pears on kitchen paper. Whisk the caster sugar and egg yolks together until thick, then stir in the cream and coffee essence. Melt the butter in a saucepan, stir in the flour and gradually beat in the milk. Return the pan to the heat, stirring until the sauce thickens. Cool slightly, then fold into the coffee mousse. Turn into the flan case and refrigerate until set. Arrange the pear halves on the flan round side up. Blend the cold pear juice with the arrowroot. Put in a saucepan and bring to the boil, stirring all the time until the sauce is clear and thickened. Strain over the pears and decorate with angelica stalks. Serves six.

PEACH WHIRL TORTE

The ingredients are simple but the success of the recipe depends on the skill in filling and decorating. It is vital to chill the small pastry circles to prevent them from becoming misshapen when baked. Serve cold.

One recipe (225 g (8 oz) flour etc.) Biscuit crust (p. 49)
410 g (14½ oz) can peach slices, drained, reserving 2 teaspoonsful
1 generous tablespoon apricot jam
150 ml (¼ pint) double cream, whipped
1 teaspoon Cointreau *or* similar liqueur
2–3 glacé cherries, chopped

Roll out three-quarters of the pastry to a 20 cm (8 in) diameter circle. Flute the edges between the thumb and forefinger (as in a rope) so that a raised border is formed. Roll out the remaining pastry thinly and cut out six to eight circles. Put the pastry on a baking tray and chill. Bake in a moderate oven, 180°C/350°F/Gas 4, for 25–30 minutes until crisp. Cool on a wire rack. Arrange the peaches in a cartwheel with the curved edges at a 45° angle on the pastry case, leaving a 1 cm (½ in) border. Insert the pastry circles equally around the flan between the fruit, tilted upwards and using the peaches for support. Warm the jam with two teaspoons of the peach juice and brush carefully over the pastry and peach slices. Fold the Cointreau into the cream which should be stiff enough to pipe and put into a forcing bag fitted with a star tube. Pipe cream rosettes around the border of the flan and pile a pyramid of the remaining cream in the centre. Sprinkle with the chopped cherries. Serves six.

Bran Pastry

Hearing all this talk about fibre in the diet, I decided to try and make a pastry using bran and I was pleasantly surprised to find that it was neither chewy nor heavy and had a particular nutty flavour and a crisp texture. Though wholesome it is nevertheless light. Bran is sold at health-food shops and in chemists, but don't confuse it with wheatgerm. Wheatgerm usually comes in a smaller packet, sometimes a green and white one, while bran is much more bulky and you will find that you seem to be buying an enormous quantity. Store bran in the refrigerator tightly sealed in a polythene bag and it will keep for a long time, but I wouldn't recommend keeping it in the larder, just in case little creepy crawlies develop. Those who haven't seen bran probably think that it is very heavy, but in fact it is light and flaky and blends well with the flour when making pastry. You could, if you wanted to, make pastry using a high-fibre filling and these will include vegetables such as parsnips, tomatoes, spinach and cauliflower. Baked beans come out way on top. Nearly all fruit is high in fibre so you can choose whatever you like best. Of the dried fruits select dates and use plenty of nuts.

The fillings that go well with bran pastry are those with a fairly strong flavour. The dough is rather wet and should be rolled out on a generously floured surface and the fat should be cold, preferably straight from the refrigerator. A flan case baked blind will take 20–30 minutes. The pastry is a rather deep gold colour when cooked. The recipe provides enough pastry for an 18–20 cm (7–8 in) flan.

Ingredients for Basic Recipe

100 g (4 oz) plain flour
Pinch of salt
20 g (¾ oz) bran
75 g (3 oz) solid vegetable cooking fat
2 tablespoons cold water

Sieve the flour and salt into a mixing bowl and stir in the bran. Add the lump of fat and cut in until the pieces are about the size of hazelnuts. Stir in the water and as soon as the pastry comes together, knead lightly with the fingertips to form a ball. Turn out on to a generously floured surface and turn the dough over, so that it has a light coating of the flour. Roll to the desired shape. Rolled-out pastry will have small patches of white fat showing through, so that you may find that you need to flour the rolling pin once or twice to prevent sticking. Bake in a fairly hot oven, 200°C/400°F/Gas 6, until golden brown unless there is a filling which requires slower cooking.

CELERY AND CHEESE FLAN

If you enjoy celery you will like this flan. It is a grand combination of thinly rolled bran pastry and celery, whose pungency is reduced both by the frying process and the mild cheese. Serve hot.

One recipe (100 g (4 oz) flour etc.) Bran pastry (above)
1 small onion, chopped
75 g (3 oz) margarine
1 small bunch celery, scraped and sliced
25 g (1 oz) cornflour
300 ml (½ pint) milk
75 g (3 oz) mild Cheddar cheese, grated
Salt

Pepper
Garlic powder (optional)

Roll out the pastry and use to line a 20 cm (8 in) flan dish. Bake blind in a fairly hot oven, 200°C/400°F/Gas 6, for 15 minutes, then remove the weights and continue baking for a further 5 minutes or until golden brown. Fry the onion in 50 g (2 oz) margarine until translucent, then add the celery and continue frying gently until tender but not brown. Drain. Now make a white sauce. Melt the remaining margarine in a pan over medium heat, stir in the cornflour and cook for ½ minute. Gradually add the milk, beating thoroughly between each addition. Bring to the boil, stirring all the time until the sauce thickens. Stir in three-quarters of the cheese and season to taste with salt and pepper and a squeeze of garlic powder. Stir in the onion and celery and pour into the baked flan case. Sprinkle the remaining cheese on top and brown under the grill. Serves four to five.

LAZY ASPARAGUS FLAN

Why not be even lazier and use one of your stored ready-made pastry cases and cut the baking time to 25 minutes. Serve hot.

One recipe (100 g (4 oz) flour etc.) Bran pastry (p. 55)
425 g (15 oz) can asparagus spears
1 large egg
1 tablespoon single cream
Salt
Pepper

Roll out the pastry and use to line an 18 cm (7 in) flan dish. Arrange the asparagus spears on the pastry in an attractive pattern. Beat the egg with the cream and make up to 150 ml (¼ pint) with liquid from the can. Season with salt and pepper. Don't throw away any remaining liquid as it is very good in soups and sauces. Pour the mixture over the asparagus and bake on the centre shelf of a moderate oven, 180°C/350°F/Gas 4, for 40 minutes or until the filling is set. Serves four.

RATATOUILLE PIE

A colourful and appetizing dish, particularly when cut. It is suitable for light suppers, as a vegetable to accompany chops or steaks or as a vegetarian main course, hot or cold. Ratatouille freezes well so double up on the filling and freeze the surplus for another time.

Double recipe (200 g (8 oz) flour etc.) Bran pastry (p. 55)
Vegetable cooking oil
1 medium onion, sliced
1 large green pepper, cored, deseeded and sliced thinly
1 medium aubergine, peeled and sliced in 5 mm (¼ in) thicknesses
1 × 198 g (7 oz) can tomatoes
Milk to glaze

Heat 2–3 tablespoons oil in a large frying pan and fry the onions until translucent. Add the green pepper rings, tossing them so that both sides are evenly cooked. Push these vegetables to one side of the pan while frying the aubergine slices, a few at a time. You will need to add more oil in between each batch, as the aubergines absorb a considerable quantity. As soon as the aubergines are browned and soft, mix in the tomatoes, crushing them slightly. Switch off the heat but leave in the pan while dealing with the pastry. Roll out half the pastry and use to line a 20 cm (8 in) pie plate and, using a slotted spoon, spread the vegetables in the centre, leaving a 1 cm (½ in) border. Roll out the remaining pastry to form a pie lid, moistening the under-edge to obtain a better seal. Flute or crimp the edges of the pie and brush the top with milk. Bake the plate pie in a fairly hot oven, 200°C/400°F/Gas 6, for 20 minutes, then reduce the heat to 190°C/375°F/Gas 5 to enable the bottom crust to cook through. Serves four.

SULTANA FLAN

The flavour of the filling is not unlike a baked cheesecake with a strong tangy taste. Use muscavado sugar if you have it. Serve warm or cold.

> One recipe (100 g (4 oz) flour etc.) Bran pastry (p. 55)
> 1 size-3 egg
> 25 g (1 oz) soft dark brown sugar
> 200 ml (7 fl oz) natural yogurt
> Grated rind of one lemon
> 100 g (4 oz) sultanas

Roll out the pastry and use to line an 18 cm (7 in) fluted flan ring. Bake blind in a fairly hot oven, 200°C/400°F/Gas 6, for 15 minutes. Meanwhile beat the egg and sugar together until thick, then fold in the yogurt and lemon rind and lastly the sultanas. Pour into the pastry case and bake in a moderate oven, 180°C/350°F/Gas 4, for 30 minutes or until the filling has set. Serves four.

Cheese Pastry

Cheese pastry is very short because the fat in the cheese is additional to any fat that has been put into the mixture. It is better to use a hard, finely grated cheese such as farmhouse Cheddar or a dry cheese such as Parmesan. The softer cheeses like Edam are not as effective in cheese pastry. Although cheese pastry is used mainly for savoury dishes, it can be used in sweet dishes, particularly when making an apple flan, because apples go so well with cheese, but choose eating rather than cooking apples. Cheese pastry is made in the same way as shortcrust pastry, that is by rubbing the fat into the flour, but the cheese should never be rubbed into the mixture, as it would make the pastry oil out. Use half lard and half margarine and the proportion of cheese to flour is one-third. A few drops of fresh lemon juice are added to the water to counteract the soft effect that the cheese would produce. The following quantity is sufficient for a 20 cm (8 in) flan.

Ingredients for Basic Recipe

200 g (6 oz) plain flour
Pinch of salt
50 g (1½ oz) lard
50 g (1½ oz) margarine
70 g (2 oz) strong hard cheese, grated
Pinch of Cayenne pepper
¼ teaspoon lemon juice
2–3 tablespoons cold water

Sieve the flour and salt into a mixing bowl. Put the lard and margarine into the bowl, cut up to sugar lump size, then rub in finely. Stir in the cheese and Cayenne pepper. Mix the lemon juice with 2 tablespoons of the water, pour into the bowl all at once and mix with a knife to a lumpy dough. If the mixture seems too dry and there are crusty masses on the outside, add the remaining water. Knead gently, then cover and leave to rest for about 10 minutes. Roll out the pastry on a well-floured surface and if possible chill before baking. Bake the pastry in a fairly hot oven, 200°C/400°F/Gas 6.

BEEF SLICE

A transportable picnic dish for hot or cold consumption. Should you buy the best mince often described as steak tartare you may have to add a little oil for frying.

> One recipe (200 g (6 oz) flour etc.) Cheese pastry
> (p. 59)
> 350 g (12 oz) raw minced beef
> 25 g (1 oz) flour
> 1 onion, chopped
> 1 carrot, sliced
> 1 small turnip, diced
> 1 stalk celery, sliced
> 300 ml (½ pint) beef stock
> Milk to glaze

Roll out just over half the pastry and use to line a 20 cm (8 in) square tin. Chill while preparing the filling. Fry the meat in its own fat until brown. Tip the saucepan, pushing the meat to one side and spoon away all but one table-spoon of the accumulated fat. Leaving the meat in the pan, stir in the flour and cook for ½ minute. Add the vegetables and the stock, bring to the boil, then simmer for 20 minutes, adding a little more stock or water if the mixture is too dry. Remove from the heat and cool rapidly. Turn into the pastry case. Roll out the remaining pastry to form a lid. If for any reason you have made this too big, tuck the sides under and into the tin. Brush with milk and bake in a fairly hot oven, 200°C/400°F/Gas 6, for 20–25 minutes until the pastry is golden. Serve from the tin. Serves four.

HAM AND EGG QUICHE

The predominant flavour in this dish is the ham, so choose the type you prefer. You could use the slightly sweet Virginia ham, a more smoked ham or the cheaper shoulder. Where there is a small portion of weighty filling a quiche will puff up considerably during baking, but inevitably will flatten when cold. Serve hot.

One recipe (200 g (6 oz) flour etc.) Cheese pastry
   (p. 59)
4 size-3 eggs
150 ml (¼ pint) milk
3 tablespoons single cream
Pinch of salt
Pinch of pepper
100 g (4 oz) cooked ham, sliced finely and cut into
   strips
Powdered paprika

Roll out the pastry and use to line an 18 cm (7 in) flan ring. Bake blind in a fairly hot oven, 200°C/400°F/Gas 6, for 10 minutes. Remove the weights and reduce the temperature to 180°C/350°F/Gas 4. Quickly beat three of the eggs with the milk, cream, salt and pepper. Stir in the ham and pour into the flan case. Bake for 30–35 minutes until set. While the flan is cooking, hard boil the remaining egg and chop finely. Sprinkle over the quiche and add a shake of paprika. Serves four to five.

PASTRY PIZZA

This is intended as a quick supper snack. The pastry base makes a change from a bread or scone base. There is plenty of cheese for extra goodness and this will appeal to the younger generation. Serve hot.

One recipe (200 g (6 oz) flour etc.) Cheese pastry (p. 59)
2–3 tablespoons vegetable oil
1 medium onion, chopped
10 cm (4 in) strip of green pepper, chopped
3 rashers back bacon, derinded and chopped
75 g (3 oz) mushrooms, sliced
1 tablespoon tomato purée
1 teaspoon dried oregano
Salt and pepper
2 tomatoes, thinly sliced
75 g (3 oz) grated cheese

Divide the pastry into three and roll out to 13 cm (5 in) circles 5 mm (¼ in) thick. Pinch round the edges so that they are slightly raised. Heat the oil and fry the onion, pepper and bacon until soft, then add the mushrooms, cooking for a few more minutes. Drain and mix in the tomato purée and oregano. Season with salt and pepper to taste. Cover the pastry circles with the mixture and top with sliced tomatoes and grated cheese. Place on a baking tray and bake in a fairly hot oven, 200°C/400°F/Gas 6, for 25–30 minutes. Serves three.

TAUNTON APPLE PIE

The pie is on the sharp side which is just right with the cheese pastry. If you find it too tart, serve with plenty of thick cream. Serve hot or warm.

Double recipe (400 g (12 oz) flour etc.) Cheese pastry (p. 59)

¾ kg (1½ lb) dessert apples
6–8 tablespoons cider
1 generous tablespoon caster sugar
¼ teaspoon powdered cloves

Peel, core and slice the apples. Put in a saucepan with the smaller quantity of cider, the sugar and cloves and stew gently without covering until very soft. Add the remaining cider if necessary but the mixture should be on the dry side. Roll out half the pastry and use to line a 20 cm (8 in) ovenproof plate. Roll the remaining pastry to a circle fractionally larger. Using a slotted spoon put the apple pulp on the pastry base and moisten the edges with water. Put on the pastry lid easing in the sides to fit. Press the edges to seal and finish and decorate as desired. Bake in a fairly hot oven, 200°C/400°F/Gas 6, for 25–30 minutes until the pastry is crisp and appetizing. Serves four to six.

TRULY CHEESY YOGURT FLAN

Serve thin slices as a starter or prepare for vegetarians as a supper dish. A crisp green salad is a natural accompaniment. Serve warm.

One recipe (200 g (6 oz) flour etc.) Cheese pastry (p. 59)
175 ml (6 fl oz) natural yogurt
1 size-2 egg
100 g (4 oz) mature Cheddar cheese, grated
1 teaspoon caster sugar

Roll the pastry and use to line a 20 cm (8 in) flan dish. Beat all the remaining ingredients together, pour into the pastry and bake in a fairly hot oven, 200°C/400°F/Gas 6, for 10 minutes, then reduce the temperature to 180°C/350°F/Gas 4 for a further 25–30 minutes until the filling is set. Serves four to six.

Choux Pastry

Choux pastry gets its name from the French word meaning cabbage because of the shape it resembles when baked. It is the egg yolks that give the pastry its yellow colour. Choux pastry is best known for its use in éclairs and cream buns, although it is very good when stuffed with savoury fillings. It can be shaped into rings, sticks or round buns and it can be baked or mixed with other ingredients and deep fat fried. It can be poached but then it can hardly be called pastry.

Choux paste is similar to hot water crust in that the fat and the liquid have to be boiling rapidly when the flour is added. Use an 18 cm (7 in) saucepan for the water and butter so that when the liquid nears boiling point, it can rise up the sides of the pan. The flour is added all in one go as the saucepan is removed from the heat. If it does not form a ball when briskly stirred with a wooden spoon, return the pan to the heat, holding it just above the flame, so that the starch grains have a chance to burst. Leave the mixture to cool a little before whisking in the eggs, a little at a time. You can add the eggs whole one by one and stir very briskly with a wooden spoon or beat with an electric mixer, but you will find you have a very slimy mass to work with and until this slimy mass thickens up you can't add the second egg. If, however, you beat the eggs with a fork first, you can add them more quickly, although you must still beat thoroughly after each addition. Perfect choux pastry should be of a dropping consistency similar to soft toothpaste and have a silky sheen. It may not be necessary to add all the egg. If you are undecided, have a softer rather than a firmer mixture. Cover the pastry and leave it until it is cold before piping. You can mix the entire pastry in the saucepan if you prefer, but if you are using a metal whisk in a metal saucepan, it tends to make the pastry go grey and this is particularly so when using a non-stick pan. Therefore you may prefer to transfer the dough to a mixing bowl before adding the eggs.

The difference between choux pastry and hot water crust is that eggs are *beaten* into choux pastry and this gives them the lightness that puffs the pastry up so beautifully. It is because the air has to be distributed evenly that the eggs have to be beaten in one at a time and very briskly.

Choux should not be frozen before baking as it softens when stored whether filled or empty. Although it is convenient to freeze after baking, you will find it to be tougher than when freshly made. Unfilled and frozen choux buns should be put briefly into a hot oven to thaw.

The baking results are better if you cover the pastry when it is in the oven. Use a Pyrex dish or even a large biscuit tin. This prevents the gluten on the outside of the pastry becoming set too quickly. The air inside the pastry then gradually gets warm and expands to its fullest extent, because of the elasticity of the outside. Take care not to uncover the pastry before it is cooked, although this is difficult if you use a tin, since you can't see through it. If you do take the cover off you will allow the steam to escape and the pastry then flops and loses its shape, because the gluten has not set. Short of baking the pastry in a microwave oven, it will never regain its shape. When baking choux pastry without the 'tent' do not open the oven door for at least the first half of the cooking time. If your oven has a glass door you will be able to see when the pastry is brown.

An important factor in the making of choux pastry is steam. You will notice that the pastry itself is a cross between a batter and a soft dough. The steam which occurs when the pastry is put into the hot oven forces the batter up and out, so that there is a large hollow in the middle. Once this has happened the pastry should have a firm wall, so that when it is removed from the oven and the steam escapes, it will still hold its shape. It is important to start baking in a very hot oven so that all these processes can take place.

If the pastry is correctly cooked, it should dry out thoroughly inside, however you may find that when the pastry is finished and the buns are split open there is a gungy mass inside. If the pastry is hard enough it will be possible to remove this with the tip of a teaspoon, leaving the buns intact. If you do find that the pastry is hard on the outside and soft on the inside, it means either that the flour was not thoroughly cooked in the first place or that not enough egg was added. An oven that is too hot will also cause this, as the warm air inside will be unable to expand once the pastry wall is set. For best results use strong rather than plain flour and the fat should be at room temperature and not refrigerator hard.

Don't make up more than a double quantity at a time.

Ingredients for Basic Recipe

65 g (2½ oz) plain *or* strong plain flour
125–150 ml (4½–5 fl oz) water
50 g (2 oz) butter *or* margarine
2 size-4 eggs
Few drops vanilla essence (optional)

Sieve the flour on to a piece of greaseproof paper. Put the water and butter in a medium-sized pan and heat slowly until the butter is melted, then bring roughly to the boil. Throw all the flour in at once. Remove the pan from the heat and beat furiously until a soft ball is formed that leaves the sides of the pan. Continue beating until the mixture is smooth. Then return the saucepan to the heat, holding it above the flame and beat for another few minutes. Leave to cool slightly. Whisk the eggs together, then gradually beat into the pastry, continuing to beat until all is incorporated and a smooth glossy paste results. If you are going to make a sweet choux, add a few drops of vanilla essence at this stage. Cover the pastry and leave until quite cold before using. Bake preferably in the centre of a hot oven, 220°C/425°F/Gas 7, for the first 15 minutes, then reduce the temperature to 190°C/375°F/Gas 5 until the pastry is brown and crisp. Small puffs or éclairs will take 25 minutes in all, but larger items may take up to 40 minutes to bake.

SAVOURY CHEESE CHOUX PASTRY

This pastry is suitable for savoury fillings. Use it in main courses, such as gougères, as a savoury instead of dessert, as small buns, or piped into tiny dots for use as cocktail savouries.

Ingredients for Basic Recipe

65 g (2½ oz) plain *or* strong plain flour
Pinch of salt
⅛ teaspoon Cayenne pepper
25 g (1 oz) strongly flavoured hard cheese, grated
125–150 ml (4½–5 fl oz) water
50 g (2 oz) butter *or* margarine
2 size-4 eggs

Sieve the flour, salt and Cayenne pepper on to a large sheet of greaseproof paper and mix in the cheese. Put the water and butter in a medium-sized pan and heat slowly until the butter is melted, then bring to the boil. Wait until the water rises up the sides of the pan, then throw in the flour mixture all at one time. Beat vigorously at the same time removing the pan from the heat and continue beating until a soft ball is formed that leaves the sides of the pan and the mixture is smooth. Leave to cool slightly. Whisk the eggs together, then gradually beat into the pastry in small quantities and continue beating until the mixture is smooth and glossy. Cover and leave until quite cold before using. Bake in a hot oven, 220°C/425°F/Gas 7, reducing the temperature after the first 15 minutes in the same way as for ordinary choux pastry. Leave the oven open and wait for 5 minutes before removing the baking tray. This will prevent the buns from sinking when hit by a blast of cold air.

CHOCOLATE ÉCLAIRS

This recipe makes seven really large éclairs but if you like the very tiny ones, pipe the mixture 5–6 cm (2–2½ in) long. Serve cold or chilled.

One recipe (65 g (2½ oz) flour etc.) Choux pastry (p. 66)
100 g (4 oz) plain chocolate
150 ml (¼ pint) double cream, whipped

Grease a baking tray, sprinkle with flour, then shake off the surplus flour. Allowing ample space between the markings, draw lines with the handle of a wooden spoon 8–10 cm (3½–4 in) long to use as a guide for piping. Fit a large forcing bag with a 1 cm (½ in) plain tube and, holding the bag almost horizontally, and without pushing or stretching, pipe the mixture over the marked lines, chopping off at the ends with a knife previously dipped in cold water. Bake the éclairs on the second or third shelf from the top of the oven at 220°C/425°F/Gas 7 for 15 minutes. Then reduce the heat to 180°C/350°F/Gas 4 for a further 20 minutes or until the éclairs are well risen, brown and crisp. Transfer to a cooling wire and make a slit in the side of each. If the éclairs have been properly cooked there should be no soft pastry inside to scrape out. Melt the chocolate on a plate over a pan of nearly boiling water, making sure that the water does not touch the plate. Fill the éclairs with the cream and grasping them between the forefinger and thumb, dip the tops into the chocolate, twisting so that the chocolate does not drip down the sides.

GÂTEAU ST-HONORÉ AUX PÈCHES

Here is a variation on the St-Honoré theme. No flan rings or dishes are used, just a good heavy baking tray. The pâte sucrée is rolled out more thickly than in most recipes. Remember that choux pastry grows in the oven so pipe the buns very small.

One recipe (100 g (4 oz) flour etc.) Pâte sucrée (p. 145)
One recipe (65 g (2½ oz) flour etc.) Unflavoured choux pastry (p. 66)
4–6 ripe peaches (depending on the size)
1 generous tablespoon sugar
150 ml (¼ pint) double cream, whipped
4 generous tablespoons apricot jam, sieved
15 g (½ oz) shelled pistachio nuts, skinned and chopped

Roll out the pastry to a 20 × 10 cm (8 × 4 in) rectangle. Place carefully on a lightly greased baking tray and prick the pastry thoroughly. Flute the edges so that there is a slightly raised rim. Put the choux pastry into a forcing bag fitted with a 1 cm (½ in) star nozzle. Using just on half the paste, pipe a border on the pâte sucrée. Pipe the remaining mixture in small buns on to another greased baking tray. Bake both trays in a fairly hot oven, 200°C/400°F/Gas 6 for 20 minutes, then reduce the temperature to 180°C/350°F/Gas 4 for a further 15–20 minutes until crisp and brown, removing the small buns as soon as they are ready. While the pastry is cooking, skin and stone the peaches, then cut each into eight slices. Put in a saucepan with the sugar and just sufficient water to cover and poach for about 10 minutes until just tender. Drain. Arrange the peaches on the smooth part of the flan. Fill the separate choux buns with plenty of cream. Warm the jam and brush over the fruit and the choux border. Stick the filled buns round the edges and brush these with jam. Use any remaining cream to decorate the fruit. Sprinkle with the chopped nuts. Serves four to five.

BOURSIN BITES

Choux pastry is ideal when fried and may be either piped or spooned into hot, deep oil, but take care when dropping it in that the oil does not splash. Boursin bites are ideal party fare but since they have to be served hot, they may not be the hostess's choice. I like to pile them on a huge stainless-steel dish and serve them as a starter for a dinner party.

> One recipe (65 g (2½ oz) flour etc.) Savoury cheese choux pastry (p. 67)
> 75 g (3 oz) Boursin cheese with herbs and garlic
> Oil for deep frying

One-third fill a deep saucepan with frying oil and heat until hot enough to cook chips in. Carefully drop small teaspoons of choux pastry into the hot oil, cooking a few at a time until golden brown. As the pastry rises to the surface, flip over gently so that both sides are equally coloured. Remove with a slotted spoon and drain on kitchen paper. Holding the choux puffs with kitchen paper so that you do not burn your hands, pipe a little of the cheese inside each. Makes twenty.

CREAM CHEESE PUFFS

Here is just one suggestion for a savoury filling, but any pâté-type mixture will do. I would not advise a crumbly stuffing as it is impossible to pipe.

One recipe (65 g (2½ oz) flour etc.) Savoury cheese choux pastry (p. 67)
175 g (6 oz) cream cheese
3 level tablespoons horseradish sauce
Dash tabasco pepper sauce
½ teaspoon made English mustard
25 g (1 oz) toasted almonds, chopped

Using a 1 cm (½ in) plain or star tube, pipe twenty-four to thirty-six small or tiny buns on to a greased baking tray. Bake in a hot oven, 220°C/425°F/Gas 7, for 10–15 minutes, then reduce to 190°C/375°F/Gas 5 for a further 5–15 minutes depending on the size of the buns. Transfer to a wire rack and gash the sides immediately to let out the steam if any. Leave to cool. Blend three-quarters of the cream cheese, the sauces and mustard and chill until firm. Put into a piping bag fitted with a long-nosed, small plain tube and pipe into the buns. Spread the outside of the buns with the remaining cheese and roll in the nuts.

CROQUEMBOUCHE

A croquembouche is a magnificent edifice originating from France, where it was sometimes used as a wedding cake. It is a truly splendid centrepiece for special occasions and is not excessively difficult to make though time-consuming to erect. The component parts are small choux buns, a flat pastry base, a filling of whipped cream and nuts or fruit and caramel. It is the caramel that creates the most problems since it must be neither under- nor over-cooked. The finished cake should not be left for long in humid conditions or the caramel will melt. The buns are built up around a metal cone which is removed as soon as they are set. Few people have one of these cones, but a large conical strainer or a home-made cone shape made from four thicknesses of foil will do.

> One recipe (225 g (8 oz) flour etc.) Biscuit crust (p. 49)
>
> Double recipe (130 g (5 oz) flour etc.) Choux pastry (p. 66)
>
> 450 g (1 lb) cube sugar
>
> 190 ml (6¼ fl oz) water
>
> ½ level teaspoon cream of tartar
>
> 450 ml (¾ pint) cream, stiffly whipped with 1 table-spoon icing sugar
>
> Choice of walnuts, marron glacé, fresh strawberries, raspberries, satsuma segments, candied peel
>
> 1 cone 20–23 cm (8–9 in) high, oiled lightly on the outside
>
> 1 cake stand
>
> 1 hat pin
>
> 1 frying pan containing hot water
>
> Extra decorations of pistachio nuts, glacé cherries and whipped cream

Using the Biscuit crust recipe roll out the pastry to an 18 cm (7 in) circle and cook in a greased flan ring to maintain a good shape. Bake in a moderate oven, 180°C/350°F/Gas 4, for 20–25 minutes until the pastry is very, very crisp. Using a plain 1 cm (½ in) tube, pipe twenty-four to thirty-six small buns approximately 2 cm (¾ in) in diameter and 1 cm (½ in) high on to greased baking sheets and shape carefully with a round-bladed wetted knife. Bake in a hot oven, 220°C/425°F/Gas 7, for 15 minutes, then reduce to 190°C/375°F/Gas 5 for a further 10–15 minutes or until the buns are risen, crisp and brown. Unless you are using a fan oven where there is even heat throughout, you should use the top half of the oven only. Change the position of the baking trays after the buns have browned and set. Because of the quantity being prepared it will obviously be necessary to bake in batches. When the buns are cooked, pierce or slit, but do not make a large gash as the domed sides will show. Select only the best shaped buns and use up the others on the family. Dissolve the sugar in the water in a heavy- based saucepan over moderate heat. Add the cream of tartar, then boil steadily without stirring until a sugar ther-mometer registers 149°C/300°F but definitely not more than 153°C/308°F. At this stage brittle strands hang from a fork. Dip the base of the pan in hot water to prevent overbrowning. Stand the cone on non-stick paper. Using a sterilized hat pin or thin skewer spear each bun and quickly dip into the caramel and build up in circles around the cone until you reach the apex. The caramel is meant to coat and stick each bun to the next, but not to the cone. When the caramel is cold and set, remove the metal cone. Pile up the cream and chosen fruit or nuts on the pastry base to fit inside the cone. For extra decoration sprinkle the freshly dipped buns with chopped pistachio nuts or glacé cherries and pipe tiny rosettes of cream between the buns after the cone is erected.

POMMES DAUPHINE

Use up left-over mashed potatoes and choux pastry to make an exciting vegetable dish which must be served hot. Mix a few chopped almonds with the mixture if you like, but then you couldn't call the dish Pommes Dauphine which is its official title. Serve hot.

Half recipe (35 g (1¼ oz) flour etc.) Unflavoured choux pastry (p. 66)
225 g (8 oz) mashed potato

15 g (½ oz) butter, just melted
⅛ teaspoon grated nutmeg
Salt
Pepper
Oil for deep frying

Press the potatoes through a sieve and mix in the butter
and nutmeg, adding salt and pepper as required. Combine
with the prepared choux paste and shape into small
cylinders 3 × 1.5 cm (1½ × ¾ in). One-third fill a deep
pan with cooking oil and heat to 185°C/360°F. Fry the
potatoes a few at a time, turning them over for even
browning. Make sure that you do not put too many in the
pan at any one time or they will be pale and greasy. Drain
on kitchen paper. Serves three.

PROFITEROLES

Choux pastry buns filled with whipped cream and covered
with chocolate sauce. Save the remaining sauce to use
another time – it will freeze very well. Should you decide
to double the quantity of buns thus requiring two baking
trays, to ensure even cooking reverse their positions
during the second half of the cooking period.

One recipe (65 g (2½ oz) flour etc.) Choux pastry
(p. 66)

Sauce
100 g (4 oz) caster sugar
300 ml (½ pint) water
1 level teaspoon instant coffee powder
100 g (4 oz) cooking chocolate, broken up
2 level teaspoons cornflour
2 tablespoons milk
¼ teaspoon vanilla essence

Filling
175 ml (6 fl oz) double cream
1 rounded teaspoon icing sugar

Put the choux paste in a piping bag fitted with a 1 cm (½ in) plain or star nozzle. Pipe out twenty-five small blobs about 2.5 cm (1 in) in diameter and 1 cm (½ in) high on to a lightly greased baking tray. Smooth the tops with a wet flat-bladed knife if spiky peaks have mysteriously appeared. Bake on the middle shelf of a hot oven, 220°C/425°F/Gas 7, for 15 minutes, then reduce to 190°C/375°F/Gas 5 for a further 10–15 minutes or until the buns are well risen, crisp and brown. Remove from the oven, half split open and leave on a wire rack to cool. While the pastry is cooking make the sauce. Put the sugar and water in a saucepan and heat gently, stirring until the sugar has dissolved. Bring to the boil and boil for a further 2–3 minutes at 105°C/215°F. Cool slightly, then stir in the coffee and chocolate. Blend the cornflour with the milk, stir into the sauce and bring to the boil, stirring all the time. Continue cooking for a further minute or two. Flavour with the vanilla essence. Whip the cream and sugar until stiff and fill the buns using a teaspoon or piping bag and 5 mm (¼ in) nozzle. Arrange in a dish and pour over the sauce at the moment of serving. Serves four to five.

SMOKED HADDOCK GOUGÈRE

Use either boil-in-the-bag, frozen or fresh smoked haddock. If you prefer cod, the texture will be different but the flavour is practically the same. If you want to improve on this dish for a special occasion, add an egg yolk blended with a tablespoon of double cream to the sauce after removing the pan from the heat. Beat thoroughly. Serve hot.

Double recipe (130 g (5 oz) flour etc.) Savoury choux
   pastry (p. 67)
225 g (8 oz) smoked haddock
25 g (1 oz) butter
20 g (¾ oz) flour
300 ml (½ pint) milk
Salt
Pepper
2 teaspoons freshly chopped parsley
100 g (4 oz) freshly cooked peas
Knob of butter

Put the choux pastry in a large piping bag fitted with a
2.5 cm (1 in) plain tube and pipe a thick or double circle
round the base of a greased 18–20 cm (7–8 in) shallow
ovenproof dish. Bake in a hot oven, 220°C/425°F/Gas 7,
for 30–35 minutes until well risen and crisp. Poach the fish
in water for 12–15 minutes until the flesh flakes easily and
remove skin and bones. Melt the butter in a saucepan, stir
in the flour and cook for 1 minute. Gradually beat in the
milk, whisking continuously until the sauce thickens and
boils. Season with salt and pepper and add the parsley.
Mix the flaked fish with the sauce. Reheat, then pour into
the centre of the baked choux ring. Top with the peas and
a knob of fresh butter. Serves four.

Crumble Mix

One of the most versatile mixes is the crumble, because it is a mixture of rubbed-in flour and fat. There is no water to mix in and provided you remember to stop rubbing in as soon as no loose flour remains you can't go wrong. Oiling out is also unlikely as the quantity of fat used is half that of flour. Make crumbles with butter for a creamy flavour, but margarine gives just as good a texture. Soft margarine or the polyunsaturated kind work as well, but it is better to rub these in until the mixture resembles small peas rather than fine breadcrumbs. Use wholemeal flour for a change, but soften the fat first and then mix it in with a fork.

Make up as large a quantity as you please, using a mixer and store it in the freezer, where it will keep for several months. Add white or demerara sugar and spices to the basic crumble mix for use in sweet dishes and herbs or spices for savoury toppings. Ground nuts can be added to either. The usual quantity of added sugar is one-third the weight of the flour, but this should be increased or decreased according to the sweetness of the filling. Crumble mix is easy going and won't mind whether it is baked at 190°C/375°F/Gas 5 or 200°C/400°F/Gas 6. The baking time, of course, depends entirely upon the filling.

To prevent juice running out into the oven, due to the fact that there is no seal between the crumble and the filling, put the dish on a baking tray. When using frozen fruit let it thaw first, then drain off the juices before using with crumble mix. If you don't, you will find that the crumble sinks into the juicy fruit and becomes a sodden stodge.

Ingredients for Basic Recipe

150 g (6 oz) plain flour
Pinch of salt
75 g (3 oz) butter *or* margarine

Sieve the flour and salt into a mixing bowl and rub in the butter or margarine. Add any flavouring ingredients and store and use as required. The crumble should be sprinkled over the base and pressed down lightly. If it is pressed too hard it goes into the filling, so that it becomes soggy.

ALABAMA CHICKEN

Crumble acts as a crispy coating for the chicken, giving a pebbly golden appearance. Chicken is more filling when cooked this way and the necessity for heating a large quantity of oil for deep frying avoided. Vary the herbs or add paprika, cheese and Cayenne or curry powder if you like. Serve hot.

One recipe (150 g (6 oz) flour etc.) Crumble mix (above)
2 level teaspoons dried sage
1 tablespoon freshly chopped parsley
½ teaspoon salt
¼ teaspoon pepper
4 chicken legs (or similar sized portions)
2 size-3 eggs, beaten

Add the sage, parsley, salt and pepper to the crumble mix. Pull off the skin and dip the chicken into the beaten egg and then into the crumble mix. Press the crumble on to the chicken and refrigerate for 30 minutes. Bake in the centre of a hot oven, 220°C/400°F/Gas 6, for 30–40 minutes until golden brown and the chicken is firm. Serves four.

APRICOT AND ALMOND CRUMBLE

The flavour of this crumble is so much better if you can use butter. Serve with single cream or custard, hot or cold.

One recipe (150 g (6 oz) flour etc.) Crumble mix (p. 78)
225 g (8 oz) dried apricots
Juice of 1 lemon
75 g (3 oz) caster sugar
50 g (2 oz) flaked almonds, chopped about twice only

Soak the apricots overnight in the lemon juice with just enough water to cover the fruit. Turn into a 1 litre (1½ pint) pie dish. Stir the sugar and almonds into the crumble mix and spread over the fruit. Pat down lightly and bake in a fairly hot oven, 190°C/375°F/Gas 5, for 30–35 minutes until the crumble is cooked. Serves four to five.

DATE CRUMBLE CAKE

The sugar is optional because the dates are sweet and some types of packeted coconut contain added sugar.

One recipe Crumble mix (p. 78) made with 75 g (3 oz)
    white and 75 g (3 oz) wholemeal flour
50 g (2 oz) desiccated coconut
225 g (8 oz) block stoned dates
Juice of 1 lemon
Juice and grated rind of 1 orange
Brown sugar (optional)

Stir the coconut into the crumble mix and spread half in the base of a greased loose-bottomed 18 cm (7 in) cake tin. Press down with the head of a rolling pin. Chill. Chop up the block of dates, mix with the lemon and orange juice and orange rind in a saucepan. Cook until the dates are soft, adding a little water if necessary. When the mixture is soft spoon over the chilled crumble, keeping the mixture away from the sides of the tin. This is the moment to add the sugar for those with a sweet tooth. Top with the remaining crumble, spreading the mixture evenly. Press down firmly. Bake in a fairly hot oven, 190°C/375°F/Gas 5, for 35–45 minutes so that the lower layer of crumble has a chance to cook properly. Remove from the tin when cold. Serves six.

SAVOURY BEEF CAKE

Alternative suggestions for the flavouring could include the addition of bay leaves or basil, beef stock/consommé instead of beef stock or red wine in place of half the tomato juice. This dish may be frozen successfully. Serve hot.

One recipe (150 g (6 oz) flour etc.) Crumble mix (p. 78)
25 g (1 oz) margarine
350 g (¾ lb) trimmed chuck steak, chopped but not minced
1 medium onion, chopped
2 medium carrots, peeled and sliced
2 celery stalks, chopped
2 rounded tablespoons flour
150 ml (¼ pint) condensed canned beef consommé
150 ml (¼ pint) water
½ teaspoon Worcestershire sauce
150 ml (¼ pint) tomato juice
Salt
Pepper

Heat the margarine and fry the steak a handful at a time, stirring briskly. As soon as the meat is sealed add the onion, carrots and celery and continue frying until the meat is brown. Stir in the flour, then add the consommé and water, Worcestershire sauce, tomato juice and salt and pepper to taste. Bring to the boil, stirring all the time and when the sauce thickens, reduce the heat, cover and cook gently for 1½–2 hours until the meat is cooked. Inspect occasionally and add water if necessary. Taste and adjust the seasoning. Turn into a 1 litre (1½ pint) pie dish. Spread the crumble on top, barely patting down. Bake in a moderately hot oven, 190°C/375°F/Gas 5, for 35–40 minutes until the crumble is golden brown. Serves four.

Curd Cheese Pastry

This is my favourite pastry when I want to make quick Danish-type pastries. You don't have all the trouble of making up a yeast dough before rolling and folding the butter in and it is the simplest pastry to prepare. The proportions are easy to remember since it is an equal weight of curd cheese, unsalted butter and plain flour. Just take note of the following points and you will have absolute success: Use plain flour because it holds the other ingredients together better, unsalted butter so that there is no salt to toughen the gluten, and curd cheese, not cream cheese which would be too rich. If you have a mixer or food processor, you can make up a large quantity, then cut the piece into four balls and wrap and freeze until required. The required amount can then be thawed out at room temperature before rolling out when it is still cold and firm. For more immediate use you can mix as little as 25 g (1 oz) of each ingredient by hand and chill, covered, in the freezer for half an hour or so before rolling out. Because curd cheese pastry contains no sugar, it can be used for turnovers, puffs and flans, whether savoury or sweet. The quantity is sufficient for eighteen to twenty small puffs or a 20–23 cm (8–9 in) flan.

Ingredients for Basic Recipe

100 g (4 oz) plain flour
100 g (4 oz) unsalted butter, fridge firm
100 g (4 oz) curd cheese

Put the flour in a mixing bowl, cut the butter into eight or ten pieces and add to the flour all at once. Then using two round-bladed knives, cut the butter in, until the pieces are about the size of small cherries. Beat the cheese to soften slightly, add to the butter and flour, and mix the dough with one of the knives. When the mixture just holds together, form into a ball with both hands. At this stage you will still see the lumps of unblended butter and this is how it should be. Wrap in cling-film or seal in a polythene bag and chill for as long as you can. Even if time is short, it is preferable to chill in the refrigerator set at a low temperature than half freeze in the freezer, as that method of chilling causes the outside of the pastry balls to become hard and not of the same consistency as the centre.

Curd cheese pastry should be baked in a moderate oven, 180°C/350°F/Gas 4, when used for small puffs. This is to enable the pastry to be cooked through without the outside over-browning. When the pastry is used in flans bake in a fairly hot oven, 190°C/375°F/Gas 5.

APRICOT CRESCENTS

Unreservedly superb and so easy to prepare but these do take a while to roll and cut out. It's very difficult to say exactly how many the pastry will make but one thing is for sure, the number reaching the table will be less than the quantity taken from the oven – you won't be able to resist eating one or two . . .

One recipe (100 g (4 oz) flour etc.) Curd cheese pastry (p. 82)
225 g (½ lb) jar apricot preserve
Beaten egg yolk and milk to glaze
Glacé icing (made from icing sugar and water mixed to a thick paste for decoration)

Cut the pastry ball in half and roll each piece out on a floured surface until the thickness of a 5 pence piece. Cut out 5 cm (2 in) squares, then roll each piece into a 8 cm (3 in) square. It is much easier to obtain thinner pastry when rolling out small pieces. Put a spoonful of the preserve in one corner of the square and roll up corner to corner to form a sausage shape. You will see a triangular piece of pastry in the middle. Turn the pastry so that this is underneath and form into a crescent shape, with the open ends upturned. Put on a baking tray – there is no need to grease this, as there is sufficient fat in the pastry. Brush the whole pastry surface with the beaten egg. When the baking tray is full, chill in the refrigerator for at least half an hour or freeze until required. Bake the pastries in a moderate oven, 180°C/350°F/Gas 4, for 15–20 minutes until golden brown and crisp, but be careful not to overcook as the edges will burn and become hard. Remove from the oven and if the pastries are for immediate consumption decorate the tops with a spoonful of the glacé icing. If, however, you are going to store the pastries in the freezer, it is better to ice them after they are thawed and warmed through. Makes eighteen to twenty.

CHEESE AND CHIVE FLAN

Chives are the most common garden-grown herb after parsley and mint. It is so easy to freeze and the flavour is much better than the dried kind. Serve cold.

One recipe (100 g (4 oz) flour etc.) Curd cheese pastry (p. 82)
1 small onion, finely chopped or minced
20 fresh chives, snipped into specks with scissors
2 size-2 eggs
150 ml (¼ pint) natural yogurt
150 ml (¼ pint) milk

Salt
Pepper
100 g (4 oz) Emmenthal cheese, grated
2 level tablespoons dried breadcrumbs

Roll out the pastry and use to line a 23 cm (9 in) flan ring. Chill. Bake blind for 10–15 minutes in a fairly hot oven, 190°C/375°F/Gas 5, until the pastry is firm. Remove the weights and the flan ring. Beat the onion, chives, eggs, yogurt, milk, salt and pepper and half the cheese together and pour into the pastry case. Sprinkle with the remaining cheese mixed with the breadcrumbs. Bake in the lower part of the oven for 30–40 minutes until the filling has set and the top is a crunchy golden brown. Serves five to six.

FRUIT SALAD MERINGUE

Lovely curd cheese pastry is used here with a fruit filling topped with a meringue, which when baked in a hot oven becomes firm on the top while remaining mallowlike underneath. The flan may only be filled with canned fruit cocktail but the taste certainly belies this. Serve hot or cold with whipped cream.

Half recipe (50 g (2 oz) flour etc.) Curd cheese pastry
   (p. 82)
1 × 411 g (14½ oz) can fruit cocktail, drained
¼ teaspoon Angostura bitters *or* ½ teaspoon vanilla
   essence
2 size-2 egg whites
100 g (4 oz) caster sugar

Roll out the pastry and use to line an 18 cm (7 in) flan ring. Chill for at least 30 minutes. Bake blind in a moderate hot oven, 190°C/375°F/Gas 5, for 15 minutes, then remove the weights. Flavour the fruit with the Angostura bitters and pour into the pastry case. Whisk the egg whites until stiff, then add just under half the sugar and whisk until stiff peaks form. Fold in the remaining sugar. Pile the meringue on top of the fruit, then spread gently to the edges of the pastry. Using the tip of a knife peak the meringue like a hedgehog's back. Raise the oven temperature to 230°C/450°F/Gas 8, then bake the flan for 10 minutes. Switch off the heat and leave the flan in the oven for a further 10 minutes. Serves four to six.

GOOSEBERRY TARTLETTES

Canned gooseberries are easiest to use as there is no prior preparation. 350–500 g (¾–1 lb) frozen or fresh gooseberries should first be lightly poached in sweetened water. As this is very special pastry, re-roll and use the trimmings for they should not be wasted. Serve hot or cold.

One recipe (100 g (4 oz) flour etc.) Curd cheese pastry
 (p. 82)
2 × 290 g (10½ oz) cans gooseberries, drained
150 ml (¼ pint) double cream, whipped

Roll out two-thirds of the pastry and cut out circles to fit the inside of twelve to sixteen patty tins. Roll out the remaining pastry and cut out circles for lids. Press out a small hole in the centre of each lid using an apple corer or tiny cutter. Line the patty tins with the pastry, insert three or four gooseberries and put on the lids, sealing the edges. Chill. Bake in a fairly hot oven, 190°C/375°F/Gas 5, for 20–25 minutes until the pastry is pale golden. If you are serving Gooseberry tartlettes cold, pipe rosettes of cream on the peeping green gooseberries, otherwise serve separately. Makes twelve to sixteen.

HAM, PEAS AND ONION PIE

Curd pastry with its delicate crispness contrasted with the flavour of ham and peas. The top crust will brown quickly so you may have to cover it with greaseproof paper or foil for the remainder of the cooking time. You might prefer to bake this in ovenproof glass so that you can see when the pastry base is cooked. Serve hot.

> One recipe (100 g (4 oz) flour etc.) Curd cheese pastry (p. 82)
> 1 large Spanish onion, chopped
> 40 g (1½ oz) margarine
> 250 ml (8 fl oz) milk
> 25 g (1 oz) flour
> 200 g (7 oz) cooked ham, diced
> 150 g (5 oz) cooked peas
> Salt
> Pepper

Roll out half the pastry and use to line a 20 cm (8 in) flan dish. Roll out the remaining pastry to use as a lid. Chill both while preparing the filling. Fry the onion in 15 g (½ oz) of the margarine until it is transparent. Drain. Stir the milk, flour and remaining margarine in a saucepan and whisk over low heat until the sauce thickens, then continue cooking for a further 2 minutes. Remove from the heat and add the ham, peas and onion. Leave to cool. Season to taste, then pour the filling into the pastry case. Fit on the pastry lid and seal, finish and decorate as desired. Bake without glazing at 190°C/375°F/Gas 5 for 40–45 minutes or until the pastry is cooked underneath. Serves four to five.

Easy Puffy Pastry

Easy puffy pastry is just what it says. It is puffy but not puff. It is very short like short pastry, but flaky like puff pastry. It literally melts in the mouth and it is easy to make. The proportion of fat to flour is exactly the same as for puff pastry, but because of the way that it is mixed, the pastry, while retaining all its richness, does not rise very much and this is useful for pie crusts and double-crust pies. The pastry is very soft and yet manageable. It is rich, creamy and delicious. The recipe makes 450 g (1 lb) pastry and half this quantity will be required for an 18 cm (7 in) flan.

Ingredients for Basic Recipe

225 g (8 oz) plain flour
Pinch of salt
225 g (8 oz) hard margarine
2½ tablespoons water

Sieve the flour and salt into a mixing bowl. Put in the margarine in one lump and then cut it up with a round-bladed knife until the pieces are cherry size. Add the water and blend it with the flour, then knead with the fingertips. Do not try to break up the pieces of fat while blending the water into the flour. This may make it take a few extra moments, but it is a worth-while exercise and I prefer to knead for a little longer, rather than resorting to adding extra water. The dough will be rather on the sticky side, but it is quite amazing how satisfactorily it rolls out. Form the pastry into a ball and chill for about 10 minutes.

Roll out the pastry on a well-floured surface and when the pastry is about three times as long as it is wide, fold it into three. Cover with cling-film and refrigerate for 10 minutes, then with the open ends towards you, roll the pastry once more into an oblong shape. Once more give the pastry a 90° turn, roll out to an oblong shape and repeat this twice more, thus in all roll, fold, turn, roll, fold, turn, roll, fold, turn, roll, fold, turn, and chill for a short time. Then roll out to use as required. If during the rolling-out process the kitchen is very hot and the pastry begins to soften, do not hesitate to pop it into the refrigerator for a short time between operations. Bake in a fairly hot oven, 200°C/400°F/Gas 6, unless stated otherwise in the recipes.

ALMOND DISCS

This is a tea-time cake. Make a full recipe if you like, but don't store filled as the icing will soften the pastry.

Half recipe (100 g (4 oz) flour etc.) Easy puffy pastry
  (p. 88)
40 g (1½ oz) unsalted butter at room temperature
90 g (3½ oz) icing sugar, sieved
Few drops vanilla essence
3–4 teaspoons milk
25 g (1 oz) flaked almonds, toasted
Paper cases

Roll out the pastry to a thickness of approximately 6 mm (¼ in). Cut out sixteen or so circles using a 5 cm (2 in) fluted cutter. Space out on a baking tray and bake in a hot oven, 220°C/425°F/Gas 7, for 5 minutes, then reduce to 200°C/400°F/Gas 6 for a further 8–10 minutes. While the pastry is baking cream the butter and half the sugar together and flavour with vanilla essence. Leave the pastry to cool, then sandwich pairs together with the butter cream. Mix the remaining sugar and milk to a thin paste and spoon a little on top of each puff. Scatter with toasted almonds before the icing sets. Place in paper cases. Makes approximately eight.

BAKED PEACH CHEESECAKE

This has a light delicate flavour and a lovely golden shine. Serve cold.

   Half recipe (100 g (4 oz) flour etc.) Easy puffy pastry
     (p. 88)
   1 × 215 g (7½ oz) can peaches, drained and chopped
   225 g (8 oz) cottage cheese
   2 size-2 eggs, separated
   1 level teaspoon lemon rind, grated
   75 g (3 oz) caster sugar
   120 ml (4 fl oz) double cream, half whipped

Roll out the pastry thinly and use to line an 18 cm (7 in) flan ring. Reserve the trimmings. Liquidize the peaches, cheese, egg yolks, lemon rind and 50 g (2 oz) of the sugar or press through a sieve into a mixing bowl. Fold in the cream. Whisk one egg white until peaks form and fold into the mixture. Pour into the unbaked flan case. Decorate with strips of pastry trimmings to form a lattice on top. Use the remaining egg white to glaze the pastry and sprinkle the rest of the sugar over the top of the cake. Bake in a fairly hot oven, 200°C/400°F/Gas 6, for 10 minutes, then reduce the temperature to 190°C/375°F/Gas 5 and bake for a further 25 minutes until the cake is firm. Serves six.

BEEF AND MUSHROOM PIE

The flavour of the filling improves if it is cooked the day before. The excess fat can then be removed when cold.

Take care to seal the edges and avoid stretching the pastry before baking. Serve hot.

Half recipe (100 g (4 oz) flour etc.) Easy puffy pastry
    (p. 88)
15 g (½ oz) butter
1 medium onion, chopped
450 g (1 lb) minced lean beef
2 rounded tablespoons plain flour
100 g (4 oz) mushrooms, sliced
1 tablespoon tomato purée
Approximately 300 ml (½ pint) well-seasoned beef
    stock

Roll out the pastry to fit the top of a 1 litre (1½ pint) pie dish. Trim and chill both this and the pastry lid separately. Melt the butter and fry the onion until transparent. Add the meat a handful at a time, stirring briskly to prevent the meat juices from escaping. When the meat browns, stir in the flour, then the mushrooms and tomato purée. Gradually blend in the stock, bring to the boil and simmer gently for 30 minutes, adding more stock if the mixture becomes too thick. Turn the meat mixture into the pie dish. Fit on the trimmings and lid and finish as desired. Slit the top of the pie, put on a baking tray and bake in a fairly hot oven, 200°C/400°F/Gas 6, for 30 minutes or until the pastry is risen and crisp. Serves four.

PUFFY SAUSAGE AND BACON ROLLS

Buy skinless sausages and lean bacon so that the flavours can mingle. There are ten sausages in a 250 g pack, but I still reckon on eight to the half pound. Serve hot if possible.

Half recipe (100 g (4 oz) flour etc.) Easy puffy pastry
    (p. 88)

8 skinless slim sausages
4 rashers lean bacon, de-rinded and trimmed
Beaten egg for glazing

Roll out the pastry thinly to a rectangle 15 × 40 cm (6 × 16 in). Cut into eight 10 cm (3 in) wide pieces about the length of the sausages. Stretch the bacon with the back of a knife and cut into half lengthwise. Coil the bacon around the sausages. Place a sausage on one long edge of each pastry strip and roll up so that the pastry edges overlap, moistening the touching edges to seal. Cut each roll in half making sixteen tiny sausage rolls. Place on a baking tray, seams underneath and brush with beaten egg. Slash or snip the tops in one or two places with scissors. Preferably chill, then put into a hot oven, 220°C/425°F/Gas 7, for 5 minutes, then reduce to 200°C/400°F/Gas 6 and bake for a further 20 minutes or until the sausage meat is cooked and no longer pink.

Egg-white Pastry

This could be described as an all-white recipe. When the pastry is baked it has a pale and delicate colour, so do not overbake. Make this pastry for those who do not eat animal fats or for vegetarians, but not for vegans who would be unwilling to eat the egg white. The dough is soft and manageable and the texture of the pastry is delicate, crisp, light, open and airy. Because the pastry is mixed with egg white and water, you will find it much easier if you mix these two together first, then, if added liquid is required, it can be put in afterwards. Egg-white pastry is rolled out thinly and the quantity is sufficient for a 20 cm (8 in) flan.

Ingredients for Basic Recipe

100 g (4 oz) plain flour
Generous pinch of salt
75 g (3 oz) solid vegetable cooking fat
1 tablespoon cold water
1 tablespoon egg white

Sieve the flour and salt into a mixing bowl, then rub in the fat, which should be at room temperature. Mix together the water and egg white and stir in with a round-bladed knife until the mixture forms a soft manageable dough. Add a little extra water if necessary. Leave the ball of dough to rest for about 10 minutes before rolling out and chill the shaped dough before baking. Bake in a fairly hot oven, 200°C/400°F/Gas 6. The length of time will depend upon the filling. When baking blind don't overbrown if you are going to rebake this flan with a filling.

MARSHMALLOW MUNCH FLAN

This bright-looking flan will cheer up any table. I find children are especially fond of it but if your family doesn't like peppermint, substitute a teaspoon of rose water (obtainable from the chemist). Serve cold.

1½ recipes (150 g (6 oz) flour etc.) Egg-white pastry (p. 93)
24 large pink marshmallows
120 ml (4 fl oz) milk
⅛ teaspoon salt
1 teaspoon vanilla essence
4–6 drops peppermint essence
250 ml (8 fl oz) whipping cream, whipped
2 tablespoons crushed pink and white peppermint sweets

Roll out the pastry and use to line a 23 cm (9 in) loose-bottomed flan dish. Bake blind in a fairly hot oven, 200°C/400°F/Gas 6, for 10 minutes. Remove the weights and bake for a further 5–8 minutes until crisp. Leave until cold before removing from dish. Heat the marshmallows and milk in a saucepan over a low heat, stirring all the time until the marshmallows are melted. Remove from the heat and stir in the salt, vanilla and most of the peppermint essence. Taste before adding the remaining peppermint essence. If the mixture does not look pink enough, add a drop of red food colouring, but be careful that you do not end up with a vibrant pink unappetizing dish. Leave the mixture in the refrigerator, stirring occasionally until it forms a mound when dropped from a spoon. Fold the cream into the marshmallow mixture. Pour evenly into the baked pastry case and refrigerate for at least 12 hours. Just before serving sprinkle with the crushed sweets. Serves six.

CHEESE SOUFFLÉ BARQUETTES

I do hope you have some boat-shaped moulds to bake these in as they make the souffléd filling look so attractive. Do not add the egg yolks too soon to the hot sauce or they will scramble. Serve hot.

>   One recipe (100 g (4 oz) flour etc.) Egg-white pastry (p. 93)
>   15 g (½ oz) margarine
>   15 g (½ oz) flour
>   4½ tablespoons milk
>   2 size 3 eggs, separated
>   100 g (4 oz) Cheddar cheese, grated
>   ½ level teaspoon Cayenne pepper

Roll out the pastry and cut out to fit twelve patty tins or boat-shaped moulds. Place the margarine, flour and milk in a saucepan and heat gently, whisking continuously until the sauce thickens. Remove from the heat, leave to cool for a few minutes, then beat in the egg yolks and 50 g (2 oz) of cheese. Whisk the egg whites until stiff but not dry. Stir in one spoonful, then fold in the remainder. Three-quarters fill each boat with mixture and sprinkle the remaining cheese on top. Bake in a fairly hot oven, 200°C/400°F/Gas 6, for 15–20 minutes. Remove carefully from the moulds. Serves four as a starter.

CHICKEN AND VEGETABLE PIE

Yet another easy family supper dish making good use of condensed canned soup. You can get these double-strength soups in quite a few varieties and undiluted they make a really creamy sauce. Serve hot.

>   Double recipe (200 g (8 oz) flour etc.) Egg-white pastry (p. 93)
>   25 g (1 oz) butter, melted

100 g (4 oz) green beans, sliced
2 medium carrots, scraped and diced
2 celery stalks, chopped
1 large leek, white part only, sliced
1 level tablespoon flour
275 g (10 oz) cooked chicken, cubed
1 small can *or* 150 ml (5 fl oz) canned condensed celery
    soup
Beaten egg to glaze

Roll out just over half the pastry and use to line a 25 cm
(10 in) flan dish. Heat the butter and sauté the vegetables
until they are tender. Stir in the flour, then add the
chicken and mix in the soup. Roll out the remaining pastry
and cut into strips the diameter of the flan. Moisten the
ends of the strips, twist and secure to the edges of the
pastry in a cartwheel pattern. Brush the pastry with
beaten egg and bake in a moderate fairly hot oven,
200°C/400°F/Gas 6, for 25–30 minutes or until the filling is
thick and the pastry cooked. Serves four to six.

COTTAGE CHEESE AND SPINACH FLAN

It is important to sieve the cottage cheese to give a smooth
texture to set off the chunky spinach. Serve warm.

One recipe (100 g (4 oz) flour etc.) Egg-white pastry
    (p. 93)
175 g (6 oz) cottage cheese
4 size-3 eggs
150 ml (¼ pint) single cream
1 level tablespoon grated Parmesan cheese
⅛ teaspoon grated nutmeg
Pinch of salt
Pinch of pepper
175 g (6 oz) cooked spinach, drained, chopped and
    drained again

Roll out the pastry thinly and use to line a 20 cm (8 in) flan dish. Bake blind in a fairly hot oven, 200°C/400°F/Gas 6, for 10 minutes. Remove the weights. Sieve the cottage cheese and beat in the eggs, cream, Parmesan, nutmeg and season with salt and pepper. Stir in the spinach. Pour the mixture into the pastry case. Reduce the oven temperature to 180°C/350°F/Gas 4 for 30–35 minutes until the mixture is set. Serves four to six.

Flaky Pastry

Flaky pastry is often preferred to puff since it is easier to make and because it has fewer rollings and foldings it does not rise so dramatically, which makes it ideal for dishes where the filling is more important than the pastry. Since the ratio of fat to flour is only 3:4 it is cheaper to make than puff pastry. I would recommend making a larger quantity at a time, putting aside the amount needed for the recipe and freezing the rest in convenient portions for later use. It is important when rolling pastry from the freezer to allow sufficient thawing, so that the top layer is just soft to the touch, otherwise the layers will be pushed out of shape when rolling is attempted and result in an uneven rise. For best results use an equal mixture of lard and butter, but don't let this put you off if you only have one type of fat in your refrigerator or if for dietary reasons you can't eat butter. A large quantity of water is used to which a drop of lemon juice should be added. This is to make the dough more elastic so that it will stretch well when rolled.

Once the ingredients have been weighed out, each of the fats should be divided into four equal portions. Place the portions of fat in pairs next to each other. Rub pair No. 1 into the flour, adding the water and lemon juice to obtain a sticky dough. The remaining three pairs are added in flakes in three separate stages. The flakes of butter and lard should be put on to the dough alternately, so that when the pastry is cooked, there will be an even rise and more important a good even flavour. You will find that you are instructed by recipes to cover two-thirds of the dough with flakes of fat. If you have your fat pairs organized before starting out, this becomes a considerably less complicated procedure. Between each addition of fat, folding and rolling, the dough should be allowed to rest. This is so that it has time to relax after being stretched. If this is not done, once in the oven, the pastry will shrink badly. Contrary to the normal advice for rolling, after you have rolled to the oblong shape, roll the pin all the way back towards you (but not over the edge) for a really even surface.

Any trimmings should be carefully piled one above the other before being pressed down with the rolling pin and rolled. If they are just gathered into a ball the layers will be totally uneven, causing a higgledy-piggledy rise. The quantity is sufficient for a 23–25 cm (9–10 in) pie or for a 20 cm (8 in) double-crust plate pie.

Ingredients for Basic Recipe

200 g (8 oz) plain *or* strong plain flour
Pinch of salt
75 g (3 oz) butter
75 g (3 oz) lard
125 ml (¼ pint) ice-cold water (approx.)
2 teaspoons lemon juice

Sieve the flour and salt into a mixing bowl. Divide the butter into four pieces and the lard into four pieces and rub in one portion of each. Set aside the other six pieces of lard and butter, add the lemon juice to the water and pour into the flour all at once. Mix with the knife to form a soft elastic dough. You may find that you have to add a little extra water. When the mixture is in one lump, turn it on to a floured surface and knead until smooth. This will take about thirty-two kneads. Turn the pastry over and put it in the refrigerator for 10 minutes to enable it to relax. Press on the top at several places with the rolling pin to make the dough give a little before rolling it out. Roll out the dough three times as long as it is wide, keeping the corners square. Mark into three equal sections down the length of the dough. Using one portion of butter and one portion of lard, place dabs on the top two sections of the pastry to within 1 cm (½ in) of the sides to avoid it spurting out when rolled. Fold the plain section over the centre fat section and then fold the top fat section over the top of that. Press the edges with a rolling pin to seal them and keep the air in each time the pastry is folded. Square the edges with the hands. You may pat and press, but not pull the pastry, because if you stretch it, it then springs back into its bad shape when being baked. Give the dough a 90° turn so that the fold is to one side. Roll out to an oblong as before three times as long as it is wide. Mark into three again, then, using the next portion of fat (i.e. the third quarter), spread it in dabs over the top two sections of the pastry. Fold into three once more, turn 90° with the fold to one side, always of course turning the same way clockwise. Roll out a third time to three times the width and mark, then using the fourth and last quarter, put the dabs of fat on in the same way. Fold into three and roll out once again. You will now have eighty-one layers although of course you can't see them. Mark into three again, seal the edges with the rolling pin once more and put to relax in the refrigerator wrapped in greaseproof paper or covered in cling-film for a minimum of 30 minutes. As a check, it is roll, dab, fold, seal, turn, roll, dab, fold, seal, turn, roll, dab, fold, roll, mark, seal, wrap and refrigerate. Bake the pastry in a very hot oven, 230°C/450°F/Gas 8, and reduce the temperature to 225°C/425°F/Gas 7 as soon as the pastry is set. Reduce the temperature further if there is a filling that requires a lower temperature.

BLACKCURRANT JALOUSIE

A jalousie is a slatted cake made with any flaky or puff pastry. If you decide to use an egg glaze be careful not to get any in the cut-outs or the pastry will not rise properly. Please use the fruitiest preserve you can obtain as this is the important sole ingredient. Serve warm with cream.

> One recipe (200 g (8 oz) flour etc.) Flaky pastry (p. 99)
> 3 generous tablespoons blackcurrant preserve
> Beaten egg to glaze

Divide the pastry in two and roll out each piece to a rectangle 36 × 20 cm (14 × 8 in). Fold one piece in half lengthwise and make cuts through the double thickness at regular intervals to within 2.5 cm (1 in) of the open-ended border and 4 cm (1½ in) from the short ends. Open the pastry out to reveal a slatted appearance. Put the plain pastry on a baking tray and spread with jam leaving a 2.5 cm (1 in) border. Moisten these edges with water, then put the slatted lid on top. Press the edges to seal and trim with a sharp knife as this helps the pastry to rise evenly. Chill until firm. Brush with beaten egg. Bake in a very hot oven, 230°C/450°F/Gas 8, for 15 minutes, then reduce to 200°C/400°F/Gas 6 for 15–20 minutes until the pastry is crisp and brown. Serves six.

ECCLES CAKES

Eccles and Banbury cakes are the same except that Eccles are round and Banbury are oval. They are most exciting to make because, although rolled almost flat until the filling pokes through, the pastry puffs up when baked to form a delicious fruit sandwich. Home-made Eccles cakes are far superior to those old bits of shoe-leather you buy in the shops.

One recipe (200 g (8 oz) flour etc.) Flaky pastry (p. 99)
25 g (1 oz) butter *or* margarine
15 g (½ oz) caster sugar
75 g (3 oz) currants
25 g (1 oz) chopped mixed peel
¼ teaspoon mixed spice
¼ teaspoon grated nutmeg

Roll out the pastry to a thickness of 3 mm (⅛ in) and cut out 10 cm (4 in) circles. Beat the butter and sugar together until light and creamy, then stir in the currants, peel and the spices. Put a generous teaspoon of the mixture in the centre of each circle and damp the edges. Gather the edges together in a dolly-bag fashion and press firmly to seal, then reverse the cakes and shape them into a round about 1 cm (½ in) thick or until the fruit just begins to show through. Slash the top of the pastry twice across the top, then brush with water and sprinkle with caster sugar. Place spread out on a baking sheet and bake in a hot oven, 225°C/425°F/Gas 7, for about 20 minutes until the pastry is crisp and golden. The recipe makes about fifteen cakes including the re-rolled trimmings.

FILET DE BOEUF EN CROÛTE

Outrageously expensive and definitely a dinner party dish. The classic French recipe is long and complicated and takes hours to prepare, unlike this recipe which is quick and easy yet deliciously mouthwatering. This means that you will have plenty of energy to enjoy the evening with your guests. Make the pastry the day before and store in the refrigerator. Serve hot.

1½ recipes (300 g (12 oz) flour etc.) Flaky pastry (p. 99)
40 g (1½ oz) unsalted butter
1.75 kg (4 lb) fillet of beef

Salt
Pepper
1 size-1 egg, separated
2 teaspoons single cream
175 g (6 oz) pâté de fois gras with truffles

Heat the butter in a frying pan until sizzling and seal the meat on all sides over a fierce heat. Remove from the pan, season with salt and pepper and leave until completely cold. Unless the meat is completely cold when put in the pastry, you won't achieve a nice crisp finish. Roll out the pastry into a rectangle three times as wide and slightly longer than the meat. Cut off the edges with a sharp knife and reserve the scraps for decorations. Whisk the egg white gently with a fork and brush over the rectangle of pastry until completely covered. Cut the pâté into very thin slices and place evenly over the centre of the pastry to the same size as the meat. The pâté cannot be spread because it would pull the pastry out of shape. Place the meat over the pâté. Fold the left-hand side of the pastry over the meat until two-thirds of the meat is covered. Then fold the right-hand side so that it overlaps the left and seal with egg white. Fold the pastry flaps at either end to make a neat rectangle and again seal with egg white. Turn the parcel on to a greased baking sheet so that the folds are underneath. Carefully reroll the trimmings remembering to keep the layers even and, using a sharp knife, cut out three or four shapes to decorate the top of the meat. Dab these with egg white and carefully place them along the top of the pastry. Then make two small holes in the top. Insert into these small pieces of paper shaped like cigarettes to form chimneys through which the steam can escape during cooking. Cover the parcel with a cloth and leave to rest for an hour in the refrigerator. Mix the egg yolk with a little cream and use to glaze the parcel. Bake in a fairly hot oven, 200°C/400°F/Gas 6, for 25

minutes, then reduce the temperature to 110°C/225°F/
Gas ¼ for a further 20 minutes. Serve on a spiked carving
dish so that when you try to carve it the whole lot will not
slide off on to the floor. Serves eight to ten.

WHISKY PÂTÉ ROLL

A whisky-flavoured pork pâté wrapped in a flaky case.
Best served hot but also pleasant warm.

One recipe (200 g (8 oz) flour etc.) Flaky pastry (p. 99)
225 g (8 oz) belly of pork, trimmed and chopped
1 medium onion chopped
25 g (1 oz) butter
2 tablespoons whisky
Salt
Pepper
Beaten egg to glaze

Fry the pork and onion in the butter until the meat is light
brown. Add the whisky and blend in the liquidizer for a
few seconds only to a rough texture. Roll out the pastry to
a rectangle approximately 30 × 40 cm (12 × 16 in).
Season the pâté with salt and pepper and shape into a
large sausage to fit the centre of the pastry, leaving a 5 cm
(2 in) border at either short end. Brush the uncovered
pastry with egg and wrap up over the meat, pressing the
overlapping edges to seal in the meat. Brush all over with
beaten egg, then put, seam underneath, on to a greased
baking sheet. Chill for ½ hour. Bake in a very hot oven,
230°C/450°F/Gas 8, for 15 minutes, then reduce to
200°C/400°F/Gas 6 for a further 35–40 minutes until the
pastry is crisp and golden and the filling is cooked. Serves
four to six.

Heart Watchers' Pastry

Dietary regimes come and go and you must take advice on the current thinking from your doctor. Over the last few years, controversy has raged on whether or not a diet high in polyunsaturated fats and devoid of animal fats will help to avert heart attacks, hardening of the arteries and strokes. Be that as it may, it is reasonable to be cautious if you are a likely sufferer. In this book there are two types of pastry suitable for the cholesterol watcher, which are also delicious for the whole family. (However, remember that all pastry is high in calories, so only a small portion, please, if the problem is also one of obesity.) One is vegetable oil pastry and this follows later. The other is heart watchers' pastry which is made by rubbing the margarine into the flour and mixing with chilled skimmed milk, rather than water. Do not add salt to the dough and use a mixture of plain and self-raising flour. This dough is like a puffy shortcrust pastry. It is a real sunshine golden colour and has a crisp spongy crumb. If the pastry breaks up when you lift it into a flan ring, don't worry, just push the pieces together and as the margarine is soft and evenly distributed through the pastry, provided it is chilled before baking no one will be the wiser. There is enough pastry in this recipe for two 15 cm (6 in) or one 20 cm (8 in) flan.

Ingredients for Basic Recipe

75 g (3 oz) plain flour
125 g (5 oz) self-raising flour
100 g (4 oz) polyunsaturated soft margarine
3 tablespoons cold skimmed milk

Sieve the flour together into a mixing bowl. Add the
margarine and mix in with a fork, first cutting up with the
side, then blending with the prongs. When the mixture is
even, which looks more like flakes than crumbs, add the
milk all at once and mix to a soft dough. Gather into a ball
with lightly floured hands, wrap in cling-film, and refrigerate for 15–30 minutes until firm, then roll out and use in
the usual way. Bake in a fairly hot oven, 200°C/400°F/Gas
6, unless otherwise stated.

CHICKEN AND SWEETCORN PIE

Chicken, provided it has been skinned, is low in
cholesterol and in this recipe it is combined with a single
slice of very lean ham and sweetcorn to make a charming
supper dish made with heart watchers' pastry. These are
small portions, so serve hot with peas, beans and carrots.

>One recipe (200 g (8 oz) mixed flour etc.) Heart watch-
>   ers' pastry (p. 105)
>2 chicken quarters, cooked, skinned and diced
>1 onion, finely chopped
>2 rounded tablespoons sweetcorn
>1 slice lean ham, finely chopped
>Pepper
>1 egg white
>Skimmed milk

Roll out half the pastry to the thickness of a 10 pence
piece. Cut four rounds or rectangles to fit bases of
individual pie dishes. Foil dishes are very suitable for this.
Put the dishes in the refrigerator and also put the remaining dough in a polythene bag and refrigerate. Mix the
diced chicken, onion, sweetcorn and ham together and
season with pepper. Bind with the egg white. Remove the
pastry from the refrigerator and fill the lined dishes with
the mixture. Roll out the remaining pastry dough and use

to cut out lids. Damp the edges of the pie bases and place the pastry lids over the filling, sealing well. Mark round the edges of the pastry with a fork and knock up the edges with a sharp knife. Brush the pastry with skimmed milk and put the dishes on a baking tray and bake in a fairly hot oven, 200°C/400°F/Gas 6, for 30–35 minutes until the pastry is slightly brown. These pies may be stored in the freezer before baking. It will then be necessary to allow an extra 15 minutes' cooking time in the pre-heated oven. Serves four.

JAM AND FRUIT TARTS

Weight-watchers won't be doing themselves much good with these, but anyone unable to eat egg yolks or cream will certainly enjoy them.

> One recipe (200 g (8 oz) mixed flour etc.) Heart watchers' pastry (p. 105)
> Raspberry and strawberry jam
> 30 raspberries
> 10 strawberries
> 15–20 small patty tins or foil dishes set on a baking tray
> *Glaze* (optional)
> Arrowroot
> Polyunsaturated soft margarine

Roll out the pastry to the thickness of a 10 pence piece on a floured surface. Using a cutter or upturned wine glass, cut circles 6 mm (¼ in) wider than the tops of the patty tins and ease carefully into the tins. To do this, push in gently from the outer edges, then using a small ball of uncooked dough, dab into the bases against the corner. Put a rounded teaspoon of jam into each tart case, making sure that the jam only reaches about one-third of the way up. If there is too much jam, it will boil over during baking. Bake the tarts in a fairly hot oven,

200°C/400°F/Gas 6, for 20–25 minutes until the pastry is nicely coloured. Remove from the tins at once. An easy way to do this is to slip a grapefruit knife round the edges and underneath the pastry and lift the tarts carefully on to a cooling wire. If the patties are large they will not balance on the knife, so use a tablespoon as well. The jam will be very hot and liable to burn the fingers. Decorate the tarts with fresh or thawed and well-drained raspberries and strawberries. For a final and professional finish make a glaze with arrowroot and fruit juice, in a proportion of 1½ level teaspoons of arrowroot to 150 ml (¼ pint) juice. Blend the arrowroot with the cold liquid and bring to the boil, stirring all the time until the glaze clears. Remove from the heat and add a tiny knob of polyunsaturated margarine, then spoon a little of the glaze over each tart. This is only feasible if you have used frozen or canned fruit, since you would have to make up a special glaze, using other fruit juices if you use fresh fruit.

STEAK AND ONION PIE

Polyunsaturated margarine melts rapidly as it has not been hardened in manufacture, so you will find it hot enough to seal the meat almost immediately. I use cheap frying steak rather than the traditional chuck, because it is so much leaner. It is not as expensive as it seems when you consider how much trimming stewing steak requires. Serve hot.

One recipe (200 g (8 oz) mixed flour etc.) Heart watchers' pastry (p. 105)
275 g (10 oz) lean frying steak
15 g (½ oz) polyunsaturated margarine
1 large onion, chopped
1 rounded tablespoon flour
450 ml (¾ pint) rich beef stock

1 tablespoon soy sauce
⅛ teaspoon celery salt
1 bay leaf
¼ teaspoon pepper
Salt
1 rounded tablespoon lentils, thoroughly rinsed
Beaten egg to glaze

Trim the meat of every vestige of fat and cut into small dice. Melt the margarine and fry the meat, adding a few pieces at a time and stirring briskly until sealed. Add the onion, frying until it is translucent and the meat browns. Stir in the flour and gradually add the stock, soy sauce, celery salt, bay leaf, pepper and lentils. Bring to the boil, then lower the heat and simmer covered with a well-fitting lid for 50–60 minutes or until the meat is tender. Add more boiling water during cooking if the sauce becomes too thick. You could carry out the whole operation in the pressure cooker in about 30 minutes, but you would need to use more stock. Remove the bay leaf and add salt if required. Transfer the meat to a deep pie dish using a slotted spoon. Pour over enough of the sauce to just cover. Reserve the remainder. Roll out the pastry and fit on to the pie dish and dampen the edges before sealing. Trim, finish and decorate as desired. Brush the top of the pastry with beaten egg and bake in a fairly hot oven, 200°C/400°F/Gas 6, for 15 minutes, then slash the top and continue cooking for 15–20 minutes or until the pastry is crisp and brown. Liquidize the reserved sauce, then reheat and serve separately. Serves four.

Herb and Spiced Pastry

Herb and spiced pastry adds that extra something to make dishes even more special. Ground spices such as nutmeg, allspice and cinnamon are delightful with sweet fillings, while coriander or cardamom go well with oriental fillings. A pinch of dry English mustard can add zing to bland fish, cheese or custard fillings. The amount of spice needed depends on their strength of flavour so you would put in less cloves than nutmeg and less Cayenne than paprika.

As far as the herbs are concerned, it is much better to use fresh than dried, but if you have no choice, put the dried herbs into cold water, bring to the boil, then cool down and chill before using – the herbs are thus added with the water. This gives them a chance to soften, otherwise they would be like hard crispy specks in the pastry. As you can see, I am not very happy with dried herbs, although I know that they are convenient, because if they are left in the larder for too long, they lose their potency and become dry and uninteresting. Use a quarter the amount of dried herbs to fresh herbs. Fresh herbs should be chopped finely and added to the dry ingredients. Don't leave the pieces too large or they will become crispy if they happen to be on the outside of the pastry. Fresh parsley is nearly always available, and many of the other herbs can be bought in supermarkets either freshly cut ready for you to freeze yourself or deep frozen and ready to use. Since these are fresh herbs that have been frozen, they retain all their natural flavour and moisture. Stir in frozen herbs while still frozen or allow them to defrost on a piece of kitchen paper, so that the surplus moisture can be removed. This will also help to blend them evenly through the pastry.

Once you have mastered the art of making shortcrust pastry you should have no trouble at all making herb and spiced pastry and you will find it great fun, since you can vary the flavours to suit yourself. The recipe is sufficient for an 18 cm (7 in) flan or twelve to sixteen tartlets.

Ingredients for Basic Recipe

150 g (6 oz) plain flour
50 g (2 oz) lard
35 g (1½ oz) margarine
Pinch of salt
Herbs *or* spices
1½–2 tablespoons cold water

(If using fresh herbs 2 level teaspoons will be required, finely chopped. If using dried herbs ½ teaspoon is required. For spiced pastry use ½ level teaspoon strong spice or 1 rounded teaspoon gentle spice, sieved with the flour.)

Sieve the flour and salt and spice, if used, into a mixing bowl, add the lard and margarine. Cut up the fat with a round-bladed knife into five or six pieces, then rub in finely. Stir in the herbs, add the water, then mix to a dough with the knife, using a cutting and stirring motion. When the mixture clings together, leaving the sides of the bowl clean, knead lightly into a ball with the fingertips. Turn on to a floured surface, then cover with the upturned bowl and leave to rest while preparing the filling. Press the pastry into shape with a rolling pin before rolling out and if possible chill the shaped pastry before baking. Unless otherwise instructed bake in the centre of a fairly hot oven, 200°C/400°F/Gas 6, for 15–20 minutes, then reduce the heat according to the filling.

LAMB AND ROSEMARY FLAN

What can you do with left-over lamb looking sad and grey? Use it up this way with plenty of fresh herbs. Serve hot or cold.

One recipe (150 g (6 oz) flour etc.) Herb and spiced pastry (p. 111) (including 2 level teaspoons freshly chopped rosemary leaves and 2 teaspoons fresh thyme)
275 g (10 oz) cooked lamb, cut into tiny dice
2 tomatoes, peeled and sliced
75 g (3 oz) cooked sweetcorn kernels
2 size-3 eggs
150 ml (¼ pint) milk
2 generous teaspoons fresh rosemary leaves
1 level teaspoon salt
1 small shallot, finely chopped

Roll out the pastry and use to line an 18 cm (7 in) plain flan ring. Bake blind in a fairly hot oven, 200°C/400°F/Gas 6, for 15 minutes. Remove the weights and reduce the temperature to 190°C/375°F/Gas 5. Spread the lamb in the pastry case, cover with tomato slices and the sweetcorn. Beat the eggs, milk, rosemary leaves and salt together and pour over the top. Bake for 40–45 minutes until golden brown. Garnish with the shallot. Serves six.

ROAST CHICKEN AND PEANUT TARTLETS

These high protein tartlets make use of left-over chicken from Sunday lunch. Serve them at 'high tea-time'. Should your family dislike yogurt you could substitute soured cream or sieved cottage cheese. Single cream will be too thin. Serve cold.

One recipe (150 g (6 oz) flour etc.) Herb and spiced pastry (p. 111) (including 1 tablespoon freshly chopped herbs)

175 g (6 oz) cooked chicken, diced
25 g (1 oz) dry roast peanuts, roughly chopped
4 tablespoons salad cream
4 tablespoons natural yogurt
White pepper
2 tablespoons chopped red and green peppers to garnish

Roll out the pastry and cut out circles to fit twelve to sixteen patty tins. Ease the pastry into the tins, prick thoroughly and bake blind in a fairly hot oven, 200°C/400°F/Gas 6, for 15 minutes. Remove the weights and cook for a further 3–4 minutes to dry out the bases. Remove the patty cases to a wire rack to cool. Combine the chicken and peanuts, mix with the salad cream and yogurt, adding an extra shake of pepper. Spoon into the pastry cases and garnish with the chopped peppers.

SPICY TREACLE TART

A classic British dessert which is simple to mix but, unless you are careful in measuring the ingredients, either turns out too stodgy or too tinny. Pour the syrup into a warmed measuring jug rather than messing about with table-spoons. If you prefer a latticed flan use a 15 cm (6 in) tin and then you will have some trimmings left for decoration.

One recipe (150 g (6 oz) flour etc.) Herb and spiced
  pastry (p. 111) (including 1 rounded teaspoon mixed
  spice)
100 ml (4 fl oz) golden syrup
50 g (2 oz) fresh breadcrumbs
Grated rind and juice of ½ lemon
¼ teaspoon ground ginger

Roll out the pastry and use to line an 18 cm (7 in) flan ring. Mix together the remaining ingredients (remember that the ginger goes into the filling and not the pastry). Put into the pastry case and bake in the centre of a fairly hot oven, 200°C/400°F/Gas 6, for 25–30 minutes. The filling rises during baking but settles back on cooling. Serves four to five.

TARTE À L'ORANGE

A dessert to grace the sweet trolley. The recipe consists of a baked pastry case, filled with an enriched and flavoured custard and topped with syrupy orange slices.

1½ recipes (225 g (9 oz) flour etc.) Herb and spiced pastry (p. 111) (including ¾ level teaspoon powdered cloves)

Filling
100 g (4 oz) caster sugar
3 egg yolks
20 g (¾ oz) farina (*or* flour if you can't obtain it)
250 ml (8 fl oz) milk
¼ teaspoon vanilla essence
50 g (2 oz) ground almonds
Pinch of salt
1 tablespoon Cointreau
Very finely grated rind of 1 orange
2 tablespoons whipping cream, whipped

Topping
4 medium oranges
100 g (4 oz) granulated sugar
1 tablespoon Cointreau

Roll out the pastry and use to line a 28 cm (11 in) fluted flan dish. Bake blind in a fairly hot oven, 200°C/400°F/Gas 6, for 15 minutes. Remove the weights and bake for a further 5 minutes or until the pastry base is brown. Remove from the oven and leave to cool. Take the pastry out of the dish before filling, as it will be too heavy to remove afterwards. While the pastry is baking, prepare the filling. Beat the sugar and egg yolks until thick and the colour of pale straw. Fold in the farina. In a medium saucepan bring the milk and vanilla essence to just under boiling point. Pour on to the mixture and stir gently. Add the almonds and salt. Return the mixture to the saucepan and bring back to the boil over a gentle heat, whisking continuously. Cool for 1 more minute. Add the Cointreau and orange rind. Leave to cool, stirring occasionally to avoid lumps forming. Fold in the cream. In the meantime prepare the topping. Cut the unpeeled oranges into the thinnest possible slices, naturally removing the pips. Put the sugar in a saucepan with the Cointreau and heat gently, stirring until the sugar dissolves. This will take a long time as no extra liquid is added. When the syrup is clear add the orange slices and poach gently for 15 minutes. Remove with a slotted spoon and spread out on a non-stick paper. Leave until cold. To assemble spread the filling in the pastry case and arrange the orange slices in overlapping circles on top. Serves eight to ten.

Hot Water Crust Pastry

A glossy raised pie is often so appetizing to look at, but when a slice is cut it can be very disappointing, the pastry being hard and almost inedible. These pies were popular in Victorian times, often eaten after the hunt with game fillings. Many of the crusts were not intended to be eaten, but were just casings in which terrines were baked, but you should be able to eat them for the most part and it very much depends on how you make them as to whether they are soft and palatable or hard, chewy and leaden. The pastry is often considered to be indigestible, but that is really due to faulty preparation which results in a heavy soggy pastry. Prepared properly the pastry will remain crisp. The dough should be fairly stiff, so that it can be moulded over jars or into tins. This should be done by hand while it is still warm, but if the dough is too soft remedy this by setting it aside for a few minutes to cool down. As it cools the fat will begin to solidify and therefore the pastry will become stiffer.

Hot water crust pastry is made by heating the fat and water to boiling point and when it is added to the flour, the starch grains burst immediately and absorb the fat and the liquid. The quicker the liquid is added, the better the result. If you find that the dough is too stiff to handle, you can add more liquid, but this must be at boiling point. Although dishes made with hot water crust pastry should go into a hot oven, reduce the temperature to moderate as soon as the crust is set to ensure that the pastry will be thoroughly cooked on the inside. A hole or sizeable slit must be made in the top of the pastry to allow the steam that has accumulated in the filling to escape. Otherwise the pastry inside will have no chance of drying out and the result will be a stodgy thick crust. One way of overcoming this is to make a cigarette shape from a piece of paper and insert it into the hole. Then the steam escaping reaches well above the top of the pie, without settling on it and causing it to become damp. If you find that the pastry cracks while you are moulding it, this is due to the fat becoming set too quickly, either because the liquid wasn't at boiling point when mixed into the flour or because the pastry was set aside for too long before shaping. If this was the case the pastry could be put in a covered basin and placed over a pan of hot water for a very short time, but of course the water must not touch the bowl and must not be boiling, otherwise the pastry will start cooking and you would have to throw it away. Use milk or water to make hot water crust pastry, but the best fat to use is lard.

Raised pies must be glazed and decorated beautifully. Use beaten egg yolk and milk or cream, mixed with a touch of salt for a high brown gloss and make pastry leaves from the trimmings. After glazing the pie, attach them to the glaze, brushing them generously with the egg mixture. This recipe is enough for a 450 g (1 lb) jam jar.

Ingredients for Basic Recipe

275 g (10 oz) plain flour
½ teaspoon salt
75 g (3 oz) lard
150 ml (¼ pint) water

Sieve the flour and salt into a warmed bowl and make a well in the centre, then put the bowl in a warm place. Heat the fat and water together but do not let it boil until the fat has completely melted, because if the water boils before the fat is melted, some of it will evaporate and the proportions will be spoilt. Quickly pour the boiling liquid

into the flour, mixing briskly and thoroughly with a
wooden spoon. As soon as the mixture becomes cool
enough to handle, knead with the hands to a smooth
dough. Put in a warm bowl and cover with a hot wet cloth
so that the pastry remains manageable without drying
out. Mould or shape according to the recipe and bake in a
hot oven, 220°C/425°F/Gas 7, reducing the heat to
180°C/350°F/Gas 4 as soon as the pastry crust has set.
Continue cooking according to the directions in the
recipe.

CHICKEN AND BACON PIE

Some people achieve better shapes when moulding over
jars. In this recipe the dough is moulded inside the tin and
I think this is the easier way. Serve cold.

> One recipe (275 g (10 oz) flour etc.) Hot water crust
>   pastry (p. 117)
> 275 g (10 oz) raw boned chicken
> 175 g (6 oz) back bacon, derinded
> Salt
> Pepper
> 1 tablespoon freshly chopped parsley
> 150 ml (¼ pint) home-made chicken stock
> 1 level teaspoon powdered gelatine
> 1–2 beaten eggs and pinch of salt to glaze

Grease a 13–15 cm (5–6 in) loose-bottomed cake tin. Cut
out one-third of the dough and roll out to a circle slightly
larger than the top of the tin. Cover with a warm damp
cloth. Roll out the remaining dough to a round about
23 cm (9 in) in diameter. Fold into four to make it easier
to fit into the tin. Using the knuckles and backs of the
fingers press the dough into the corners of the base,
gradually working up the sides until it protrudes 1 cm
(½ in) above the tin. Maintain a uniform thickness with-

out stretching the pastry if you can. Chop the chicken and bacon finely, season with salt and pepper and mix in the parsley and two tablespoons of the stock. Turn into the pastry case, spreading the mixture evenly. Moisten the edge of the mould, fix on the lid and flute the doubled edges together. Trim with scissors. Roll out the trimmings and use to make pastry leaves. Brush the top of the pie with beaten egg and salt and make a small hole in the centre. Decorate with the pastry leaves around the hole and brush again with the egg. Put on a baking tray and bake in a hot oven, 220°C/425°F/Gas 7, for 15 minutes, then reduce to 180°C/350°F/Gas 4. Bake for 15 minutes, then remove the sides of the tin, leaving the pie on the base. To do this carefully balance the tin on a jam jar and gently ease the sides of the tin down. Brush the sides of the pie with beaten egg and continue baking at 180°C/350°F/Gas 4 for 30 minutes. Remove from the oven and leave to cool. Heat the remaining stock and dissolve the gelatine and gradually pour into the pie through the hole. If your hand is unsteady use a funnel or cone made out of card. Leave to set. Serves four.

GAMMON AND APPLE PIE

The pastry will be fairly thin on this soft-centre pie. Serve hot or cold with a glass of cider.

One recipe (275 g (10 oz) flour etc.) Hot water crust pastry (p. 117)
25 g (1 oz) butter
350 g (¾ lb) dessert apples, peeled, cored and sliced
1 small onion, sliced
Pinch of ground cloves
⅛ teaspoon sugar
¼ teaspoon pepper
450 g (1 lb) gammon, skinned and diced

25 g (1 oz) mixed chopped nuts
Beaten egg to glaze

First prepare the filling. Melt the butter and stir in the apples. Add the onion, cloves, sugar, pepper and bacon and cook gently for 10 minutes while preparing the pastry. Grease the inside of a 15 cm (6 in) square loose-bottomed tin. Shape two-thirds of the pastry into a square and fit into the tin, coaxing the dough evenly into the corners and up the sides until it reaches just beyond the top of the tin. Roll out the remaining pastry to form a lid. Turn the filling into the pastry case, moisten the edges of the dough and fit the lid on top. Fold the protruding pastry over the lid and press around the edges with the prongs of a fork to seal and decorate. Brush with beaten egg and pierce a hole in the centre. Put the tin on a baking tray and bake in a hot oven, 220°C/425°F/Gas 7, for 25 minutes. Remove the sides of the cake tin and brush the top and sides of the pie with beaten egg. Sprinkle the lid with the chopped nuts. Reduce the oven temperature to 180°C/350°F/Gas 4 and bake for 35–40 minutes, covering the pie with foil if the pastry becomes too brown. Serves four to six.

PICNIC PIELETS

A quick, easy filling for individual pies suitable for a picnic or a summer supper on the patio. You will need four foil 8 cm (3 in) diameter dishes but you can use patty tins if you like although these come up rather small.

One recipe (275 g (10 oz) flour etc.) Hot water crust pastry (p. 117)
450 g (1 lb) sausage meat
¼ teaspoon dried herbes de Provence
Salt
Pepper
Beaten egg to glaze

Roll out three-quarters of the pastry and use to line four greased individual dishes. Ease the pastry into the dishes so that it protrudes just above the edges. Brush with water. Mix the sausage meat, dried herbs and a shake of salt and pepper together and divide between the pastry cases. Divide the remaining pastry into four, shape into balls and flatten with the hands to make lids. Fit on to the pies and press the edges together to seal well. Trim with scissors. Brush the surface with beaten egg. Put on a baking tray and bake in a hot oven, 220°C/425°F/Gas 7, for 10 minutes, reducing to 190°C/375°F/Gas 5 for a further 35–40 minutes to cook the sausage meat. Serves four.

SMALL MEAT PIES

Use small preserves jars or straight-sided drinking glasses to mould the pastry, or vinegar bottles with suitably shaped base and sides. Serve cold.

> One recipe (275 g (10 oz) flour etc.) Hot water crust pastry (p. 117)
> 200 g (8 oz) minced raw pork, beef, veal *or* ham *or* a mixture of these
> 1 small onion, chopped
> 2 leaves sage, chopped *or* a pinch of dried sage
> Salt
> Pepper
> 150 ml (¼ pint) good beef stock
> 1 level teaspoon gelatine
> Beaten egg to glaze

First prepare the filling by mixing the meat, onion and herbs together and season with salt and pepper. Divide the pastry into four. Remove a quarter of each piece for the lids and cover with a warm damp cloth. Flour the outside of the glasses, shape the pieces of dough in a round a little wider than the base and press over the upturned glasses, working the pastry evenly up the sides to a height of 5 cm (2 in). Prepare double thickness strips of greaseproof paper 1 cm (½ in) taller than the pastry and grease one side. Wrap these collars tightly around the pastry with the greased side against the dough. Turn on to a greased baking tray. Using a twisting motion remove the glasses. Pack the pies with the filling. Shape the reserved pastry into lids, brush the edges with beaten egg and press into the pies. Seal well, fluting the doubled edges together. Brush the tops with the egg and make a hole in the centre. Roll out the trimmings to make pastry leaves. Bake in a hot oven, 220°C/425°F/Gas 7, for 15 minutes, then remove the paper collars and brush the sides of the pies with egg. Reduce the oven temperature to 180°C/350°F/Gas 4 and bake for a further 25–30 minutes. Leave to cool. Heat the stock and dissolve the gelatine and pour into the pies through the central hole. Makes four.

Low Fat Pastry

Strictly speaking it is not possible to make pastry without any fat at all, but for those on special diets it may be preferable to vary the menus by the use of some sort of crust. In this recipe a raising agent is used to puff up the flour and dried skimmed milk gives an added richness. In imperial terms, 2 oz of the dried granules mixed with 1 pint water makes the equivalent of 1 pint milk. In this pastry the milk solids become much more concentrated, since only a few tablespoons of water are added. The pastry, though sticky, is easy to roll out on a well-floured surface and needs no dampening to make the edges adhere so that it does not shrink. You will require a sharp knife to loosen the edges of the pastry crust when serving and because this is a chewy pastry, it should be eaten with a knife or spoon and fork. The flavour is delicate and although the pastry should not be compared to the conventional types, in many ways, because it is less rich, it is more appealing. However, it is much better eaten hot than cold. The given quantity is sufficient for an 18 cm (7 in) dish.

Ingredients for Basic Recipe

   100 g (4 oz) plain flour
   1 rounded teaspoon baking powder, preferably golden
   50 g (2 oz) skimmed low fat milk granules
   6 tablespoons cold water

Combine the flour, baking powder and milk granules in a mixing bowl, stirring thoroughly to blend evenly. Add the water and mix with a round-bladed knife to form a soft sticky dough. Turn on to a well-floured surface and knead briefly, then roll out to a thickness of 6 mm (¼ in). The pastry should be baked in a pre-heated fairly hot oven, 200°C/400°F/Gas 6. After the first 15 minutes, the outer crust of the pastry will brown rapidly and this is no indication of the pastry being cooked through. As soon as browning occurs, reduce the oven temperature to 190°C/375°F/Gas 5 for the remaining cooking time, which will vary according to the filling.

COD PACS

I can't wax lyrical about these, but suffice it to say that they are suitable for the dieter and the tomato sauce and marjoram bring them to life. Cod pacs look attractive served on a dish with Julienne strips of carrot and red pepper, which you could poach in grease-free stock. Serve hot.

One recipe (100 g (4 oz) flour etc.) Low fat pastry (p. 123)
2 × 90 g (2½ oz) cod steaks, thawed
2 tablespoons tomato ketchup
½ teaspoon dried marjoram
Salt
Pepper
25 g (1 oz) low fat spread
Beaten egg to glaze

Divide the pastry into two and roll out each piece to a rectangle large enough to enclose one fish steak. Place a steak in the centre of each pastry piece and spread with tomato ketchup. Sprinkle with marjoram, salt and pepper and dot with low fat spread. Moisten the edges of the pastry and wrap up the fish securely. Brush all over with beaten egg, or milk if eggs are off the menu too, and bake on a lightly greased or non-stick baking tray in a fairly hot oven, 200°C/400°F/Gas 6, for 15 minutes, then reduce to 190°C/375°F/Gas 5 for 25–30 minutes until the pastry is cooked. Serves two.

GRAPEFRUIT AND CHERRY FLAN

The flan has an attractive appearance, the yellow grapefruit and the red cherries peeping through the lattice, but treat the pastry gently as the strips are liable to crack. Serve hot or cold.

One recipe (100 g (4 oz) flour etc.) Low fat pastry (p. 123)
2 large grapefruit
10 glacé cherries
2–3 tablespoons sugar

Roll out the pastry and use to line an 18 cm (7 in) greased flan dish, reserving the trimmings. Bake blind in a fairly hot oven, 200°C/400°F/Gas 6, for 15 minutes or until the pastry is firm. Remove the weights. While the flan is cooking, roll out the trimmings and cut into thin strips the diameter of the tin. Halve the grapefruit, remove the segments and cut the cherries into quarters. Spread the grapefruit and cherries in the flan case and arrange the pastry strips in a lattice on top. Brush with any remaining grapefruit juice and sprinkle with sugar. Reduce the oven temperature to 190°C/375°F/Gas 5 for 30–35 minutes until the lattice is cooked. Serves four.

LAMB CURRY PIE

Some recipes cannot be played about with, but curries have the advantage that substitutions produce not an inferior but just a different result. Use a mixture of coriander, cumin or ground cardamom, some turmeric or a pinch of dill compound powder and if you prefer a less sweet curry, use some well-blotted lime pickle instead of the mango chutney. Serve hot.

> 1 recipe (100 g (4 oz) flour etc.) Low fat pastry (p. 123)
> 450 g (1 lb) boned leg of lamb, and well trimmed
> 1 level tablespoon curry powder ⎱
> 2 level teaspoons cornflour ⎰ mixed together
> 1 × 198 g (7 oz) can tomatoes
> 1 level tablespoon mango chutney
> 1 × 275 g (10 oz) can condensed beef consommé
> ½ level teaspoon salt
> 1 really large Spanish onion, chopped
> 1 large potato, peeled and cubed

Cut the meat into 2.5 cm (1 in) cubes and toss in the cornflour mixture until well coated. Use a large plastic bag for this. Turn into a deep narrow casserole dish and stir in the other ingredients. Cover and cook in a moderate oven, 180°C/350°F/Gas 4, for about 1½ hours, adding more liquid if required. The gravy should be of a pouring consistency but not in great quantity. Raise the oven temperature to 200°C/400°F/Gas 6. Roll out the pastry to form a lid approximately the size of the top of the casserole. Quickly cover the dish with the pastry and press the edges to seal. Bake in the centre of the oven for 15 minutes, reducing again to 180°C/350°F/Gas 4 for a further 10 minutes so that the pastry is cooked through. Serves five or six.

RAISIN AND CHEESE TART

Chop the raisins with a floured knife to prevent sticking. If a low fat diet is not vital add two egg yolks when mixing the cheese. Serve hot or warm.

> One recipe (100 g (4 oz) flour etc.) Low fat pastry (p. 123)

350 g (12 oz) cottage cheese, sieved
½ teaspoon vanilla essence
1 rounded tablespoon sugar
1 level teaspoon ground nutmeg
Pinch of salt
50 g (2 oz) seedless raisins, chopped
2 egg whites
1 generous tablespoon apricot jam

Roll out the pastry and use to line a lightly greased 18 cm (7 in) flan dish. Bake blind using non-stick paper in a fairly hot oven, 200°C/400°F/Gas 6, for 15 minutes or until the pastry is firm. Remove the weights. Reduce the oven temperature to 190°C/375°F/Gas 5. While the flan is cooking combine the cheese, vanilla essence, sugar, nutmeg, salt and raisins. Beat the egg whites until stiff but not dry and fold into the mixture. Spread the jam on the base of the flan and pour in the cheese mixture. Bake for 20–25 minutes until the filling is set. Serves six.

Melted Butter Pastry

This is the pastry to make if you really hate getting your fingers messy, because there is no rubbing in involved. The butter is first melted so that all you have to do is to stir in the other ingredients, and by all means use an electric mixer. Should you wish to increase the quantities, keep the dough warm, once mixed, for the second dish in a covered bowl over a pan of warm water. Work in a warm room and roll the pastry when it is only just cold. If it is left too long the dough will harden, crack easily and be difficult to lift.

Use melted butter pastry for tartlets, small pie crusts or two-crust patties or flans. The butter imparts a rich flavour and the pastry is very short. It is one of the few where margarine just cannot be substituted. Unsalted butter will melt without leaving a white scum, which salted butter tends to do. Do not freeze the dough before rolling, but the shaped uncooked pastry improves with freezing. One recipe is sufficient for a 23–25 cm (9–10 in) flan or two 15–18 cm (6–7 in) flans.

Ingredients for Basic Recipe

150 g (6 oz) unsalted butter
200 g (8 oz) plain flour
Pinch of salt
1 size-6 egg, beaten (*or* ½ large egg)

Cut the butter into even-sized pieces, put in a saucepan and melt over gentle heat until just clear. Don't wait until it foams and separates or it will clarify, changing the flavour. Leave to cool for a few minutes but don't let it begin to congeal. Add half the flour, the salt and the beaten egg and mix thoroughly with a wooden spoon, then work in the remaining flour. Knead very gently to a smooth dough. Roll out and use as required, preferably chilling the prepared dishes before baking. Bake in a hot oven, 220°C/425°F/Gas 7, then after 10 minutes reduce to 180°C/350°F/Gas 4 to enable the filling to cook evenly. Microwave note: Melt the butter on Defrost (about 5 minutes) in a bowl large enough to take all the flour.

GINGER CHRISTMAS PIES

Roll out the pastry more thinly than usual as covered patties should not be all crust and no filling. Beware when eating hot straight from the oven as they will burn your tongue.

One recipe (200 g (8 oz) flour etc.) Melted butter
  pastry (p. 128)
350 g (12 oz) mincemeat
4 pieces stem ginger, finely chopped
Beaten egg to glaze
Caster sugar to dust on top

Roll out half the pastry thinly and cut eight to twelve circles 1 cm (½ in) wider than the top of the patty tins. Set aside. Cut the remaining pastry into circles 2.5 cm (1 in) wider than the tins and ease into the base and sides of the tins, leaving the surplus pastry standing up like a collar. Put a spoonful of mincemeat in each pastry case so that it is no more than half full and sprinkle with the chopped ginger. Dampen the inside of the pastry collar and insert the reserved circles, curving them to form lids thus making a double collar. Roll both edges over to form a rouleau round the pies, sealing the edges. Brush the pies with beaten egg and make a small hole in the lid with a skewer. Bake in a hot oven, 220°C/425°F/Gas 7, for 10 minutes, then reduce to 180°C/350°F/Gas 4 for a further 5–10 minutes until the pastry is cooked. Sprinkle with caster sugar.

MOCHA FLAN

There is always a risk of curdling when cooking egg custards but as there is flour in the French custard filling, you should have no trouble in producing a smooth sauce. The mocha topping is soft and fudgy.

Half recipe (100 g (4 oz) flour etc.) Melted butter pastry (p. 128)

Custard
50 g (2 oz) butter
2 level tablespoons caster sugar
50 g (2 oz) flour
2 size-2 egg yolks
300 ml (½ pint) milk
½ teaspoon vanilla essence

Topping
100 g (4 oz) icing sugar
1 level tablespoon cocoa
2 level teaspoons coffee powder
40 g (1½ oz) soft white cooking fat
2 tablespoons milk
40 g (1½ oz) caster sugar

Roll out the pastry and use to line an 18 cm (7 in) flan tin. Chill until firm. Bake blind in a hot oven, 220°C/425°F/Gas 7, for 10 minutes, then remove the weights. Reduce the oven temperature to 180°C/350°F/Gas 4 for a further 20 minutes until the pastry is cooked. To make the custard, melt the butter in a saucepan, then stir in the sugar and flour. Beat the egg yolks and milk together and strain into the pan. Whisk the mixture over moderate heat until the custard thickens. Immediately remove from the heat and continue whisking for 1 minute. Flavour with the vanilla essence and pour into the pastry case. Cover the filling with a damp circle of greaseproof paper to prevent a skin forming. To make the topping sieve icing sugar and cocoa into a medium bowl. Heat the remaining ingredients gently until the caster sugar has dissolved. Bring to the boil, pour into the flavoured icing sugar and beat for a few minutes so that the topping cools. Pour over the custard and leave to set. Serves four to five.

SAVOURY PICNIC PATTIES

This is a very economical picnic or TV snack and can be served either hot or cold with sweet pickle and salad.

One recipe (200 g (8 oz) flour etc.) Melted butter pastry (p. 128)
100 g (4 oz) pork loaf, roughly chopped and divided into four
1 medium sized potato, peeled and diced
1 egg white and pinch of salt, whisked together for glazing

Roll out the pastry to 3 mm (⅛ in) thickness and cut eight 10 cm (4 in) circles. Brush four of the pastry pieces with egg white and arrange piles of mixed meat and diced potatoes in the centre. Cover with the remaining circles, cupping the hand and pressing down so that the filling is completely secure inside. You will find that the top piece of pastry is slightly smaller than the bottom, due to the fact that it has to stretch over the filling. To seal, either crimp or round with the prongs of a fork or press a 9 cm (3½ in) diameter cup over the pastry, so that it presses the two edges together, leaving an interesting rim. Press the pastry on top unless any cracks have naturally developed. Brush the tops of the pastry with the egg white glaze, place on an ungreased baking tray and bake in a hot oven, 220°C/425°F/Gas 7, for 20 minutes, then reduce to 180°C/350°F/Gas 4 for 10 minutes to cook the potatoes. Serves four.

TUNA AND SWEETCORN FLAN

A cheap supper dish that tastes more expensive. Serve warm or cold with cucumber and mushroom salad.

One recipe (200 g (8 oz) flour etc.) Melted butter pastry (p. 128)
25 g (1 oz) butter
25 g (1 oz) flour
300 ml (½ pint) milk
1 × 198 g (7 oz) can sweetcorn, drained
1 × 198 g (7 oz) can tuna fish, drained and flaked
2 size-3 eggs, beaten
1 level tablespoon tomato ketchup
Salt
Pepper

Roll out the pastry and use to line a 23 cm (9 in) flan ring. Chill while making the sauce. Melt the butter in a saucepan, stir in the flour and cook gently for 1 minute. Gradually whisk in the milk and bring to the boil, stirring continuously until the sauce thickens. Remove from the heat and add the sweetcorn, tuna, eggs, tomato ketchup and salt and pepper to taste. Pour the mixture into the flan case and bake in a fairly hot oven, 220°C/425°F/Gas 7, for 10 minutes, then reduce to 180°C/350°F/Gas 4 for a further 25–30 minutes, until the filling is set and the pastry cooked. Serves five to six.

Pâte Brisée

One of the most frequently used recipes in French cuisine is pâte brisée. It is similar to shortcrust but because top-quality waxy butter is used, the pastry is very different in texture. I replace some of the water with egg yolk, which produces a short crisp crust with an orangy brown colour. Pâte brisée is simple to mix, easy to roll and does not need much in the way of a rest. It can be transferred lightly cradled in the hands to a flan dish and is good natured enough to be cooked without needing to be baked blind. The bottom rises up a little but not so much that it will leave no room for the filling. The butter should be soft enough to cut with a spoon handle but not soft enough to spread. As soon as the dough is supple, but not soft, sufficient liquid will have been added, but do not add too little of the water or you will find that the pastry is too hard to roll out. Pâte brisée cooks particularly well in glass fluted flan dishes and the quantity given is enough for a 23–25 cm (9–10 in) dish.

Ingredients for Basic Recipe

250 g (9 oz) plain flour
125 g (4½ oz) Normandy butter, slightly soft
Pinch of salt
1 egg yolk
2½–4 tablespoons cold water

Sieve the flour into a medium mixing bowl and make a well in the centre. Put in the butter and salt and cut in with a round-bladed knife until the mixture is lumpy and the flour thickly coated. Beat the egg yolk and the smaller amount of water together and pour into the mixing bowl, continuing to stir with the knife only until the dough is of a workable and fairly soft consistency. Then add the extra water if necessary. Gather the pastry into a ball with the fingers and pat it to a round shape. Roll out to a thickness of ½–1 cm (¼–⅜ in). Chill the uncooked pastry for 10 minutes if time allows but if you haven't time, then you will find that pâte brisée behaves itself very well. Bake the pastry in a hot oven, 220°C/425°F/Gas 7, unless otherwise stated.

PISSALADIÈRE

Try to use a glass dish or a well-seasoned tin on a heavy baking tray to make sure that the pastry browns under all that heavy filling. For a change you could spread a little tomato purée over the onions before decorating. Serve hot.

> One recipe (250 g (9 oz) flour etc.) Pâte brisée (p. 133)
> Egg white
> 3 tablespoons olive oil
> 1 kg (2 lb) onions
> ¼ teaspoon salt
> ½ teaspoon pepper
> 12 anchovy fillets (about one can)
> 10 black olives
> Beaten egg yolk and milk to glaze

Roll out the pastry and use to line a greased and floured 25 cm (10 in) flan dish. Brush the base with egg white. Roll out the trimmings and cut into strips. Chill all the pastry. Chop the onions finely but do not mince or the juices will seep. Heat the oil in a large pan and 'sweat' the onions, cooking gently for 15–20 minutes until they are golden. Shake the pan occasionally so that all the onions have a chance to cook. Season to taste, adding more salt if you prefer it, but remember that anchovies are salty. Transfer the onions to the flan dish with a slotted spoon so that the mixture is not too oily. Spread evenly. Make a lattice on top of the flan with the rolled out strips, securing them to the edges with water. Roll up the anchovy fillets and arrange alternately with the olives on the onion mixture in between the lattice. Brush the pastry with the beaten egg yolk mixture and bake in a hot oven, 220°C/425°F/Gas 7, for 20–30 minutes. Serves six.

QUICHE À L'AUBERGINE

Aubergine is on the bitter side and these unpleasant juices are usually removed by *dégorgement*. Salt is sprinkled on the cut surfaces which are then left in a colander for about 30 minutes. The blackened fluid can then be rinsed away. Blanching is equally good depending on the recipe you are using – it is also quicker and less messy. Serve this lovely quiche hot.

One recipe (250 g (9 oz) flour etc.) Pâte brisée (p. 133)
2 medium aubergines
Oil for frying
1 medium Spanish onion, sliced into rings
1 clove garlic, finely sliced
½ green pepper, cut into strips
Salt
Black pepper
2 bay leaves
1 whole egg *plus* 1 egg white
6 tablespoons milk
50 g (2 oz) grated Cheddar cheese

Roll out the pastry and use to line a 23 cm (9 in) flan dish. Prick the base well with a fork. Bake in a hot oven, 220°C/425°F/Gas 7, for 15–20 minutes until the pastry is golden and shrinks from the sides of the dish. Meanwhile peel and slice the aubergines, put into boiling water and cook for 3 minutes, then drain thoroughly. Pat dry on kitchen paper if it is available. Put about 1 cm (½ in) good quality frying oil in a shallow pan and lightly fry the onion and garlic. As soon as they soften add the aubergine, green pepper and a good shake of salt and black pepper. Put in the bay leaves and sauté gently until the vegetables are soft. Beat the eggs and milk together and season lightly, then pour into the flan case. Remove the vegetables from the pan with a slotted spoon and arrange on the beaten egg mixture. Sprinkle the cheese on top leaving a 5 cm (2 in) border. Return to the oven reducing the temperature to 180°C/350°F/Gas 4 for a further 15 minutes. Serves four to five.

TARTE AU CAMEMBERT

For me this ranks among the specials and I save it as an alternative to a dessert. Choose the cheese carefully – it should be just ripe – an over-ripe Camembert has an acrid aroma and tastes like ammonia. It is quick to prepare and should be ready within the hour. Serve warm if you can but it is also pleasant cold.

One recipe (250 g (9 oz) flour etc.) Pâte brisée (p. 133)
4 size-3 eggs
2 generous tablespoons yesterday's double cream
Salt
Pepper
1 whole Camembert cheese
1 rounded tablespoon finely grated
   dried breadcrumbs   } mixed
1 level tablespoon finely ground   } together
   toasted hazelnuts

Roll out the pastry and use to line a 23–25 cm (9–10 in) flan tin. Prick thoroughly and chill until firm. Beat the eggs until thick, then add the cream and salt and pepper to taste. Scrape away the crust and divide the Camembert into eight wedges. Arrange in the pastry case leaving a 1 cm (½ in) border. Pour the egg mixture over the cheese, making sure that there is a coating over each piece. Bake in a hot oven for 35–40 minutes or until set. Cover with a fine layer of crumbs and hazelnuts. Serves six to eight.

TARTE TATIN

I was given this recipe by a pâtissier in Avoriaz in the Haute-Savoie in France. The pastry is traditionally baked over the filling and then reversed for serving. Either cook the entire dish in a 5 cm (2 in) deep round flameproof dish suitable for use on the hob and in the oven or first cook the apples in a shallow pan and transfer to a 20 cm (8 in) cake tin before fitting on the pastry lid. Serve warm.

One recipe (250 g (9 oz) flour etc.) Pâte brisée (p. 133)
1 kg (3 lb) cooking apples
150 g (5 oz) butter
200 g (7 oz) granulated sugar
½ teaspoon vanilla essence

Keep the pastry cool while preparing the filling. Peel, core and cut the apples into eighths. Melt 120 g (4 oz) butter in the dish or pan and stir in two-thirds of the sugar and vanilla essence. Arrange the apples in the base of the pan, leaving no spaces between. Cover with the remaining sugar and the butter cut into small cubes. Leave to cook over a low heat for 20–25 minutes until the sugar on the base caramelizes, but remains light brown. If you have cooked the apples in a separate pan, transfer to the cake tin now. Roll out the pastry to a thickness of 6 mm (¼ in) and a little wider than the dish. Place over the apples, tucking any surplus pastry underneath and into the dish. Pierce the pastry in several places with a pointed knife. Bake in a hot oven, 220°C/425°F/Gas 7, for 15 minutes, then reduce the heat to 190°C/375°F/Gas 5. Cover the pastry with greaseproof paper and bake for a further 10 minutes. Remove from the oven, stand the dish on a damp dish cloth and leave for 10 minutes. Reverse on to a warm serving dish. Serves six.

Pâte Sablée

The name comes from the French word *sable*, 'sand',
which is how the mixture should look, when the flour is
being incorporated. Use this pastry for small tartlets or for
tarts, which can be served directly from the tin. The pastry
is very delicate and may break if unmoulded, so use solid
dishes or loose-bottomed tins rather than flan rings. For
the same reason, roll the pastry no thinner than 5 mm
(¼ in) thick. Bake the pastry blind and put in a light
filling such as well-drained strawberries or raspberries,
with a jam glaze or a pre-cooked filling such as lemon curd
or that adorable white whipped cream cheese, beaten with
a spot of sugar and chopped raisins. Watch the baking
carefully as pastry with a high sugar content burns easily.
15–20 minutes is an average time to allow, but unfortunately ovens do vary considerably in temperature. It is
safer to be sure than sorry. The quantity given is sufficient
for one 25 cm (10 in) tart or twenty individual small
tartlets.

Ingredients for Basic Recipe

> 125 g (4½ oz) caster sugar
> 1 size-3 egg
> Pinch of salt
> 250 g (9 oz) plain flour, sieved twice
> 125 g (4½ oz) butter, softened to mashing point but not
>   oily

Put the sugar, egg and salt in a mixing bowl and beat until
thick white and doubled in volume. Add the flour all at

once and stir with a wooden spoon only until all the flour is mixed in. Rub the mixture between the fingertips until it looks and feels like sand. Make a well in the centre, put in the butter and knead with the fingers spread crablike, so that all the flour is clawed in at one time. There will then be less likelihood of the butter oiling out, which can happen if the flour is added a little at a time. The resulting dough will be very, very soft, but don't be tempted to remedy this with flour. As soon as the dough reaches this stage, cover it with foil or cling-film and give it a rest in the refrigerator for at least 15 minutes. The pastry should be rolled out evenly on a well-floured surface so that it is not less than 6 mm (¼ in) thick. Carefully transfer to the tin or tins and leave to rest for a further 10 minutes once again preferably in the refrigerator. Bake blind on the centre shelf of a moderate oven, 180°C/350°F/Gas 4, until set and cooked but not coloured.

ALMOND SYLLABUB

A sweet and sour sherry-flavoured cream dessert in a delicate pastry case. For a change smother the surface with finely chopped pistachios.

One recipe (250 g (9 oz) flour etc.) Pâte sablée (p. 139)
2 level teaspoons powdered gelatine
300 ml (½ pint) double cream
75 g (3 oz) icing sugar, sieved
5 tablespoons sherry
Grated rind and juice of 1 lemon
2 generous tablespoons flaked almonds, toasted
2–3 tablespoons whipped cream for decoration

Roll out the pastry and use to line a 23 cm (9 in) flan dish. Bake blind in a moderate oven, 180°C/350°F/Gas 4, for 15 minutes, then remove the weights and continue cooking for a further 5–10 minutes until the pastry is crisp. Leave to cool. Meanwhile dissolve the gelatine in 2 tablespoons very hot water. Whip the cream very slightly and while still of a pouring consistency, beat in the icing sugar and the sherry until the mixture thickens slightly, then beat in the lemon rind and juice. Fold in the dissolved gelatine and leave the mixture until it is just showing signs of setting before pouring it into the flan case. Spike a 5 cm (2 in) border of the mixture with the toasted almonds standing up hedgehog fashion and fill the centre with whirls of whipped cream. Serves four to six.

BLACK CHERRY TARTLETS

Gelatine is helpful in thickened cream mixtures but unless it is carefully measured, that wobbly cream could turn into a rigid block.

One recipe (250 g (9 oz) flour etc.) Pâte sablée (p. 139)
100 g (4 oz) plain chocolate
2 level teaspoons powdered gelatine
150 ml (¼ pint) black cherry yogurt
150 ml (¼ pint) cream
1 × 396 g (14 oz) can pitted black cherries
1½ level teaspoons arrowroot

Roll out the pastry and cut out circles to fit into sixteen to twenty greased patty tins. Prick thoroughly and bake blind in a moderate oven, 180°C/350°F/Gas 4, for 10–15 minutes or until the pastry is crisp and dry. Remove carefully from the tins while still warm. Melt the chocolate in a bowl over a pan of steaming water or in the microwave oven. Dip the bottoms of the tarts in the chocolate and leave to set on waxed or non-stick paper. Meanwhile dissolve the gelatine in 2 tablespoons of very hot water. Mix the yogurt, cream and dissolved gelatine together and leave to thicken slightly, then spoon into the tartlet cases. Arrange the cherries on top when the filling is set. Put the arrowroot in a measuring jug and gradually stir in 150 ml (¼ pint) of the cherry juice. Pour into a saucepan and heat gently, stirring constantly until the mixture thickens and clears. Spoon sparingly over the cherries.

PISTACHIO CITRUS FLAN

Freeze the flan if you like and then it will be similar to an ice cream. The milk will whip to greater volume if the can is chilled for several hours before opening.

One recipe (250 g (9 oz) flour etc.) Pâte sablée (p. 139)
1 × 170 g (6 oz) can condensed milk
215 ml (7½ fl oz) double cream
3 tablespoons fresh lemon juice
3 tablespoons fresh orange juice
40 g (1½ oz) peeled pistachio nuts, skinned and chopped
Icing sugar to decorate

Roll out the pastry and use to line a 23–25 cm (9–10 in) flan dish. Bake blind in a moderate oven, 180°C/350°F/Gas 4, for 15 minutes, then remove the weights and continue cooking for a further 5–10 minutes until the pastry is crisp. Leave to cool. Whip the condensed milk until thick, then add the cream and whip until soft peaks form. Stir in the lemon and orange juice and the chopped pistachios. Pile into the pastry case and chill for 1 hour. Dredge generously with the icing sugar. Serves six.

TARTLETTES FROMAGE BLANC PRALINE

Use the real French Fromage Blanc, but if you can't obtain it, Jockey or Speiselquark will do. When making the praline the mixture must be handled carefully as it reaches an exceedingly high temperature of 185°–195°C/

360°C–380°F. If the syrup turns dark brown plunge the base of the saucepan into a pan of HOT water. If it turns black it will be too bitter to use and more to the point it will burn emitting clouds of black smoke. I am sure this won't happen but if it does use an oven glove to clamp on a tight lid and move the pan to an unheated part of the cooker.

One recipe (250 g (9 oz) flour etc.) Pâte sablée (p. 139)
200 g (8 oz) Fromage Blanc
5 tablespoons double cream
½ teaspoon vanilla essence
1 rounded tablespoon icing sugar, sieved

Praline
50 g (2 oz) almonds with skins on
50 g (2 oz) granulated sugar
2½ tablespoons water

Roll out the pastry and cut out circles to line sixteen to twenty greased patty tins. Bake blind in a moderate oven, 180°C/350°F/Gas 4, for 10–15 minutes or until the pastry is crisp. Remove from the tins while still warm and put on a wire rack to cool. Half whip the cream, then beat in the cheese, vanilla essence and sugar. Pile into the pastry cases.

To make the praline, put the sugar and water in a small heavy-based saucepan and stir over low heat until the sugar has dissolved. Raise the heat and add the almonds and boil without stirring until the mixture turns a rich brown colour. Pour on to a baking tray lined with a non-stick paper and leave to cool. Crush finely or pulverize in a liquidizer. Sprinkle the tarts with a generous coating of praline just before serving.

Pâte Sucrée

I never have to look up the recipe for pâte sucrée because it is so easy to remember. It is 4, 2, 2, 2, and as easy to make as it is to remember. All the ingredients are mixed together on a floured surface. The pastry is best kneaded lightly but won't mind too much if it's treated with a heavy hand, so long as it is a cool one. The pastry must be rested in the refrigerator before shaping. When using for small flans and tartlets, pâte sucrée may be baked without the filling without baking beans or foil to weight it down. It is economical in that it is rolled out very thinly and as the title suggests, it is only suitable for sweet dishes. Pâte sucrée is crisp, short and a pale yellow colour. Although the cooked pastry will break if treated unkindly, it has a great resistance to wet fillings, which do not seep into the pastry making it soft. Use pâte sucrée for small tarts or to line loose-bottomed flan rings, when the rings can be removed, leaving the pastry on the tin base for support. The tins should be greased – it's a delicate pastry and the sugar tends to make it sticky. Pâte sucrée is very soft until it cools down, so do not attempt to remove the pastry from the tins straight from the oven. Leave it to cool a little first. Use a curved grapefruit knife to slide small tartlets out of the tins. Unfilled tartlets or patty cases store well in an airtight tin. If you have difficulty in rolling the pastry, because it is too soft, roll it between two sheets of greaseproof paper. When fitting into the tins do not worry too much because the pastry can be moulded by hand should it crack. This quantity is sufficient to fill twelve to fifteen patty tins or an 18 cm (7 in) flan.

Ingredients for Basic Recipe

100 g (4 oz) plain flour
Pinch of salt
50 g (2 oz) caster sugar
Generous 50 g (2 oz) butter
2 egg yolks

Sieve the flour and salt in a huge pile together on to a cool surface. Make a well in the centre and add the sugar, butter and egg yolks. Using the fingertips, pinch and work together until all the ingredients are well mixed. Knead the pastry lightly until smooth and rest in the refrigerator for at least an hour before shaping. Prick baking cases well and bake in a moderate oven, 180°C/350°F/Gas 4, for 7–10 minutes for small tartlet cases depending upon the thickness of the pastry.

LOVERLEY LIME PIE

If you can't obtain limes, lemons may be substituted. Measure the quantity of juice as lemons tend to be larger than limes. When using lemons substitute yellow fruit colouring. Serve this tangy summer dessert cold.

One recipe (100 g (4 oz) flour etc.) Pâte sucrée (above)
4 size-3 egg yolks
100 g (4 oz) caster sugar
Pinch of salt
5 tablespoons fresh lime juice (2–3 limes)
2 drops green food colouring
250 ml (8 fl oz) whipping cream
Grated rind of 1 lime

Roll out the pastry and use to line a 25 cm (10 in) flan dish. Prick thoroughly and bake in a moderate oven, 180°C/350°F/Gas 4, for 15–20 minutes or until crisp and dry. Leave to cool in the dish. Beat the egg yolks until light and fluffy. Mix in the sugar, salt and lime juice and turn into a saucepan. Cook over a medium heat, stirring all the time until the mixture thickens. This will take about 5 minutes. Take care not to cook over a too strong heat or the mixture will curdle. Cool, then stir in the food colouring. Whip the cream until soft peaks form, then fold into the cooled lime mixture together with the grated rind. Spoon into the pastry case and shake the dish to evenly distribute the mixture without spoiling the surface. Leave in the refrigerator for 3–4 hours until cold and set. Serves six.

MAGALI

These petit fours are a real fiddle to make, but if you can face it, the effort is well worth while. They freeze beautifully so that you may as well double up on the quantities. Make sure that you bring the apricot mixture to the boil, otherwise you may find it goes mouldy.

One recipe (100 g (4 oz) flour etc.) Pâte sucrée (p. 145)

Crème Ganache
150 g (5 oz) plain chocolate
4 level tablespoons double cream
50 g (2 oz) butter
2 size-3 egg yolks
1 tablespoon rum

Toppings
100 g (4 oz) marzipan
Generous tablespoon apricot jam
25 g (1 oz) pistachio nuts, skinned and chopped

Roll out the pastry and use to line sixteen to twenty 2.5 cm (1 in) diameter patty tins. Prick thoroughly and bake in a moderate oven, 180°C/350°F/Gas 4, for 8–10 minutes. Remove from the oven and leave until cold, then remove from the tins.

To make the Ganache, break up the chocolate, put into a bowl over a pan of simmering water, making sure the water does not touch the bottom of the bowl and stir until melted. Add the cream and cook until thick, stirring all the time. Remove from the heat and beat in the butter a little at a time. Beat in the egg yolks and rum. Leave the mixture until it becomes quite thick, stirring occasionally.

Fill the tartlets with the Ganache right up to the rim. Roll out the marzipan very thinly. This is best done using icing sugar rather than flour to stop it sticking. Using the upturned tartlet moulds or a cutter cut out enough rounds for the number of tartlets. Cover the Ganache with the marzipan lids and press down lightly. Mix the jam with 1 tablespoon water, put in a small saucepan and bring to the boil. Pour through a strainer to remove any lumps of fruit. Brush the tops of the tartlets with the glaze and sprinkle with the pistachio nuts.

NAPOLEON TRIFLE

Use fresh or frozen raspberries but I prefer the frozen ones because they are juicier. I use a solid flan dish because the filling, being somewhat soft and weighty, might break down the pastry walls if the flan has to wait more than a few hours. Serve cold.

One recipe (100 g (4 oz) flour etc.) Pâte sucrée (p. 145)
600 g (1¼ lbs) raspberries
4 tablespoons brandy
600 ml (1 pint) milk
1 size-2 egg
1 heaped tablespoon caster sugar
1 teaspoon vanilla essence
25 g (1 oz) flour

300 ml (½ pint) whipping cream
2 level tablespoons roasted hazelnuts, chopped

First soak the raspberries in the brandy for 3 hours, gently stirring occasionally taking care not to break up the fruit. To make the custard, blend a few tablespoons of the milk with the egg, sugar, vanilla essence and the flour. Heat the remaining milk to steaming but not to boiling point, whisk into the paste and return to the saucepan. Stir over gentle heat until the sauce thickens sufficiently to coat the back of a wooden spoon. Leave to cool. Meanwhile roll out the chilled pastry and use to line a 25 cm (10 in) flan dish. Prick thoroughly and bake in a moderate oven, 180°C/350°F/Gas 4, for 15–20 minutes until the pastry is pale yellow. Leave to cool. Using a slotted spoon so that most of the juice is drained, arrange the raspberries in the flan to completely cover the base. Spoon the custard on top. Whip the cream until soft peaks form and put in a piping bag fitted with a 1 cm (½ in) star nozzle. Starting at the outside pipe in ever-decreasing circles until the custard is entirely covered. Sprinkle the chopped hazelnuts on top. Serves eight to ten.

NORWEGIAN TART

The finished result depends upon your skill in piping. Pipe the mixture in large rosettes as close as possible to the edges of the pastry, then fill in the centre. Take care not to overcook the sugar syrup as the temperature rises rapidly after reaching 230°C/450°F and continues to heat after removal from the cooker. Serve cold.

Double recipe (200 g (8 oz) flour etc.) Pâte sucrée (p. 145)
4 size-3 eggs, separated
150 g (5 oz) caster sugar
40 g (1½ oz) plain flour, sieved

250 ml (bare ½ pint) milk
Grated rind of one lemon
2 level teaspoons powdered gelatine

Roll out the pastry and line a 25 cm (10 in) flan dish. Prick thoroughly and bake in a moderate oven, 180°C/350°F/ Gas 4, for 15–20 minutes or until crisp and dry. Leave to cool in the dish. Beat the egg yolks with half the sugar until it is dissolved, then mix in the flour thoroughly. Heat the milk to boiling point and pour into the mixture with the lemon rind. Pour back into the saucepan and bring to the boil, stirring all the time. As soon as large bubbles appear, remove from the heat. Sprinkle the gelatine on to 2 tablespoons hot water and stir until dissolved. Pour into the custard, stirring thoroughly, then leave to cool, stirring occasionally to prevent lumps forming. When cold the mixture should be very thick. Beat the egg whites until stiff and dry. Put the remaining 65 g (2½ oz) sugar into a saucepan with 4 tablespoons water. Stir to dissolve, then bring to the boil and cook until the temperature reaches 130°C/260°F when half a spoonful of the syrup forms a hard ball when dropped into cold water. Pour from a height into the beaten whites, whisking frantically until the mixture cools. Fold into the thickened custard. Put the mixture into a forcing bag fitted with a large star nozzle and pipe decoratively into the pastry cases. Put in a fairly hot oven, 200°C/400°F/Gas 6, for a few moments to brown. Serves six.

Potato Pastry

'You wouldn't know it had potato in it,' one of my tasters said to me when eating one of the sweet dishes made with potato pastry. So please don't be put off by the name and give it a try. Potato pastry is easy to make, but requires careful handling when lifting on top of pies. It is economical and quite crusty as a pie topping, although soft and cakey when used to line flan dishes. Use butter for sweet dishes and margarine in savoury dishes and choose firm floury and not waxy potatoes. There is no liquid in the recipe. If you decide to use instant potato, reconstitute it with the minimum of water – you will have to calculate the quantity according to the directions on the packet as these vary.

The recipe calls for 100 g (4 oz) mashed potato, so you would need to use 150–175 g (5–6 oz) potato to allow for peeling and loss of fluid during cooking. Boil the potatoes in slightly salted water until soft but not mushy, then drain thoroughly before mashing. For best results put the potatoes through a ricer or press through a sieve. Leave until cold before using, but do not store for any length of time or the potato will discolour. Use potato pastry as an alternative to shortcrust or suet pastry or instead of serving potatoes separately. An attractive potato crust on top of meat casseroles or hot-pots will add variation and appeal. I particularly like to use potato crust on deep, individual oval pottery dishes. When cooked on top of a casserole, the potato pastry absorbs some of the moisture of the meat cooking which gives it a suet pastry texture. It is filling and quick to prepare. It may also be used to top sweet dishes such as fruit cobblers and looks good when brushed with milk and sprinkled with sugar before cooking. The recipe is sufficient for an 18–20 cm (7–8 in) square or round tin and makes six to eight small lids when the pastry should be rolled out to about 1 cm (¼–½ in) thick. The pastry is easy to roll and cuts into clean well defined shapes.

Ingredients for Basic Recipe

100 g (4 oz) plain flour
Pinch of salt
50 g (2 oz) butter *or* margarine
100 g (4 oz) cold well-mashed potato

Sieve the flour and salt into a mixing bowl and rub in the fat until the mixture resembles breadcrumbs. Add the potato, preferably pushed through a sieve first, and work in with a wooden spoon until the mixture forms dough. The dough should be firm yet manageable, but if it is too hard, add a little milk and if too soft to roll, add a little more flour. Mould into a ball with the hands and roll out on a lightly floured surface to a depth of about 1 cm (¼–½ in) depending upon the use. Bake in a fairly hot oven, 190°C/375°F/Gas 5, for 35–40 minutes or according to the directions in the recipe. If you are apprehensive about using potato pastry, try the griddle scones (p. 153) first, which are made in a frying pan.

BAKED CHEESECAKE

When cooked the pastry becomes a crunchy case to support the lemon-flavoured filling.

One recipe (100 g (4 oz) flour etc.) Potato pastry (above)
50 g (2 oz) butter

100 g (4 oz) caster sugar
2 size-3 eggs, separated
Grated rind and juice of 1 lemon
250 g (10 oz) curd cheese
50 g (2 oz) sultanas
65 g (2½ oz) ground almonds

Roll out the pastry and use to line a greased 18 cm (7 in) square loose-bottomed tin. Beat the butter and sugar together until light and fluffy, gradually beat in the egg yolks, then stir in the lemon rind and juice, cheese, sultanas and ground almonds. Whisk the egg whites until stiff but not dry and fold into the cheese mixture. Pour into the pastry case and bake in a fairly hot oven, 190°C/ 375°F/Gas 5, for 40–45 minutes until the cake is golden and firm to the touch. Serves eight.

CHEESE AND TOMATO PIE

A pretty flan which belies the simple ingredients. Ideally the tomatoes should be skinned but then again why bother; this is supposed to be a filling supper dish. Serve hot with an accompanying green salad.

One recipe (100 g (4 oz) flour etc.) Potato pastry
   (p. 151)
175 g (6 oz) mature Cheddar cheese, grated
1 level tablespoon fresh *or* 1 teaspoon dried marjoram
4 medium tomatoes, skinned and thinly sliced
Salt
Pepper
Beaten egg to glaze

Roll out two-thirds of the pastry and use to line a 20 cm (8 in) greased flan ring. Fill with two layers of grated cheese, herbs and well-seasoned tomatoes. Roll out the remaining pastry, cut into thin strips and arrange on top in a lattice design. Press the ends well into the sides of the pastry to seal. Brush the pastry with beaten egg and bake in a fairly hot oven, 190°C/375°F/Gas 5, for 35–45 minutes until the pastry is golden and cooked through. Serves four.

LIDDED PIES

Potato pastry should not be cooked for hours on end while waiting for the filling to become tender. For best results partially cook meat fillings, then cool rapidly before putting on the potato lid. Use your favourite casserole or stew for fillings. Subsequently bake in a fairly hot oven, 200°C/400°F/Gas 6, for 20 minutes, then reduce the heat to 160°C/325°F/Gas 3 for the remainder of the time the filling requires.

Fish fillings, which obviously require no prolonged cooking, may be baked in the raw pie pastry.

SULTANA GRIDDLE SCONES

Make these when you have left-over potatoes. The fruit spreads evenly through the soft scone mixture. Serve freshly cooked.

One recipe (100 g (4 oz) flour etc.) Potato pastry (p. 151)
100 g (4 oz) sultanas
1 rounded teaspoon baking powder
1 generous tablespoon golden syrup, warmed

Knead the sultanas and baking powder into the unrolled potato dough and mix in the syrup. Roll out on a floured surface to a thickness of 5 mm (¼ in) and cut out 6 cm (2½ in) circles. Well grease a griddle or heavy based frying pan. Bring to moderate heat and cook for 7–10 minutes on each side. Makes twelve to sixteen.

Puff Pastry

It must be admitted that of all the pastries, puff is the most difficult to make and unless everything is done correctly, you will have a failure on your hands. Of course it is easy to pop down to the shops and buy frozen puff pastry (the cost is about the same), but the flavour will not be as good as in the pastry you make yourself, since you will be using superior ingredients.

Once you get the hang of it, puff pastry is great fun to make. Since there are several rollings, foldings and restings, it can be done in stages throughout the day, in between your chores. It will keep for about two months in the freezer so make up a reasonably large quantity. It can also be kept for a short time in the refrigerator, though you may find that after a couple of days black specks appear and the pastry is unusable. This is because damp uncooked flour starts to go mouldy very quickly.

When puff pastry is made the total weight will be double the quantity of flour that you have put in, because you have to add the weight of the flour to the weight of the butter. Few recipes require this amount of pastry, but since the pastry takes a long time to bake, it would be better to make the full amount and then cut away the surplus vertically with a sharp knife and store. Although baked pastry refreshes well in a hot oven, it is never as good as when it has been freshly made.

Puff pastry is exceedingly versatile and can be used with savoury or sweet dishes, pie crusts, pastry cases or baked in a slab and used as mille feuilles. It is often used for sausage rolls, although I feel that it rises too much for this. It is excellent for patty cases and vol-au-vents, which as their name 'gone with the wind', suggests, have to be very light and the trimmings can be made into sacristans or cheese straws.

Puff is a very rich pastry since it has equal quantities of fat and flour. Use 300 ml (½ pint) ice-cold water, ½ teaspoon salt and 2 level teaspoons lemon juice to every 500 g (1 lb) flour. If you prefer you can substitute ½ level teaspoon cream of tartar for the lemon juice, sifted in with the flour. To chill water quickly, place ice cubes in a jug of water, then measure the quantity required. For the best results use strong plain flour that is well sifted and cool. Put the mixing bowl in the refrigerator while weighing out the other ingredients. For the best flavour use butter. My choice is for the slightly salty English butter because I find the continental butters are too creamy and give sticky results. If you decide to use margarine you will find the cheaper ones, such as Echo, excellent. Keep to the correct quantities of lemon juice and salt since, as I have pointed out before, they are very vital ingredients in pastry making. Mix the lemon juice with approximately two-thirds of the water, so that if you do not require all the liquid, you will be sure that the correct amount of lemon juice has gone into the mixture.

Puff pastry rises for the same reasons as do other flaky types of pastry, where a large quantity of liquid is used: the water turns to steam, the fat melts in layers to force the gluten in the flour to rise and set. Made correctly and with its full number of rollings and foldings it can rise to six times the thickness of the rolled-out pastry. Unless the recipe says otherwise, bake puff pastry in a very hot oven, 230°C/450°F/Gas 8. If the oven were cooler the fat would run out and destroy the flaky layers.

In the making of puff pastry one-quarter of the fat is rubbed into the flour, formed into a dough with the water and lemon juice, then it is kneaded thoroughly and firmly, so that the gluten, as it strengthens, will help to form a barrier against the fat when all the folding and rolling starts. The remaining fat is put in in one lump and must be of the same consistency as the dough. It must be cool and firm, malleable without being soft. If the butter is too hard, it will not roll or will break through the surface of the paste. On the other hand if the dough is too stiff, you won't be able to get even distribution of the fat when rolling. To achieve an equal consistency first beat down the fat with a fork, shaping it into an oblong about 1 cm (½ in) thick. You may find it easier to do this by putting it between two layers of greaseproof paper. Now enclose the butter in the pastry wrapping. Lightly punch to flatten, but do not roll. This movement keeps the air trapped in and prepares the dough for the rolling process.

When rolling make sure that you have even pressure on the pin, so that the layers do not go out of shape. The pastry should be folded and rolled seven times, no more or you may destroy the formation of the delicate layers. After seven rollings there will be 2,187 layers and I checked this by folding up a very large piece of brown paper. There are two methods of folding after rolling the pastry to an oblong; for the double roll and fold the top and bottom edges are both folded to a central point and then folded over one another, so that only two thicknesses are visible. In the single roll and fold, the pastry is rolled to an oblong and marked into three sections. Then the top one is folded over the middle and the bottom one over that, so that only one piece of pastry will be visible along the narrow end. Both are good methods.

There are a few rules that should be observed when rolling. Use strong firm pressure in one direction only and do not roll over the edges. It is important to keep the shape, particularly the corners, square. Use a pinching action if necessary but don't be tempted to pull the corners with the fingers, because the pastry will invariably shrink back, so you will have an uneven rise when baked. The best method of keeping it square is to put pressure in the middle of the oblong and then roll to the outside, so that an even thickness is achieved. Don't push so hard that the butter comes up through the dough. I use a sprinkling of flour although this is against the rules. The best plan is not to roll too thinly in the first place. If the fat does come through, stop rolling and chill the pastry for ten minutes. Don't treat the pastry too roughly or you will be pushing out the air that you have so carefully put in. Each time the pastry is rolled out, a certain amount of extra flour will have to be used, on the pin and on the surface of the pastry. Before folding, make sure that this is brushed off, using a dry pastry brush. The chunky kind is the best for this. It is also important to give the pastry a minimum of 15 minutes' rest in between each rolling, preferably in the refrigerator. If the pastry is left to rest at room temperature the fat may soften too much. The rolling of puff pastry is much more important than when rolling out the rubbed-in pastries.

Rest and chill in a polythene bag lightly dredged with flour. Trim the edges with a sharp knife, cutting, but not dragging the pastry, so that an even rise will be ensured. If you are using cutters such as for vol-au-vent cases, keep them well within the perimeter of the pastry. The trimmings can only be used for cheese straws or small biscuits. For larger trimmings it is essential to place one on top of the other and not gather the pastry into a ball. Prick puff pastry thoroughly with a skewer before baking, so that the hot air can blow through. Put the pastry on a damp baking tray so that the steam that immediately forms will push the layers apart. Bake in a very hot oven. If the oven is not hot enough, the fat will melt and when the pastry goes in, it will not rise at the bottom, so that a hard thick layer will result. Bake in the centre of the oven and don't open the door for the first three-quarters of the cooking time, because any sudden draught will cause the delicate layers to collapse and they will not rise again unless the pastry is transferred to the microwave oven.

Puff pastry should feel lighter when it is cooked than when you put it in the oven, so if it feels heavy, it isn't ready. Beware of starting to cook puff pastry in cold fan ovens. Make sure the oven is pre-heated to the correct temperature and lower the heat if the pastry becomes too brown. If the pastry rises unevenly and this is not caused by uneven rolling or the wrong temperature of the oven, it could be that one side of your oven is hotter than the other. The pastry on the hotter side will rise more quickly. If you have a glass door on the oven, you can see this happening, but you will still have to wait until the pastry is golden before turning the baking tray. Raise the oven temperature for a few moments beforehand, then open the door slowly and lower the temperature after you have turned the pastry. If the pastry does not rise very much, this is probably due to it having a very close texture, showing that the original dough was too stiff, so that it was not possible to get the fat evenly rolled in. In the event of the pastry rising badly and being unsuitable for the dish you propose, wait until the pastry is cold and crumble the flakier parts which can be used as toppings for meat or fruit pies. You will have to look at the individual recipes for dish sizes since it all depends upon the thickness to which you roll out the pastry.

Ingredients for Basic Recipe

250 g (8 oz) plain *or* strong plain flour
¼ teaspoon salt
250 g (8 oz) butter
1 measured level teaspoon fresh lemon juice
Approximately 150 ml (¼ pint) ice-cold water

Sieve the flour and salt into a mixing bowl and rub in a quarter of the butter finely. Add the lemon juice, mix with most, but not all, the water. Mix to a soft malleable dough, adding more water if necessary, and turn out on to a barely floured surface. Knead vigorously until the dough is smooth and pliable, this being necessary for the even distribution of the moisture, then put in a lightly floured polythene bag and leave in a cold place to rest for at least 30 minutes. Beat the remaining butter with a fork to soften. The butter should have been firm but not at refrigerator temperature. If the butter is too hard, put it between two sheets of greaseproof paper and beat with a rolling pin to flatten. Shape into an oblong about 1 cm (½ in) thick. Remove the dough from the polythene bag and brush off any surplus flour. Roll the dough into a square sufficiently large to wrap up the butter, like a well-sealed parcel to be sent through the post. There should be sufficient dough to allow an overlap of about 1 cm (½ in) on each side. Shape the butter as square as possible, though this is not vitally important, and put centrally on the pastry square. Fold the top and bottom edges of the dough over the butter and then enclose the sides and turn upside-down before rolling. You should now be looking down on a smooth square surface. Flour the rolling pin and, before rolling, using even pressure, press ripples into the dough to start it moving. Roll out the pastry to a strip three times as long as it is wide, making sure that the corners are square. You may have to encourage this by rolling diagonally from about 2.5 cm (1 in) below the edges, but do not roll over the edges. If this does not work, pinch the dough between the thumb and forefinger, but do not pull. Mark the pastry evenly into three sections and folding top to bottom and bottom over top, a threefold piece of dough will be formed. That completes the first roll and fold. So that you will remember how many rolls and folds you have given the pastry, press with a finger on the top of the pastry to make an indentation, but make sure that your fingernail doesn't poke through.

Pop the pastry back into the floured polythene bag and rest in the refrigerator for 15 minutes. Repeat the rolling and folding, mark with two fingerprints and rest for a further 15 minutes. Roll and fold again and mark with three prints. At this rolling the dough will be 1½ times the length of the rolling pin and approximately 15 cm (6 in) wide. Leave to rest again. Repeat until the pastry has had seven rolls and seven folds with a rest in between each. If the pastry is sufficiently cold you can give it two rollings and foldings at a time after the third one, but you must then increase the resting time to 30 minutes. After the seventh roll and fold, the pastry must be once more rested and again for 30 minutes after shaping and before baking. Remember that each time you roll, the flap sides should be underneath and the triple layer or open ends towards you. Don't forget to brush off the surplus flour each time and press the open edges with the flat of the rolling pin before rolling. It also helps to press the dough in the ripple fashion previously described at each rolling.

Bake in a very hot oven, 230°C/450°F/Gas 8, then reduce according to the instructions in the recipes. Small items take 15 minutes, medium-sized 20 minutes and large-sized about 30 minutes in a very hot oven.

CHERRY PURSES

The pastry is rolled out fairly thinly so that you don't get too much of a mouthful of pastry in these tea-time treats. If you are having a special afternoon tea, include one or two of these in the selection on the cake-stand. It isn't always possible to obtain cans of stoned cherries, so if you haven't a cherry stoner, cut the fruit in half and arrange them so that the shiny side shows.

Half recipe (125 g (4 oz) flour etc.) Puff pastry (p. 158)
1 × 280 g (10½ oz) can red cherries, drained and stoned
175 ml (6 fl oz) double cream
1 level tablespoon icing sugar
¼ teaspoon vanilla essence
Milk for glazing
Icing sugar for dusting
Paper cake cases

Roll out the pastry to a thickness of approximately 5 mm (¼ in). Cut out circles using a 5 cm (2 in) fluted cutter (you can sometimes buy plastic ones singly). Arrange on two dampened baking trays and chill until firm. Bake on the second and third shelves of a very hot oven, 230°C/450°F/Gas 8, for 8–10 minutes or until the pastry is puffed up and is pale golden. Cool on a wire rack. Whip the cream until thick and fold in the icing sugar. Cut horizontally through each puff so that it does not completely separate into halves. Open up the puffs like clams and when they are absolutely cold, fill with the cream and cherries. Dust the tops with icing sugar. Put into paper cases. Makes eighteen to twenty.

CROÛTES

Use croûtes as a garnish with meat served in sauces or thick gravies. They store well in a tin and if you are not fussy can be made from carefully stacked trimmings.

Half recipe (125 g (4 oz) flour etc.) Puff pastry (p. 158)
Beaten egg to glaze

Roll out the pastry to a 5 mm (¼ in) thickness. Cut out 5 cm (2 in) diameter circles. Now three alternative shapes are possible – crescents, coins and rings. To make crescents, use the same cutter and press out one or two crescent-shaped curves. Re-roll the trimmings. To make rings, simply cut out the centres with a 2.5 cm (1 in) cutter, these being the coin shapes. Brush the tops with beaten egg or egg yolk and milk and bake in a very hot oven, 230°C/450°F/Gas 8, for 8–10 minutes until puffed up, crisp and just golden. Makes twenty to twenty-four coins or forty crescents.

COCKTAIL TWISTS

Make these delicious and far-too-appetizing cocktail biscuits long enough to fan out comfortably in tall glasses for the buffet table. Use a very sharp knife to cut out the pastry strips.

    Half recipe (125 g (4 oz) flour etc.) Puff pastry (p. 158)
    75 g (3 oz) mature Cheddar cheese, grated
    75 g (3 oz) salted peanuts, chopped
    ⅛ teaspoon Cayenne pepper
    1–2 beaten eggs to glaze

Divide the pastry into two and roll out each half to a 25 × 30 cm (10 × 12 in) rectangle. Brush the top surface of one piece with beaten egg. Mix the cheese, peanuts and Cayenne pepper together and sprinkle over the egg-brushed pastry. Cover with the other pastry rectangle and roll out to seal in the filling. Cut into thin strips lengthwise (to fit into the glasses) and 1 cm (½ in) wide. Twist the strips and place on a baking tray and chill until firm. Brush the upper surfaces with beaten egg. Bake in a very hot oven, 230°C/450°F/Gas 8, for 8 minutes, then carefully reverse the strips and brush the tops with the remaining egg. Bake for a further 4–6 minutes until golden brown and crisp. Makes forty to fifty.

FILLINGS FOR PUFF PASTRY COCKTAIL CASES

Make up a good white coating sauce and mix 150 ml

(¼ pint) of the sauce with any of the following to fill six medium patties, one large vol-au-vent or ten small bouchées.

Neptunes

    100 g (4 oz) cooked white fish, flaked
    40 g (1½ oz) shrimps, chopped and shelled
    1 teaspoon anchovy essence
    2 teaspoons fresh lemon juice
    ½ level teaspoon paprika pepper
    Lemon butterflies for garnish

Sea Urchins

    150 g (6 oz) lobster *or* salmon, flaked
    ½ teaspoon Cayenne pepper
    1 teaspoon fresh lemon juice
    Whole prawns for garnish

Chickolatas

    100 g (4 oz) cooked chicken, chopped
    25 g (1 oz) mushrooms, chopped ⎫ sautéed together in
    2 tomatoes, thinly sliced   ⎰ 15 g (½ oz) butter
    ¼ teaspoon curry powder
    Chopped parsley for garnish

Jambonettes

    50 g (2 oz) Virginia ham, very finely chopped
    2 eggs, hard boiled and sieved
    2 small mushrooms, chopped and sautéed in 6 g (¼ oz)
      butter, chopped
    Pinch of Cayenne pepper
    Hard-boiled egg yolk, sieved for garnish

Parmigiani

2 tomatoes, skinned, de-pipped and chopped
75 g (3 oz) grated Parmesan cheese
½ teaspoon English made mustard
Pepper
Fresh chives, chopped for garnish

PATTIES AND BOUCHÉES

Because of the small diameter, patties and bouchées must be cut from pastry that is no more than 8 mm (⅓ in) thick. If the pastry is too thick the bouchées will rise and topple over. Should you see this happening, briefly open the oven and flatten the offending side with a palette knife. There are two methods of making patties. Either you can roll out the pastry thinly and cut two or three rounds, removing the centres of two with a small cutter. Then using beaten egg, join the circles together with the solid one at the bottom. Bake the lids at the same time on the same baking sheet. Another method is to cut two-thirds of the way through the pastry with a small cutter, then with great care, remove this part and bake separately or mark as for vol-au-vents removing the lid later on. Be extra careful when brushing with egg, so that it doesn't run down the sides and prevent the pastry from rising. Remember to prick well round the outside and bake on a damp baking sheet as before. Try to avoid putting too many round the outside of the baking sheet, as the ones that are nearest to the heat are the most likely to topple over. Vol-au-vent and patty cases will not be as successful if they are out of shape when cut, not turned over before baking or insufficiently rested before baking, or if you have twisted the cutter when cutting out. The oven temperature must be even on both sides.

TARTE FRANÇAISE

A pastry case filled with crème pâtissière, fresh fruit and glazed with apricot jam. The initial shaping of the pastry is important – but the recipe is in fact much simpler than the long instructions make it seem. Serve as soon as possible after the pastry has cooled, but if this is not feasible, flash the case in a hot oven and leave until cool but not cold before filling.

One recipe (250 g (8 oz) flour etc.) Puff pastry (p. 158)
Beaten egg and milk to glaze
50 g (2 oz) butter
40 g (1½ oz) flour
225 ml (7½ fl oz) milk
40 g (1½ oz) sugar
1 egg yolk
2 as-they-come tablespoons double cream
3 drops almond essence
2 teaspoons Kirsch
4 tablespoons apricot jam
Mixed fresh fruit: 2 satsumas, sectioned
    2 bananas, sliced and dipped in lemon juice
    2 oz black grapes, de-pipped
    2 oz green grapes, de-pipped
    3 rings fresh pineapple, each cut into eight
    12 cherries, stoned

Roll out the pastry to a long strip about 30 × 15 cm (12 × 6 in). The pastry will be about 1 cm (¼–½ in) thick. Lightly dust the surface with flour and fold the pastry over lengthwise. Using a sharp knife cut out a rectangle from this double piece, leaving three sides of one long and two short all 4 cm (1½ in) wide so that when you open it up again you have a picture-frame. Now roll out the pastry that you have cut out to the same size. Put the plain pastry rectangle on to a dampened baking tray, moisten the edges and, without distorting, put the 'frame' on top. Trim all the edges. If you are afraid of scratching the baking tray you could slip a sheet of thick paper underneath each edge as you cut. Criss-cross the border to make an interesting design. Knock up the edges horizontally so that the sides resemble a stack of writing paper and prick the base thoroughly and pierce the border at several places with a skewer. Refrigerate for at least ½ hour until firm. Brush the border with beaten egg and milk and bake in the centre of a very hot oven, 230°C/450°F/Gas 8, for 25–30 minutes until the border is golden brown. Flatten the centre with a knife or fork if it rises during baking. Transfer the pastry case with two fish slices to a wire rack and leave to cool.

Meanwhile prepare the filling. Melt the butter in a saucepan over moderate heat, stir in the flour and cook for 1 minute. Gradually add the milk, beating all the time to remove lumps before the sauce boils and thickens. Cool slightly. Add the sugar blended with the egg yolk. Return the saucepan to the heat and cook over the lowest possible heat, stirring all the time until the sauce becomes even thicker. Remove from the heat and leave to cool. Stir in the cream and flavour with almond essence and Kirsch. Spread the cold filling in the cooked pastry case. Arrange the fruit in lines down the length of the tart. Warm the jam and brush over the fruit. Serves eight to ten.

VOL-AU-VENTS

To make vol-au-vents roll the pastry to a thickness of 1–2 cm (½–¾ in). The traditional vol-au-vent cases are oval and made with an 18 cm (7 in) cutter but this can be done using a sharp knife and an oval pie-dish as a guide. Most people nowadays use an ordinary round cutter for savouries and a fluted cutter for sweet fillings.

One recipe (250 g (8 oz) flour etc.) Puff pastry (p. 158)

Choose the heaviest baking sheet that you have, making sure that it is not buckled, and wet with a smear of cold water. Light the oven. Roll out the pastry to 2 cm (¾ in) thick, dip the cutter in hot water, shake off any spare droplets and, making sure not to twist the cutter, press out the required shapes. Cut within the outer edges so that you get even rising, then turn the pastry upside-down. Using a smaller cutter but of the same shape and leaving a border of about 1 cm (½ in), cut two-thirds of the way through the pastry. Make a few decorative slashes in what will later be the pastry lid. Prick through the outside rim at several points. Refrigerate for at least 30 minutes. Bake in a very hot oven, 230°C/450°F/Gas 8, for 15–30 minutes depending upon the size and when the pastry is well risen and brown, reduce the heat to 200°C/400°F/Gas 6. The vol-au-vent cases should be crusty on the outside but are often softer on the inside. Remove the pastry lid, discard the bottom half and scrape out any soggy part inside the case. Brush the lid and edges of the pastry cases with beaten egg into which you have mixed a little salt. Brush carefully from outside to inside and not down the sides or this will prevent rising. Put the cases and the lids back in the oven for another few minutes until browned and well dried out. Put in hot filling if the pastry is to be eaten hot or wait for it to cool down before putting in a cold filling. Makes six to eight 6 cm (2½ in) patties or one 18 cm (7 in) oval vol-au-vent or twelve 5 cm (2 in) patties.

Quick Flaky Pastry

Quick flaky pastry bakes up golden and crisp so that when bitten through you hear an audible crack. Tiny layers of crisp flakes tucked close together are clearly visible. You can prepare this recipe fairly speedily using one large mixing bowl. The ratio of fat to flour is two to three and hard margarine is the best fat to use. This should be refrigerator firm and the water must be ice cold. Strong plain flour absorbs more water than plain flour so you may have to add a little more than stated. You should be able to make this pastry from start to finish in 10 minutes. Because it is such a quick pastry to make, I have given recipes for dishes which are similarly quick. The quantity is sufficient for two double-crust pies or four 20–23 cm (8–9 in) flan dishes.

Ingredients for Basic Recipe

350 g (12 oz) strong plain flour
3 pinches of salt
225 g (8 oz) hard margarine (just under one packet)
225–275 ml (7½–9 fl oz) ice-cold water

Sieve the flour and salt into a mixing bowl. Grate or flake in a quarter of the margarine. Add the smaller amount of water in one go and mix to a soft, almost sticky dough, adding the remaining water if necessary. Knead firmly until the dough is stretchy. Still in the bowl, pull or chop the dough into small pieces. Cut the remaining margarine into 1 cm (½ in) dice, add to the bowl and gather together in one large ball. The lumps of fat will not be mixed in at all at this stage. Roll out on a well-floured surface to a rectangle about 25 × 20 cm (10 × 8 in). Fold the sides to the middle, then the top over the bottom. Give the pastry a 90° turn. Firmly punch down the pastry with the side of a rolling pin so that it slightly flattens. Repeat the process three times. At this point refrigerate or freeze the pastry for 5 minutes, then roll out and use as required. In all, that is roll, fold, turn, roll, fold, turn, roll, fold, turn, roll, fold, chill. If you are only going to use half the pastry, cut vertically and wrap and store the remainder in the freezer or for short-term storage the refrigerator. Bake the pastry in a very hot oven, 230°C/450°F/Gas 8, then reduce according to the filling you are using.

ALMOND GALETTE

A round puff filled with almond paste, so simple to do, but impressive to see. Use a wire tea strainer when you only have a little sugar to sieve. Serve hot if possible or re-heat briefly in a hot oven if it has to wait.

    Half recipe (175 g (6 oz) flour etc.) Quick flaky pastry
        (p. 168)
    100 g (4 oz) ground almonds
    75 g (3 oz) caster sugar
    1 tablespoon undiluted orange squash
    1 tablespoon water
    1 egg, separated
    1 tablespoon icing sugar

Cut off a third of the pastry and roll it out to a 20–23 cm (8–9 in) circle. Roll out the larger piece to form a lid twice as thick and slightly larger. Thoroughly mix the almonds, caster sugar, squash, water and egg white to form a thick paste. Spread over the thinner circle leaving a 1 cm (½ in) border. Brush the edges with water and put on the pastry lid, easing in the sides to prevent pressing out the filling.

Press the edges to seal, then knock up and finish as desired. Beat the egg yolk with a little water and brush over the top of the galette. Bake in a very hot oven, 230°C/450°F/Gas 8, for 10 minutes, then reduce to 200°C/400°F/Gas 6 for a further 15–20 minutes until puffed up and brown. Remove from the oven and sieve the icing sugar over the top. Serves four.

PILCHARD PIE

While personally I am not too fond of pilchards, they do seem to be popular, as all grocers stock them. You can substitute herrings or mackerel, but if these are not canned in tomato sauce add a tablespoon of tomato ketchup and cut the vinegar down drastically. This economical pie should be served hot.

Half recipe (175 g (6 oz) flour etc.) Quick flaky pastry
   (p. 168)
425 g (15 oz) can pilchards in tomato sauce
1 tablespoon vinegar
¼ teaspoon lemon juice
Salt
Pepper
Milk

Halve the pastry and roll out each piece to a 20 cm (8 in) circle. Mash the pilchards, their sauce, vinegar and lemon juice together and season with salt and pepper. Put one piece of pastry on an ovenproof plate. Spoon the pilchard mix in the centre and dampen the edges. Cover with the reserved pastry lid, pressing the edges firmly together to seal. Brush the pastry with milk and bake in a very hot oven, 230°C/450°F/Gas 8, for 15 minutes, then reduce the temperature to 200°C/400°F/Gas 6 for 15–20 minutes until the pastry is golden and well risen. Serves four.

FLAKY BACON AND EGG PIE

No-time-to-spare people, who prefer not to live on sandwiches, could use these frozen pastry circles that they have been storing. Serve hot with mayonnaise.

> Half recipe (175 g (6 oz) flour etc.) Quick flaky pastry
> (p. 168)
> 8 rashers back bacon, de-rinded
> 6 size-4 eggs
> Milk

Roll each half of the pastry to a 23 cm (9 in) circle and use one to line a shallow round pie dish. Halve the bacon rashers cross-wise and arrange ten pieces over the pastry. Break the eggs separately and place well spaced out, around the edges of the bacon. Loosely curve a piece of bacon over each yolk. Moisten the edges of the pastry and cover with the pastry lid, pressing the edges firmly together to seal. Trim and decorate if you wish. Chill while heating the oven. Brush the pastry with milk and bake in a very hot oven 230°C/450°F/Gas 8, for 15 minutes, then reduce the temperature to 200°C/400°F/Gas 6 for 20–30 minutes until the pastry is crisp and brown. Serves four to six.

MARMALADE FLAKY SQUARES

Most people have marmalade in the larder and it goes well with dried fruit, but any jam will do. Fewer people have pastry cutters in the drawer and they will be pleased to know that here is one recipe which does not require anything special at all. Can be served hot or cold, but if served hot, the marmalade will be very hot indeed so watch the roof of your mouth.

> Half recipe (175 g (6 oz) flour etc.) Quick flaky pastry
> (p. 168)

4 heaped tablespoons mixed dried fruit
¼ jar marmalade
Milk for glazing
2–3 tablespoons demerara sugar

Cut the pastry in half, and roll one piece to a 23 cm (9 in) square and the other fractionally larger. Mark the smaller piece of the pastry into approx. 8 cm (3 in) squares. Mix the dried fruit and marmalade together and place a heaped teaspoon of the mixture centrally on each square. Using a clean finger, brush cold water over the uncovered sections of the pastry. Place the pastry lid on top and press firmly between the fruit mounds to seal. Brush with milk, sprinkle with the sugar and, using a sharp knife and without dragging the pastry, cut out the nine squares. Bake in the centre of a very hot oven, 230°C/450°F/Gas 8, for 10 minutes, then reduce the temperature to 200°C/400°F/Gas 6 for 5 minutes or until the bottom half of the pastry is well risen. Makes nine.

Quick-mix Shortcrust

The method of making quick-mix shortcrust differs considerably from the usual method of making shortcrust pastry. The fat is first mixed with the water and then the flour is stirred in with a fork and mixed for no longer than half a minute. The reason that it is possible to make shortcrust pastry by this method, is due to the fat that is used. All makes of whipped-up soft white cooking fat are similar in appearance, being white, opaque and easily cut with a spoon or fork. They are made from a highly refined blend of fats and oils, mostly of vegetable origin. In this book I describe this as soft white cooking fat. The ingredients are similar to those used in margarine, but there is a 100% fat content and no water, milk solids or added flavour. The fats are odourless. During manufacture, air is passed through the mixture at a high pressure in order to give a light texture. The fats with the most air beaten into them, break down more easily, even if taken straight from the refrigerator. They are ideal for modern methods of pastry making. Soft white cooking fat has a very good plasticity and this makes it possible to spread it over a large area of flour, so that each tiny speck of flour is coated with a film of fat. When blending the water and fat together, they will not completely emulsify, but the broken-up fat globules will coat each tiny drop of water. When the flour is stirred in each grain will then have a covering, firstly of fat and then of water, each separated from the other by air. The pastry should not be overmixed in order to keep in the air already trapped in the soft white cooking fat. This recipe is sufficient for a 20 cm (8 in) double-crust pie or for two 15–18 cm (6–7 in) flans.

Ingredients for Basic Recipe

100 g (4 oz) soft white cooking fat
3 tablespoons cold water
200 g (8 oz) plain flour ⎫
½ teaspoon salt   ⎬ sieved together
                           ⎭

Stir the fat and cold water together in a mixing bowl, then add one tablespoon of the salted flour. Stir with a fork until thoroughly mixed, then stir in the remaining flour and knead lightly to a stiff dough. Unless otherwise stated, bake in a fairly hot oven, 200°C/400°F/Gas 6, reducing the temperature after 15 minutes if there is a filling that requires slower cooking.

CUSTARD TARTS

The soft filling sweetened with muscavado sugar gives a richness which overrides the rather flavourless, but quick-to-make pastry. Did you know that mace is the outer layer of the nutmeg but it is usually grated away by the time it gets to you? Serve hot or cold.

Half recipe (100 g (4 oz) flour etc.) Quick-mix short-
    crust pastry (above)
300 ml (½ pint) milk
2 size-3 eggs
20 g (¾ oz) light muscavado sugar
¼ teaspoon vanilla essence
⅛ teaspoon ground mace

Roll out the pastry thinly and cut out circles with a fluted cutter to fit deep patty tins. Bake blind in a fairly hot oven, 200°C/400°F/Gas 6, for 6 minutes. Remove from the oven and take out the weights. Heat the milk to steaming but not boiling point. Beat together the eggs, sugar and vanilla essence. Pour on the milk, beat thoroughly, then strain into a jug. Half fill the patty cases (still in the tins) with the mixture, sprinkling a little mace on each. Return to the centre shelf of the oven, reducing the temperature to 180°C/350°F/Gas 4 and bake for 15–20 minutes until the filling has set. Remove carefully. Makes twelve to fifteen.

SAVOURY WALNUT FLAN

Shelled walnuts are bitter when stale. To refresh them put them into cold water and bring to the boil. Repeat this three times, then refrigerate covered in cold water overnight. You might be unable to resist eating them, instead of putting them in the pastry – they are so good. Serve the flan hot or cold.

Half recipe (100 g (4 oz) flour etc.) Quick-mix shortcrust pastry (p. 174)
25 g (1 oz) shelled walnuts, finely chopped
1 small onion, finely chopped
1 clove garlic, crushed
25 g (1 oz) butter
1 size-3 egg plus 1 further yolk
150 ml (¼ pint) double cream
25 g (1 oz) fresh white breadcrumbs
Salt
Pepper
4 small tomatoes, skinned and chopped
½ green pepper, diced
½ box cress

Roll out the pastry to a 15 cm (6 in) circle. Sprinkle the nuts evenly over the surface then roll out to fit an 18 cm (7 in) plain flan ring. Refrigerate while preparing the filling. Fry the onion and garlic in the butter until just soft. Beat the egg and egg yolk together in a medium bowl and stir in the cream and breadcrumbs and season with salt and pepper. Drain the fried onion and mix with the tomatoes and green pepper. Spread evenly over the pastry and cover with the breadcrumb mixture. Bake in a fairly hot oven, 190°C/375°F/Gas 5, for 20 minutes, then reduce the temperature to 180°C/350°F/Gas 4 for a further 20 minutes or until the mixture has set. Garnish with cress. Serves four to six.

SPEEDY APPLE FLAN

Use up all your windfalls if you are lucky enough to have an apple tree. Otherwise use Bramleys because of their tangy fresh flavour. This dessert is best served warm.

Half recipe (100 g (4 oz) flour etc.) Quick-mix shortcrust pastry (p. 174)
60 g (2½ oz) butter
¼ teaspoon ground cinnamon
1 heaped tablespoon demerara sugar
350 g (¾ lb) cooking apples, peeled, cored and sliced
1 heaped tablespoon sultanas

Roll out the pastry and fit into an 18 cm (7 in) fluted flan dish. Bake blind in a fairly hot oven, 200°C/400°F/Gas 6, for 15 minutes. Remove the baking beans or foil and bake for a further 10 minutes. Switch off oven and close door to keep in the heat while preparing the filling. Melt the butter in a large frying pan, then stir in the cinnamon and the demerara sugar. Cook over gentle heat until the sugar is dissolved. Add the apples and cook a few at a time, removing and draining each batch on kitchen paper. Then arrange the apples in the pastry case. Stir the sultanas into the mixture remaining in the pan, then spoon over the apples. Do not remove the flan from the oven until the filling is ready. Serve with thick unwhipped cream or custard. Serves four.

TUNA AND TOMATO SCATTER PIE

Roll out the pastry in advance and the filling can be whipped up in moments. Try using salmon and add a few chopped capers for a change. Serve hot.

One recipe (200 g (8 oz) etc.) Quick-mix shortcrust
   pastry (p. 174)
2 size-2 eggs
150 ml (¼ pint) milk
1 × 198 g (7 oz) can tuna, drained and flaked
450 g (1 lb) tomatoes, skinned and chopped
¼ teaspoon lemon juice
Few drops Worcestershire sauce
Salt
Pepper
25 g (1 oz) hard cheese, grated
¼ teaspoon Cayenne pepper

Roll out just over half the pastry and use to line a 23 cm (9 in) flan dish. Roll out the remaining pastry to a thickness of 6 mm (¼ in). Beat the eggs and milk together lightly, then stir in the tuna, tomatoes, lemon juice, Worcestershire sauce and salt and pepper to taste. Pour into the pastry case. Bake both the pastry case and the misshapen pastry piece in a fairly hot oven, 200°C/400°F/Gas 6, for 15 minutes, then reduce to 160°C/325°F/Gas 3. Remove the unfilled pastry and crush with a rolling pin. Leave the pie to cook for another 30–35 minutes until the filling has set. Mix half the crumbled pastry with the cheese and Cayenne pepper and sprinkle over the pie. Store the remaining crumbs for another time. Brown briefly under a moderately hot grill. Serves four to five.

Quick Rough Puff Pastry

Quick rough puff and its sister rough puff both use the same ingredients, yet quick rough puff is a little heavier and a little more solid. This is because of the easy way that it is mixed. Quick rough puff pastry rises to about double the height of the rolled-out dough and is very useful for pie crusts. You can use either butter or margarine, but I find that butter gives a better colour. Give the pastry a little longer in the oven than you expect so that it becomes a really crisp golden brown. Strong plain flour is a better choice than the plain flour, because it makes the dough stretch more quickly which hastens the rolling and folding process. The butter or margarine should be firm but not hard. A little lemon juice is added to improve the dough. Use quick rough puff pastry as pie crusts or trim the edges and bake it in a large oblong, cutting it into half, quarters or fingers and serve with meat dishes which will be cooked separately. This is a very good catering ploy. This recipe is sufficient for one 30 cm (12 in) or two 20 cm (8 in) pie crusts.

Ingredients for Basic Recipe

200 g (8 oz) strong plain *or* plain flour
Pinch of salt
150 g (6 oz) firm butter *or* margarine
½ teaspoon lemon juice
125 ml (¼ pint) ice-cold water

Sieve the flour and salt into a mixing bowl, then cut the fat in with a round-bladed knife until the pieces are walnut-sized. Mix quickly with the water to prevent over-working the dough, which could cause starchiness, then gather into a ball and turn on to a floured surface. Roll the pastry to an oblong, fold into three and turn it round so that the open ends are towards you. Then repeat this twice, so that the pastry has had three turns in all. In other words, roll, fold, turn, roll, fold, turn, roll, fold then cover and chill for 10 minutes. Remove from the refrigerator and give one more roll and fold if the pastry looks streaky. Otherwise you can roll out and use at once. Roll quick rough puff to a thickness of 1 cm (⅜ in) so that the layers are not over-flattened. Bake in a very hot oven, 230°C/450°F/Gas 8, for 20–25 minutes. Reduce the temperature as soon as the pastry is brown if there is a filling being cooked underneath. Should the pastry become very brown during cooking, cover with a piece of greaseproof paper or foil, but make certain the paper does not wave about and get burnt.

CHICKEN AND HAM PLAIT

Why not use left-over chicken which is great, but if you have to start from scratch, boil a small bird with an onion, carrot and bay leaf, using a few of the chicken pieces and use the liquid for soup or stock. Serve hot or cold.

One recipe (200 g (8 oz) flour etc.) Quick rough puff pastry (p. 178)
300 ml (½ pint) milk
25 g (1 oz) flour
25 g (1 oz) butter *or* margarine
25 g (1 oz) dry thyme and parsley packet stuffing
225 g (8 oz) cooked chicken, diced
75 g (3 oz) ham, chopped
Beaten egg to glaze

Roll out the pastry into a rectangle 23 × 30 cm (9 × 12 in) and put on a greased and floured baking tray. With a well-used sharp knife make diagonal cuts about 8 cm (3 in) long and 2.5 cm (1 in) apart down both short sides of the pastry, leaving a plain 8 cm (3 in) strip in the middle. The diagonals must of course be sloping in the same direction. Chill while preparing the sauce. Put the milk in a saucepan and blend in the flour, then add the butter or margarine. Cook over gentle heat, whisking all the time until the sauce thickens. Cook for one more minute, then remove from the heat and stir in the dry stuffing, chicken and ham. Spread in an even mound down the centre panel of the pastry but not over the triangular shaped piece at either end. Brush these ends with egg and fold up over the stuffing. Fold all the strips from one side up and over the stuffing, spacing them out evenly and brush the tips with egg. Fold up the strips from the other side to overlap the glazed pastry edges by 1 cm (½ in). Press together to seal. There should now be a plait effect. Brush all the pastry with beaten egg. Return to the refrigerator to firm up the pastry again. Bake in a very hot oven, 230°C/450°F/Gas 8, for 15 minutes. then reduce to 200°C/400°F/Gas 6 for a further 20–30 minutes until the pastry is golden brown. Serves five to six.

CÔTELETTES EN CROÛTE

There is no need to make much fuss when wrapping the pastry round the chops. All the edges will be hidden underneath. Make sure that the chops are properly sealed, which is important if they are not to toughen during baking. Serve hot.

One recipe (200 g (8 oz) flour etc.) Quick rough puff pastry (p. 178)
4 cutlets of lamb with long bone
100 g (4 oz) mushrooms
50 g (2 oz) ham

15 g (½ oz) butter, softened
1 tablespoon freshly chopped parsley
2 teaspoons tomato purée
Salt
Pepper
Beaten egg to glaze

Rapidly brown the chops on both sides under a fierce grill and cook for 2–3 minutes only. Leave to cool. Finely chop the mushrooms and ham and mix with the butter, parsley and tomato purée. Salt and pepper to taste. Divide into four. Divide the pastry into four and roll each piece thinly to a rectangle large enough to wrap around a chop. To assemble damp the edges of the pastry, spread some stuffing over the centre, put the meaty end of the chop on top and spread with the remaining stuffing. Fold the pastry over the chop leaving the bone protruding. Seal well. Place the chops on a damp baking sheet, smooth side uppermost. Brush with beaten egg and slash the top with scissors. Bake in a very hot oven, 230°C/450°F/Gas 8, for 20–25 minutes until puffed and golden brown. Serves four.

DANISH APPLE SLICE

I have taught this recipe numerous times and not one student has gone home feeling disappointed. The main point to note is to seal the ends of the pastry strips securely or they come adrift during baking. Serve warm or cold.

Half recipe (100 g (4 oz) flour etc.) Quick rough puff pastry (p. 178)
350 g (¾ lb) cooking apples
50 g (2 oz) caster sugar
50 g (2 oz) sultanas
100 g (4 oz) marzipan
Beaten egg and milk for glazing

75 g (3 oz) icing sugar, sieved
Knob of butter, soft
3 glacé cherries, halved

Roll out the pastry to an oblong 30 × 18 cm (12 × 7 in).
Peel, core and chop the apples and mix with the sugar and
sultanas. Roll out the marzipan (on a little sieved icing
sugar) to an 8 cm (3 in) width. Place the marzipan strip
down the centre of the pastry and spread with the apple
mixture, leaving a 2.5 cm (1 in) border at either end. Fold
up the ends, then wrap one long side of the pastry over the
fruit and brush the long upper edge with beaten egg. Fold
up the other side overlapping by about 1 cm (½ in). Press
lightly to seal. Turn over to hide the join and place on a
damp baking tray. Brush all the exposed surfaces with
beaten egg yolk and milk. Bake in a very hot oven,
230°C/450°F/Gas 8, for 15 minutes, then reduce to
190°C/375°F/Gas 5 and bake for a further 20–30 minutes
until the pastry is crisp. If you like a crisp all-round crust,
you can turn the slice over and bake upside down for 10
minutes before reversing once more to complete the
cooking, but this results in a flattened top which is less
attractive. Transfer to a wire rack to cool. Mix the icing
sugar with a little water to a coating consistency, stir in the
butter and pour over the cake, allowing the icing to
dribble down the sides. Place cherry halves round side up
along the top. Serves six to eight.

FRUITY SUGAR RING

Sweet and delicious – serve at tea-time when still warm
from the oven or as a hot dessert with custard or whipped
cream. For an ever-so-special occasion ice with glacé icing
and shower with freshly chopped citrus peel.

One recipe (200 g (8 oz) flour etc.) Quick rough puff
    pastry (p. 178)

225 g (8 oz) mixed dried fruit
25 g (1 oz) brown sugar
½ teaspoon mixed spice
2 tablespoons sherry
Milk to glaze
Caster sugar to decorate

Divide the pastry in two. Roll out each to a 30 × 15 cm (12 × 6 in) rectangle. Mix together the remaining ingredients and spread half over each. Roll up the pastry from the long side to form two long rolls. To make two rings join the ends together, using water or beaten egg to help them stick. Brush with milk and slash at intervals around the tops of the rings. Dredge generously with caster sugar. Bake in a very hot oven, 230°C/450°F/Gas 8, for 10 minutes, then reduce to 200°C/400°F/Gas 6 for 25 minutes. Dredge again with sugar while still hot. Makes two.

Rich Pie Pastry

This pastry, having a high fat content, is very rich and tasty, crisp outside and flaky yet soft inside. Unusually it is mixed with boiling water. Follow the directions carefully, making sure than when the pastry pieces are piled on top of one another, the sides are square. If they overlap uneven rising will result. Rich pie pastry is really fabulous as a crust for savoury and rich meaty pies. This recipe is sufficient for a 20 cm (8 in) double-crust pie or to cover a small roasting tin.

Ingredients for Basic Recipe

6 tablespoons *boiling* water
Pinch of salt
150 g (6 oz) hard margarine
150 g (6 oz) plain flour

Bring the water and salt to the boil in a saucepan, add 50 g (2 oz) of the margarine, then bring back to the boil until the fat has melted and the water is just bubbling. Stir in the flour until the mixture forms a ball, turn on to a scarcely floured surface and knead thoroughly. Cover or wrap in cling-film and leave until cool but not cold. Roll out the pastry to a square about 5 mm (¼ in) thick on a floured surface and divide into four equal pieces. Chill for 30 minutes. Cut the remaining margarine into slices to a thickness of 3 mm (⅛ in) and divide into three portions. Arrange one portion over the surface of each of three pastry pieces and pile up the pastry, finishing with a pastry section. Press down with a rolling pin, then roll out the pastry thinly. Fold into three, giving the pastry a 90° turn, then roll and repeat the folding and rolling process twice. That is: roll, fold, turn, roll, fold, turn, roll, fold. Chill for 10 minutes, then roll out and use as required. Bake the pastry in a very hot oven, 230°C/450°F/Gas 8, then reduce to 190°C/375°F/Gas 5 until the filling is cooked. Although this pastry is pleasant cold, it is even more delicious when served hot.

GOULASH PLATTER

All you need to provide a well-balanced one-dish meal. Serve a side salad of cucumber and carrot matchsticks, bean sprouts and shredded lettuce tossed in a mere spoonful of vinaigrette. Serve hot or cold.

One recipe (150 g (6 oz) flour etc.) Rich pie pastry (p. 184)
2 tablespoons vegetable cooking oil
450 g (1 lb) minced veal
1 large onion, chopped
2 cloves garlic, crushed
½ green pepper, chopped
2.5 cm (1 in) strip red pepper, chopped
25 g (1 oz) flour
300 ml (½ pint) well-flavoured chicken stock
50 g (2 oz) mushrooms, sliced
¼ level teaspoon chilli compound powder
1 level tablespoon paprika
¼ teaspoon celery salt
2 bay leaves, crushed
1 generous teaspoon tomato paste
50 g (2 oz) any hard cheese, grated
¼ teaspoon freshly ground black pepper
Salt

Heat the oil in a large saucepan and fry the veal for 5

minutes, stirring all the time until the meat is sealed. Add the onion, garlic, green and red pepper and cook for a further 10 minutes until they are soft. Stir in the flour, add the stock and bring to the boil, stirring all the time. Add the mushrooms and all the remaining ingredients and season to taste with salt. Reduce the heat and cook gently for 10–15 minutes to allow the flavour to develop. Add a little more water if the sauce becomes thick and dense. Cool rapidly. Roll out half the pastry and use to line a 20 cm (8 in) round pie dish. Allow the pastry to overlap the lip of the dish. Moisten the edges and pour the filling into the dish. Roll out the remaining pastry to form a lid. Seal, finish and decorate as desired. Bake in a very hot oven, 230°C/450°F/Gas 8, for 20 minutes, then make a slit in the lid and reduce the heat to 190°C/375°F/Gas 5 for a further 10–15 minutes to make sure the bottom crust is cooked through. Serves six to eight.

ITALIAN MINCE PIE

A variation on the usual mince. The pimiento gives colour and an extra special flavour. You could cook a double quantity of filling before separating into one to eat and one to freeze. Serve hot.

Half recipe (75 g (3 oz) flour etc.) Rich pie pastry (p. 184)
275 g (10 oz) fresh minced raw beef
50 g (2 oz) streaky bacon, de-rinded and chopped
3 level tablespoons flour
1 × 198 g (7 oz) can pimientos, drained and cut into strips
1 medium onion, chopped
300–450 ml (½–¾ pint) beef stock
Pinch of mixed herbs
Salt

Rich Raised Pastry

This pastry is similar to hot water crust pastry in that it is used for raised pies. Frequently these are savoury and it is a popular pastry to use with game pies. The pastry is moulded by hand either round a jar or inside a greased cake tin or a special pie mould. These are called spring form moulds and are made so that it is easy to remove the sides without disturbing the shape of the pastry, but they are very expensive to buy. Rich raised pastry is more like the French croûte in that it is softer and creamier-tasting than hot water crust and is no more difficult to make. A raised pie pastry takes longer to prepare than other types of pastry, so you may prefer to make up a larger quantity and make a bigger pie, but since raised pies are usually eaten cold, left-overs will be just as pleasant to eat as when freshly made. Where a recipe states 'half recipe', halve the ingredients before making up the pastry and produce two pies. Baking times are the same whether you put two, four or six items in the oven, provided they are the same size. Take care with the decoration of the pies, because raised pies should be rich brown, golden and shiny, to really catch the eye and start the old salivary juices working. The pastry is also suitable for picnic flans when they need to be held in the hand without the pastry falling apart. The quantity is sufficient for two 13 cm (5 in) deep cake tins or two 1 kg (2 lb) jars or one 1 kg (2 lb) loaf tin.

Ingredients for Basic Recipe

400 g (1 lb) plain flour
1 level teaspoon salt

150 g (6 oz) lard
125 ml (generous ¼ pint) milk
2 egg yolks

Sieve the flour and salt into a warmed bowl and make a
well in the centre. Cut the lard into small pieces and put
into a saucepan with the milk. Bring to steaming, but not
boiling point, over gentle heat. Immediately pour the
liquid into the flour and mix with a wooden spoon. Beat
the egg yolks together and add to the mixture as soon as
part of the flour has been mixed in. Stir vigorously with a
wooden spoon, then as soon as the dough is cool enough
to handle, knead with the hands until a soft, but not
sticky, dough is formed. Shape the dough into a ball, put it
into a warm bowl and cover with a damp hot cloth. Raised
pies are usually enclosed, so cut off the portion required
for the lid, usually one-third, and keep it warm under the
bowl while rolling out the remainder of the pastry. Raised
pie pastry is rolled out thickly to 1 cm (just under ½ in),
but if you are moulding pastry around empty jam jars,
there is no need to roll out at all. Flour the jam jar on the
outside, then stand it on the ball of warm dough and
carefully mould the pastry, working it up the sides of the
jar with the fingers. As the pastry cools, it will harden into
shape and the jar should not be removed until this has
happened. You will find it easier to remove the jar using
an unscrewing motion. Put the filling into the cavity, roll
out the remaining dough for the lid and seal well. Decorate with the trimmings, brush the pastry top with beaten
egg and make a hole in the centre of the lid. Wrap a
double thickness of foil around the sides of the pie to
prevent it collapsing during baking and tie loosely with a
piece of string. Start the pastry off in a very hot oven,
230°C/450°F/Gas 8, then as soon as the pastry has set,
remove the foil wrapping and continue baking at a reduced temperature according to the instructions given in

the recipe. Small pies are differently timed to large pies. Leave raised pies to set until completely cold, then pour jellied stock through the hole in the lid. Since raised pastry is unaffected by the fat melting, it is a suitable pastry for hot-handed children to mould. You can also use raised pastry with sweet fillings and these need not necessarily be jellied.

BRANDY AND ORANGE MINCE PIE

What a surprise to cut the raised pie and find a rich fruity filling. Serve this dessert hot or cold with custard or whipped cream and I would suggest that it could follow a lightly sauced chicken main course. The quantity makes two pies but you could freeze the other provided you let it return to room temperature in a warm kitchen before serving.

One recipe (400 g (1 lb) flour etc.) Rich raised pastry (p. 189)
450 g (1 lb) mincemeat
Grated rind and juice of two small oranges } filling
5 tablespoons brandy
Beaten egg and cream to glaze

Have ready the filling ingredients mixed together. Divide the pastry in half and evenly mould two-thirds of each piece around the base and down the sides of an upturned floured Kilner jar (approx. 10 cm (4 in) diameter) to a depth of 8 cm (3 in). Keep the remaining dough warm. Fold a strip of double thickness greaseproof paper the depth of the pastry plus 1 cm (½ in) and grease one side. Wrap the greased side inwards tightly around the pastry and secure with pins. Use the remaining dough to shape two lids slightly larger than the diameter of the base of the jars. Reverse the jar on to a greased baking sheet and, cupping the paper collars in one hand, twist and lift out the jars. Put the filling in the pies and fix in the lids close to the mixture. Moisten the joining edges of the protruding sides of the pastry and press the double thickness together to seal. Flute the edges and trim with scissors. Roll the trimmings into a thin rope and wind round the edges of the pastry lid. Brush with the beaten egg mixture and bake in a very hot oven, 230°C/450°F/Gas 8, for 15 minutes. Remove the paper collars and brush the tops and sides of the pastry with the egg mixture. Reduce the oven temperature to 180°C/350°F/Gas 4 and bake for 25–30 minutes until the pastry is crisp and brown. Makes two pies, each serving three to four.

CHICKEN AND MUSHROOM PIE

Leave this pie with its smooth good-looking lines undecorated. Serve hot.

Half recipe (200 g (8 oz) flour etc.) Rich raised pastry
  (p. 189)
20 g (¾ oz) butter
50 g (2 oz) flour
225 ml (7½ fl oz) milk
5 sprigs fresh tarragon
Salt
Pepper
225–250 g (8–10 oz) boned raw cubed chicken
100 g (4 oz) small button mushrooms, washed
Beaten egg to glaze

Put the butter, flour and milk into a large saucepan and whisk together over gentle heat until the sauce thickens. Mix in two sprigs of tarragon and season with salt and pepper and cook for one more minute. Leave to cool while shaping the pastry. Roll out two-thirds of the pastry and use to line an 18 cm (7 in) greased flan ring standing on a greased baking tray. Roll out the remaining pastry to form a lid slightly larger than the diameter of the tin and moisten the upper edge. Mix the chicken and mushrooms into the sauce, pour into the flan case and put on the pastry lid, tucking the sides in to seal and establish a good fit. Brush the surface with beaten egg, taking it right to the edges. Pierce a 5 mm (¼ in) hole in the top. Bake in a very hot oven, 230°C/450°F/Gas 8, for 15 minutes, then remove the flan ring. Brush once again with the beaten egg. Reduce the heat to 180°C/350°F/Gas 4 for a further 35–45 minutes. Plant two or three more sprigs of tarragon in the centre hole. Serves three.

EASTER BONNET SUNDAY DINNER

The decorations on the bonnet are purely for effect and may be too brittle to eat, but the casing round the joint should be pleasant since the moisture from inside will soften the pastry. Serve hot.

One recipe (400 g (1 lb) flour etc.) Rich raised pastry (p. 189)
1 medium onion, finely chopped
25 g (1 oz) butter
100 g (4 oz) mushrooms, thinly sliced
Salt
Pepper
600 g (1½ lb) rolled bacon joint, string removed
Plenty of egg yolk beaten with 1 tablespoon milk for glazing

Fry the onion in the butter for 5 minutes until golden, then stir in the mushrooms and cook for a further 5 minutes. Season lightly with salt and pepper. Roll out three-quarters of the pastry to a circle large enough to wrap round the bacon joint. Spread the onion and mushroom mixture over the surface leaving 1 cm (½ in) border and place the bacon in the middle. Brush the edges with beaten egg and gather up the sides, joining at the top dolly-bag fashion. Seal the edges well and reverse on to a greased baking tray so that the seams are underneath. Brush with beaten egg. Roll out 2.5 cm (1 in) strip of pastry the circumference of the joint and wrap round to form a ribbon. Using the remaining pastry, shape a brim, fixing it to the crown with the beaten egg and form the remainder into grape-sized balls. Still using the beaten egg fix about eight balls on the crown and the remainder on the brim. Brush once again with the beaten egg. Bake in a very hot oven, 230°C/450°F/Gas 8, for 15 minutes, then lower to 160°C/325°F/Gas 3 for 2–2¼ hours. If the pastry becomes too brown cover in greaseproof paper or foil. Serves four to five.

VEAL AND HAM PIE

This traditional recipe has hard-boiled eggs tucked inside. Lightly flour the eggs before bedding them into the mixture and put them in horizontally, so that an even ring of yolk shows when the pie is cut.

  Half recipe (200 g (8 oz) flour etc.) Rich raised pastry
    (p. 189)
  225 g (8 oz) trimmed veal, chopped
  100 g (4 oz) cooked ham, chopped
  1 level teaspoon dried mixed herbs
  Salt
  Pepper
  2 hard-boiled eggs, shelled
  150 ml (¼ pint) rich chicken stock
  1 level teaspoon gelatine
  Beaten egg and cream to glaze

Grease a 450 g (1 lb) loaf tin and line with two-thirds of the dough, pressing it into the corners and sides of the tin, maintaining an even thickness. With the thumbs press up

the pastry from just under the rim until it protrudes 1 cm
(½ in) above the rim. Mix the veal, ham and herbs
together and season sparingly with salt and generously
with pepper. Spread half the mixture into the pastry case
and press an indentation between the centre and either
end to receive and cradle the eggs. Cover with the
remaining mixture. Roll out the reserved dough to make a
lid slightly bigger than the top of the tin. Moisten the
inside edge and press firmly on to the meat. Pinch the
double edges of the pastry together to seal and flute
attractively. Trim with scissors. Brush with the beaten egg
mixture and make two holes in the lid and use the
trimmings to make pastry leaves. Brush a second time
with the egg. Put the tin on a baking tray and bake in a
very hot oven, 230°C/450°F/Gas 8, for 15 minutes, then
reduce to 160°C/325°F/Gas 3 for 1½ hours. Turn out
carefully on to a clean teacloth, then reverse back on to
the baking tray. Brush the sides of the pie once again and
raise the oven temperature to 200°C/400°F/Gas 6 for about
15 minutes until the pastry walls are golden. Remove from
the oven and leave until cold. Heat the stock and dissolve
the gelatine, pour the liquid carefully through the holes in
the lid, tipping the pie so that the set jelly fills up any
spaces there may be. Serves four to five.

Rough Puff Pastry

Rough puff is probably the plainest of the flaky-type pastries which have a large quantity of fat and water and rise in layers. A little lemon juice is added, but be sure to measure this, because if you add too much, it will make the dough acid and more indigestible. Although the ingredients are similar to those in quick rough puff pastry, the method is more like puff pastry. Rough puff will rise much higher than quick rough puff, so you should get about three times the height of the rolled-out pastry. Rough puff is lovely as pie crusts and also as turnovers and little vol-au-vent cases, because it does not rise so much that the cavity is too small to hold the ingredients. Trim the edges of the pastry before baking, so that the hot air can penetrate through the cut surface more quickly. Greater heat is needed for rough puff than suet or shortcrust pastry, owing to the extra fat that the starch has to absorb. Rough puff pastry is ideal for frying.

If the pastry is too hard, you may have added too much water, changing the proportions. Another cause could be either under- or over-rolling so that the fat is unevenly distributed, and a frequent error is to put the pastry into too cool an oven. Falt melts at a lower temperature than the one at which starch will cook, so in an oven that is not hot enough, the fat will not be absorbed by the starch in the flour and will ooze out on to the baking tray and make the pastry hard. You can see if this is happening by looking through the glass oven door, if you have one. If after a few moments you see that the pastry is becoming oily, you will know that the temperature was not hot enough. There may be little that you can do for this pie,

but you can, of course, put it right for the next one. If the
pastry seems to be brown and crispy on the outside, yet,
when you cut into it, it is soft and gooey, it means that the
oven was too hot and the gluten set forming a hard crust,
so that the steam and air could not force up the layers. I
am sorry to say that further cooking won't help the situa-
tion at all and this could also be the case if you decide to
fry the pastry at too hot a temperature.

The quantity in this recipe is sufficient for a 30 cm
(12 in) flan dish or a 1 litre (1½ pint) pie crust.

Ingredients for Basic Recipe

200 g (8 oz) plain *or* strong plain flour
Pinch of salt
150 g (6 oz) butter *or* hard margarine
½ teaspoon lemon juice
125 ml (¼ pint) ice-cold water

Sieve the flour and salt into a mixing bowl and rub in 25 g
(1 oz) of the butter or margarine. Blend the lemon juice
with the water and mix in all at once, adding extra water
only if necessary to form a workable dough. Knead
thoroughly, then leave to cool down but do not refrigerate. This will take about 15 minutes. Beat the remaining
fat flat between two sheets of greaseproof paper, so that
the consistency is the same as the dough. Roll the dough
into a large rectangle, put the slab of fat in the middle and
form it into a parcel, sealing the edges with a spot of
water. Turn the dough over on a floured surface and roll
into a rectangle approximately 30 × 10 cm (12 × 4 in),
keeping the edges straight. If you see the butter through
the pastry, this is quite all right, but if the butter breaks
through the surface of the pastry, then you will need to
sprinkle it with a little flour and put it in the refrigerator
for a short time to firm up. Fold the pastry into three and

give it a 90° turn, then press the open sides with the rolling pin to seal them and roll out again. Repeat the rolling and folding three times, giving the pastry a quarter turn between each rolling. That is to say in all: roll, fold, turn, roll, fold, turn, roll, fold, turn, roll, fold. If the fat is hard, then you must increase the number of rollings and foldings by two. Chill for 10 minutes. Then making sure that the open edges are towards you, roll out and use as required. Bake rough puff pastry in a very hot oven, 230°C/450°F/Gas 8, then reduce the oven temperature as soon as the pastry is golden and set, depending upon the filling used.

CHOCONUT WHEEL

Serve this for a special tea using the best china or as a dinner party dessert. You could make and shape the pastry the day before and store in the refrigerator or freezer. The filling can also be made beforehand either in one or two stages. Serve cold.

> Half recipe (100 g (4 oz) flour etc.) Rough puff pastry
> (p. 197)
> 50 g (2 oz) shelled unskinned almonds
> 50 g (2 oz) caster sugar
> 450 ml (¾ pint) double cream
> 50 g (2 oz) plain chocolate, grated
> A few flaked almonds for decoration
> Beaten egg to glaze

Cut the pastry vertically in half and roll out each piece to an 18 cm (7 in) diameter circle. Trim the edges. Divide one circle into eight triangular pieces. Brush the pastry triangles with beaten egg and place all the pastry on baking trays and bake in a very hot oven, 230°C/450°F/Gas 8, for 15–20 minutes until gold and crisp. Cool on a wire rack. Put the almonds and sugar in a heavy-based pan and heat gently, stirring occasionally until the sugar caramelizes to a mid-tan colour. Pour quickly on to a baking tray lined with non-stick paper. Leave to cool, then crush or pulverize in the liquidizer. Whip the cream until soft peaks form and fold in the pulverized mixture and half the chocolate. Pipe or spread the cream without flattening on to the pastry circle. Discard one of the pastry triangles and arrange the others on the cream. This is necessary to leave a gap for the filling to peep through. Sprinkle with the remaining chocolate and decorate with flaked almonds. Serves seven.

DEVILISHLY DELICIOUS CRAB HORNS

This recipe originates from Cornwall where fresh crab and shellfish are easily obtainable. These horns can be served either as a first course or a light supper dish. Serve cold piled upon a serving dish garnished with sprigs of fresh thyme.

One recipe (200 g (8 oz) flour etc.) Rough puff pastry
    (p. 197)
2 level teaspoons powdered gelatine
1 tablespoon tomato ketchup
1 tablespoon soured cream
1 tablespoon mayonnaise
½ teaspoon Dijon mustard
¼ teaspoon Cayenne pepper
2 teaspoons lemon juice
1 teaspoon Worcestershire sauce
1 small onion, finely chopped
1 stick celery, finely chopped
1 × 75 g (3 oz) canned crabmeat
75 g (3 oz) peeled prawns
Beaten egg to glaze
Sprigs of fresh thyme to garnish

Roll out the pastry and trim to a 30 cm (12 in) square. Cut twelve strips of pastry each measuring 30 × 2.5 cm (12 × 1 in). Dampen along one edge with water. Grease the outside of twelve pastry horn tins. Starting at the pointed ends wind the pastry strips round the outside of the tins, each spiral overlapping the dampened edge of the previous one by 5 mm (¼ in). Place the tins on a dampened baking sheet with the pastry ends underneath. Brush with the beaten egg. Bake in a very hot oven, 230°C/450°F/Gas 8, for 15 minutes, then slide the pastry off the tins and continue baking for a further 5 minutes until golden brown. Meanwhile dissolve the gelatine in 2 tablespoons hot water, stirring until clear. Mix the remaining filling ingredients together and stir in the gelatine. Spoon the mixture into the cooled pastry horns.

GAMMON AND PINEAPPLE SURPRISES

As with all patties these surprises are marvellous for picnics. You can take them hot with you by preparing and leaving them uncooked in the refrigerator and then popping them into the oven 40 minutes before leaving. Wrap individually in double thickness foil and pack in an insulated box or wrap them round with newspaper.

1½ recipes (300 g (12 oz) flour etc.) Rough puff pastry (p. 197)
4 × 13 cm (5 in) diameter gammon steaks
2 tomatoes, skinned and thinly sliced
100 g (4 oz) bacon pâté
1 × 235 g (8½ oz) can of pineapple, drained and chopped finely
Beaten egg to glaze

Roll out the pastry to a 50 × 25 cm (20 × 10 in) rectangle and cut out eight 13 cm (5 in) circles using a cutter or upturned saucer. Place a gammon steak topped with two tomato slices on four of the pastry pieces. Mix the pâté and the pineapple together and spread a quarter of the mixture over the gammon. You may find it easier to smooth if you use a wet knife. Brush the uncovered edges of the pastry with beaten egg and cover with the remaining pastry lids and seal. Knock up the edges and decorate as desired. Brush with beaten egg. Put the surprises on a baking sheet and bake in a very hot oven, 230°C/450°F/Gas 8, for 10 minutes, then reduce the heat to 190°C/375°F/Gas 5 for 20–30 minutes to cook the gammon. Makes four.

SARDINE PYRAMIDS

Sardine and cottage cheese! 'Ugh!' you may say, but if you like sardines you'll make these pyramids again and again. Serve hot or cold.

One recipe (200 g (8 oz) flour etc.) Rough puff pastry (p. 197)
2 × 133 g (4¾ oz) tins sardines in oil, drained
200 g (7 oz) natural cottage cheese
1 very small onion, chopped finely until the juice runs free
2 teaspoons lemon juice
2 teaspoons tomato purée
1 teaspoon freshly chopped parsley
1 size-3 egg, beaten
Salt
Pepper
2 tablespoons milk

Roll out the pastry to a rectangle 5 mm (¼ in) thick. Trim the edges, then cut out sixteen squares approximately 8 × 8 cm (3 × 3 in). Mash the sardines and cottage cheese and mix in the onion, lemon juice, tomato purée and parsley. Bind with half the egg and season with salt and pepper if desired. Put a teaspoon of filling in the centre of each square and brush the edges with water. Draw up the corners to the centre and press the four seams together to seal, making sure that there are no gaps at the lower corners. Flute the edges. Brush the pyramids with milk mixed with the remaining egg. Chill for ½ hour if the pastry seems to be soft. Bake in a very hot oven, 230°C/450°F/Gas 8, for 10 minutes, then reduce to 200°C/400°F/Gas 6 for 15–20 minutes until the pastry is cooked and the filling set.

Shortcrust Pastry

Shortcrust pastry is the best known and most widely used of all the pastries. Personally I do not feel that it is necessarily the best for every dish, nor do I think that it is the easiest to make, but it is certainly the most popular.

The proportions are half fat to flour. Purists use half hard margarine and half lard. In imperial measurements, one level teaspoon of salt is required for every pound of flour and one teaspoon of cold water to each ounce of flour or 4–5 tablespoons to each pound of flour, but you may need to use a little more, depending upon the amount of water the flour absorbs. Use plain flour, preferably sifted with the salt. The water should be ice cold, so that the fat remains waxy and has no chance to melt during the rubbing-in process. For most efficient rubbing in, first add the fat to the flour and cut in with a round-bladed knife until the pieces are quite small. Then, when you come to rubbing in the fat, your fingers, which may be hot, will not melt it. Keep everything as cool as possible and work in a dry cool kitchen.

One of the problems with shortcrust pastry is that because so little water is used, the pastry is difficult to knead to a smooth dough, but it is preferable to over-knead rather than to add more water, which would make the pastry very hard. If you are not a very good short pastry cook, leave the shaped dough in the refrigerator or freeze before baking. This will enable the gluten to recover and, surprisingly, very little harm is done by this over-kneading.

Shortcrust is a sort of neutral pastry suitable for use in nearly every dish, but it is plain and unsophisticated, adding little to the filling except a delicious short texture. It can be used for pastry crusts, tarts, flans, pasties and may also be deep fat fried. The flavour and to some extent the colour are governed by the fat of your choice and the finish on the glaze that you use. If you are a shortcrust pastry fan, you can use most of the fillings found in recipes elsewhere in the book.

Shortcrust pastry stores very well, wrapped and frozen in a ball. If frozen it must be left to thaw out completely before you attempt to roll it out. Freeze it shaped or store it in the refrigerator for one or two days. Do not store in the refrigerator in a polythene bag, because the hot air trapped in the bag will make the pastry go slimy and little black dots may appear, which means that the pastry is going off. If you are clever with pastry, you can store the rubbed-in mixture in either of the ways described and add ice-cold water when required. If you are new to the pastry-making game, note down carefully how much water will be required for that quantity.

If you have been getting poor results with your short-crust pastry, it could be due to a number of reasons. If the pastry is hard, sufficient fat may not have been added or the mixture was not rubbed in properly. You may have added too much water, which would have altered the proportion of fat. Blistering on top of pastry lids is caused by adding the water too slowly, so that some parts of the pastry are more moist than others. In these parts steam caused by the heat of the oven will blow the thin upper surface of the gluten out to form a blister. If the pastry has a speckled appearance, this may be due to the sugar that you have sprinkled on top, but personally I do not find this unattractive. If the pastry on the top crust sinks, and this is particularly pertinent to fruit tarts, it could mean that you have not put in enough filling, or that you have slit the top of the pastry and all the steam collected while the fruit is cooking has escaped, when what it should have done is raise the pastry from underneath. If the pastry is put into the oven at the correct temperature, it should rise and set well above the fruit. When cooking meat pies, there is no need to slit the top if the mixture is dry, but if the mixture is wet, you may find it better to insert a glass pastry funnel, which lets the steam escape, but the pastry rises and stays crisp. When cooking a plate or double-crust pie, the mixture inside may seep into the pastry underneath, making it heavy and sodden. To extract as much steam as possible and avoid this, as soon as the top crust is set and firm on the outside, slit the pastry in two places off centre so that the steam will be able to escape.

The recipe is sufficient for a 1 litre (1½ pint) pie dish or for a double-crust 15 cm (6 in) pie or to line an 18–20 cm (7–8 in) flan dish.

Ingredients for Basic Recipe

200 g (6 oz) plain flour
Just under ½ teaspoon salt
50 g (1½ oz) lard
50 g (1½ oz) hard margarine *or* butter
2–2½ tablespoons ice-cold water

Sieve the flour and salt into a mixing bowl, add the fat and cut with a round-bladed knife into thin slices. Rub in with the fingertips, keeping the hands well above the bowl, so that the flour will gather plenty of air. As soon as the mixture resembles fine breadcrumbs, stop rubbing in, then shake the bowl. Any large lumps that escape notice will appear on the surface of the mixture. Sprinkle most of the water evenly over the flour and mix in with a round-bladed knife. As soon as the mixture clings together, finish kneading with the fingers. If the dough won't hold together and floury bits cling to the outside, add more water. Knead the pastry lightly into a round ball, then cover and leave to rest while preparing the filling. Properly mixed shortcrust dough is easy to shape. Put the dough on a floured board, lightly flour a rolling pin and press the pastry into shape before rolling. While shaping the pastry, remember the old maxim to turn the pastry and not the rolling pin. Loosen the pastry from the board with the blade of a palette knife as you go. In keeping with other pastries shortcrust will benefit from a short stay in the refrigerator before baking. Bake in a fairly hot over 200°C/400°F/Gas 6 for 15–20 minutes, then reduce the heat according to the filling. Bake pastry flans blind if the recipe says so.

BAKED STUFFED APPLE DUMPLINGS

Pears or apples can be stuffed and wrapped in pastry. These are typical English recipes such as 'Mother' used to make. Vary the fillings to suit your personal taste.

One recipe (200 g (6 oz) flour etc.) Shortcrust pastry (p. 205)
3 medium cooking apples
1 heaped tablespoon currants
1 generous tablespoon brown sugar } mixed together
Grated rind of 1 lemon
Beaten egg and a teaspoon milk to glaze

Roll out the pastry and cut 3 rounds sufficiently large to enclose the apples. Peel and core the apples, place one in the middle of each pastry round. Fill the apples with the currant mixture. Draw up the pastry around the apples, shaping smoothly. Damp the edges and squeeze together so that the pastry completely conceals the apple. Place the dumplings upside down on a greased baking tray. Shape the remaining pastry into leaves, moisten and fix round the top of the dumplings. Brush the pastry plentifully with the beaten egg mixture. Pierce a small hole in the tops and bake the dumplings in a fairly hot oven,

200°C/400°F/Gas 6, for 15 minutes, then reduce to
180°C/350°F/Gas 4 for a further 30 minutes. Serves
three.

BAKEWELL TART

Whenever you add egg to a mixture of fat and sugar beat
in only a little at a time or curdling will occur. This is
because during beating, the fat and sugar will have
become warm and the sudden addition of the cold egg can
cause curdling. To prevent this all ingredients for cake
making should be warmed evenly to a temperature of
about 20°C/70°F, i.e. warm room temperature. Serve hot
or cold.

   One recipe (200 g (6 oz) flour etc.) Shortcrust pastry
      (p. 205)
   2 as-they-come tablespoons raspberry jam
   50 g (2 oz) butter *or* margarine
   50 g (2 oz) caster sugar
   1 size-3 egg, beaten
   ⅛ teaspoon almond essence
   ⅛ teaspoon vanilla essence
   40 g (1½ oz) ground almonds
   25 g (1 oz) self-raising flour, sieved
   40 g (1½ oz) flaked almonds

Roll out the pastry and use to line an 18 cm (7 in) fluted
flan ring. Spread the jam over the base of the pastry.
Beat the butter and sugar together until light and fluffy,
then beat in the egg a few drops at a time. Mix in the
essences, ground almonds and flour. Pile on top of the
jam and spread the mixture to the edges of the flan.
Scatter with flaked almonds and bake in a fairly hot
oven, 200°C/400°F/Gas 6, for 25–30 minutes or until
golden brown and firm to the touch. Serves five to six.

CHEESE AND ASPARAGUS FLAN

Keep a can or two of asparagus in the larder – it always adds an air of luxury to any dish, but remember, there are different sorts and on the whole the lower the price, the tougher the stems. Serve hot or cold.

> One recipe (200 g (6 oz) flour etc.) Shortcrust pastry (p. 205)
> 1 × 298 g (10½ oz) can green cut asparagus, drained
> 1 size-3 egg, beaten
> 150 ml (¼ pint) single cream
> 50 g (2 oz) Lancashire cheese, grated
> Salt
> Pepper
> 1 rounded tablespoon fresh brown breadcrumbs

Roll out the pastry and use to line an 18 cm (7 in) flan tin. Bake blind in a fairly hot oven, 200°C/400°F/Gas 6, for 15 minutes. Remove the weights. Arrange the asparagus in the base of the flan, Beat the egg, cream and three-quarters of the cheese and season with salt and pepper. Pour over the asparagus. Reduce the oven temperature to 190°C/375°F/Gas 5 and bake the flan for 20 minutes or until the custard is just set. Combine the remaining cheese with the breadcrumbs, sprinkle over the flan and brown under the grill. Serves four to six.

LAMB AND LEEK PIE

Use 450 g (1 lb) lean lamb, cubed, instead of the chops if you prefer. Serve hot.

> One recipe (200 g (6 oz) flour etc.) Shortcrust pastry (p. 205)
> 8 thick lamb cutlets
> 1 rounded tablespoon flour seasoned with salt and pepper

300 ml (½ pint) chicken stock
1 medium onion, finely chopped
450 g (1 lb) leeks, white part only, sliced
1 teaspoon fresh rosemary leaves

Trim away the fat and dip the chops in the seasoned flour. Pour the stock into a deep pie dish and put in the chops so that the meaty parts are evenly distributed. Add the onion, leeks and rosemary leaves. Cover with foil and bake in a moderately hot oven, 190°C/375°F/Gas 5, for 40 minutes. While the meat is cooking roll out the pastry roughly the shape of the dish and chill. When the meat is nearly tender, damp the edges of the dish and fit the pastry lid on top, tucking the trimmings under the edges. Finish and decorate rapidly before the pastry starts to soften. Raise the oven temperature to 200°C/400°F/Gas 6 and bake for 25–30 minutes, slashing the top of the pastry after 15 minutes. Serves four to five.

QUICHE LORRAINE

The oldest recorded open flan case from Lorraine which was made using a bread dough. You may care to use this filling with a yeast pastry case. Traditionally ingredients are bacon, cream and eggs but nowadays cheese is frequently included and the pastry used is shortcrust. Serve preferably hot.

One recipe (200 g (6 oz) flour etc.) Shortcrust pastry (p. 205)
4 rashers bacon
300 ml (½ pint) single cream
3 egg yolks
1 whole egg
Salt
Pepper

Roll out the pastry and use to line a 20 cm (8 in) plain flan ring. Bake blind in a fairly hot oven, 200°C/400°F/Gas 6, for 15 minutes, then remove the weights. Reduce the oven temperature to 160°C/325°F/Gas 3. While the flan is cooking grill the bacon rashers lightly. The reason for this is not to make the rashers crisp but to remove all the fat. Remove the rinds, chop the bacon and spread in the base of the flan. Beat the cream and all the eggs together and season well, depending on the flavour of the bacon. Pour the mixture over the bacon and bake for 30–35 minutes until the filling is puffed up and golden brown. Serves six.

SUNSHINE FLAN

You can make your own custard from milk, cornflour, vanilla essence and a little yellow food colouring, but somehow custard powder, which should be the same, tastes different. Use a rounded tablespoon of custard powder and a level tablespoon sugar to 300 ml (½ pint) milk. Serve cold.

One recipe (200 g (6 oz) flour etc.) Shortcrust pastry
    (p. 205)
½ tangerine jelly
300 ml (½ pint) freshly made thick custard (made from
    custard powder)
50 g (2 oz) icing sugar
Milk
Orange food colouring
3 satsumas

Dissolve the jelly in 225 ml (7½ fl oz) near-boiling water (according to the directions on the packet) and leave until nearly set. The refrigerator will hasten this. Roll out the pastry and use to line a 20 cm (8 in) fluted flan ring. Bake blind in a fairly hot oven, 200°C/400°F/Gas 6, for 15 minutes, then remove the weights and metal ring. Bake in the oven for a further 5 minutes until the pastry is golden and crisp. Leave to cool. Pour the jelly into the pastry case. Leave until completely set, then pour over the custard. Leave until cold. Mix the icing sugar to a coating consistency with one or two teaspoons milk. Add a few drops of orange food colouring. Pour over the custard and arrange a circle of satsuma segments around the edge. Serves five to six.

Strudel

Strudel pastry comes from Hungary where it was a challenge to be able to make it properly and you really had the accolade as a first-rate cook if you could make the pastry so thin that you could read a book through it. It is a very popular pastry in Austria and Germany and it is used to make the famous apple strudel which you can buy in most continental pâtisseries in this country. It is rather difficult to make at home, because it takes such a long time and you have to be very careful not to tear the dough. The mixing of the ingredients, however, is not so difficult and strudel is one of the few pastries where everything has to be warm to guarantee success. The dry ingredients are sieved into a bowl and mixed with the liquid ingredients to form a dough. After that the dough must be kneaded for a considerable time until it is soft, silky and stretchy. After resting the dough is rolled out on a large table covered with a clean cloth, which has been generously dusted with flour. The dough is then stretched by hand from underneath until it is wafer thin and transparent. The filling should be ready to put on directly the pastry is stretched. The strudel is then rolled up and baked.

Any strudel dough that is not going to be used should be brushed generously with melted butter, covered with a piece of greaseproof paper and rolled up Swiss roll fashion. Overwrap in a double thickness of foil and it will freeze for up to a month. The pastry should be left to thaw while still wrapped at room temperature and the filling should be ready to put on immediately the pastry has thawed. The recipe is the minimum that I would recommend as to make less would not be worth the effort.

Ingredients for Basic Recipe

200 g (8 oz) strong plain flour
½ level teaspoon salt
1 size-3 egg
1 teaspoon lemon juice
2 tablespoons vegetable oil (not olive)
125 ml (generous ¼ pint) warm water
Melted butter

Sieve the flour and salt into a mixing bowl and make a well
in the centre. Beat the egg, lemon juice, oil and most of
the water together and pour into the centre. Stir, gradually drawing the flour in from the sides and beat until the
dough forms a soft ball. Turn on to a floured surface.
Lifting the dough well above the surface, throw it down
about 100 times or for about 15 minutes until it is smooth
and silky. Knead the dough into a round and dust with
flour, then cover with an upturned warm mixing bowl,
making sure that the top of the dough does not touch the
bowl and leave in a warm place for 30 minutes. Meanwhile
prepare the table for rolling out the dough. Cover a table
or two-sided work surface (so that it is possible to reach
the dough from two angles) with a square metre (yard) of
clean cloth. Dredge the cloth generously with flour. To
shape the dough, divide it in half, leaving one piece under
the bowl. With a well-floured rolling pin, roll out the
dough to the size of a large plate. Brush the top with
melted butter, then putting your hand underneath the
dough with the backs of the hands uppermost, keeping the
thumbs and fingers well tucked in, stretch the dough until
it is wafer-thin and transparent. When doing this, imagine
that you are putting on a bath hat with your hands inside it
as you would if protecting a new hair-do. Keep the dough
to an even thickness. From time to time brush with melted
butter to prevent drying out. When the dough is thin

enough to see through and about 45 × 38 cm (18 × 15 in) cut off the edges with scissors until it measures 38 × 30 cm (15 × 12 cm) and immediately fill. Stretch the other piece of dough, then fill or store as desired. Bake in a very hot oven, 230°C/450°F/Gas 8, for 10 minutes, then reduce to 200°C/400°F/Gas 6 until the pastry is a light brown colour.

ALMOND, APRICOT AND CHERRY STRUDEL

Cut off the pastry flaps with a sharp knife before serving. Substitute fresh peaches if they are cheaper but they must be first peeled due to their tougher skins. Serve warm or cold.

Half recipe (100 g (4 oz) flour etc.) Strudel pastry (p. 213)
100 g (4 oz) ground almonds
Finely grated rind of 1 orange
75 g (3 oz) caster sugar
450 g (1 lb) fresh apricots, stoned and sliced
50 g (2 oz) (10) glacé cherries, chopped
Melted butter for brushing
Icing sugar

Leaving the pastry on the floured cloth, trim the edges with scissors and brush the whole surface with butter. Combine the almonds, orange rind and sugar in a large polythene bag, put in the apricots and cherries and shake the bag to evenly coat the fruit. Spread over the pastry leaving a 5 cm (2 in) border. Roll up from the long end Swiss roll fashion, using the cloth as a guide. Lift carefully on to a greased baking tray, keeping the seam underneath. Curve the ends of the roll to form a horseshoe shape. Brush all over with melted butter. Bake in a very hot oven, 230°C/450°F/Gas 8, for 10 minutes, then reduce to 200°C/400°F/Gas 6 for 20 minutes or until the pastry is crisp and golden brown. Transfer carefully to a serving dish and dredge generously with icing sugar. Serves five to six.

APPLE STRUDEL

This is the best known of all the strudel pastries, so what can I say about apple strudel – only that there are two types, one made with a more solid pastry in a single roll and this one, which looks more like a thin parchment and is in a class of its own. Serve hot or cold with whipped cream or a glass of Liebfraumilch.

Half recipe (100 g (4 oz) flour etc.) Strudel pastry (p. 213)
225 g (½ lb) cooking apples, peeled, cored and thinly sliced
75 g (3 oz) butter ⎫ fried together until the
75 g (3 oz) fresh breadcrumbs ⎭ butter is absorbed
75 g (3 oz) granulated sugar
50 g (2 oz) sultanas
Melted butter for brushing
Icing sugar

Combine the apples, fried crumbs, sugar and sultanas. Trim the pastry to a rectangle 38 × 30 cm (15 × 12 in). Sprinkle the fruit mixture in an 8 cm (3 in) band over the length of the pastry, leaving a 5 cm (2 in) border at either end. Brush the uncovered dough with butter, then roll up the pastry from the filled side using the cloth as a guide in the same way as a Swiss roll. Seal all the edges with water and transfer to a greased baking tray with the edges underneath. You will find that you will have to curve the pastry into a horseshoe. Brush the dough all over with melted butter and bake in a very hot oven, 230°C/450°F/Gas 8, for 10 minutes, then reduce to 200°C/400°F/Gas 6 for 20 minutes more or until the pastry is crisp and golden, an average time being 30–40 minutes in all. Remove

carefully with two fish slices to the dish from which you
are going to serve and sprinkle the pastry with icing sugar.
Serves four to six.

BAKLAVA

You can make Baklava with puff pastry splitting the
baked pastry into four and filling with nut mixture below
and coating with the syrup. A double recipe of strudel
pastry is enough for a modest-sized Baklava but the best
way to make this gooey Greek pâtisserie is to buy strudel
leaves or phyllo. Phyllo is obtainable in all specialist
grocers and is sold in fresh or frozen 450 g (1 lb) packs –
the amount required for a large baking tray which will
serve about thirty. I find it is better to make up the large
quantity and freeze in batches for future use. You must
pour cold syrup over the hot pastry, so make this first.

450 g (1 lb) phyllo
200 g (8 oz) unsalted butter, melted
150 g (6 oz) walnuts, finely chopped ⎫
100 g (4 oz) blanched almonds, finely
    chopped   ⎬ mixed
½ level teaspoon ground cinnamon   together
½ teaspoon ground nutmeg
50 g (2 oz) caster sugar   ⎭

Syrup
200 g (8 oz) sugar
2 generous tablespoons clear honey
2 teaspoons fresh lemon juice
1 tablespoon orange juice

First make the syrup. Dissolve the sugar in 150 ml
(¼ pint) water over gentle heat, stir in the honey and fruit
juices and bring to the boil. Reduce to simmering for
three or four minutes until the syrup thickens sufficiently

to coat the back of a spoon (103°C/218°F). Cool and refrigerate.

Have ready a deep roasting tin and a pastry brush. Brush the base and sides of the tin with butter. Lay two pastry leaves in the tin and brush with butter. Repeat until you have used about half the pastry. Unless you are working quickly, keep the waiting pastry covered with cling-film to prevent it drying out. Sprinkle with two-thirds of the nut mixture (you may need to fold over the pastry leaves if the tin is too small, but this doesn't matter at all. In fact the middle layer can even be made up with any broken phyllo). Layer and butter another four leaves and cover with the remaining nuts. Layer the remaining pastry as before and pour over any surplus butter. Using a sharp knife and cutting through the top layers of pastry only, criss-cross the pastry to mark out diamond-shaped portions. Bake in a cool to moderate oven, 160–180°C/325–350°F/Gas 3–4, for 30 minutes. Raise the oven temperature to 230°C/450°F/Gas 8 for 12–15 minutes or until the pastry is golden and puffy. Switch off the oven leaving the pastry inside. Remove the tin from the oven, pour the syrup over the pastry and cut completely through to separate the portions. Leave in the tin until the syrup is well soaked in. Serve from the tin or transfer to a wire rack or serving dish. Makes thirty to thirty-five pieces.

CHESHIRE MUSHROOM STRUDEL

For people with plenty of time but little money. Don't use other kinds of fish but do add a few chopped scallops when poaching the fish, if you feel like lashing out. Serve hot.

Half recipe (100 g (4 oz) flour etc.) Strudel pastry (p. 213)
225 g (½ lb) cod *or* haddock fillet
250 ml (½ pint) milk

Salt
Pepper
50 g (2 oz) button mushrooms, sliced
50 g (2 oz) butter
25 g (1 oz) plain flour
1 hard-boiled egg, chopped
50 g (2 oz) Cheshire cheese, chopped
Grated rind of 1 lemon
Melted butter for brushing

Garnish
1 oz Cheshire cheese, crumbled
1 egg, hard boiled and chopped

Poach the fish in the milk seasoned with salt and pepper until flaky (about 10–15 minutes). Remove the fish with a slotted spoon and discard the skin and bones. Sauté the mushrooms in butter for 2 minutes – just enough to give them flavour – then stir in the flour. Gradually add the poaching liquid, straining if necessary and bring to the boil stirring continuously. Simmer for 3 minutes, then remove from the heat and stir in the fish, egg, cheese and lemon rind. Leave to cool. Spread the filling over the trimmed pastry to within 5 cm (2 in) of the short end and 10 cm (4 in) along the long end. Brush the exposed surfaces with the butter, then roll up tucking in the edges. Seal the seams with water. Shape into a horseshoe and place seamed sides down on a greased baking tray. Brush all over with melted butter. Bake in a very hot oven, 230°C/450°F/Gas 8, for 10 minutes, then reduce to 200°C/400°F/Gas 6 for a further 30 minutes until crisp and a light brown. Remove to a heated serving dish and garnish with chopped cheese and hard-boiled egg. Serves four.

Suet Crust Pastry

Suet crust pastry can be used in either sweet or savoury dishes, but it is best known as the pudding in steak and kidney pudding. Roly poly pudding is another favourite.

Suet crust pastry can be either steamed or boiled. Use self-raising flour or plain flour plus baking powder, so that the pastry will be less heavy. Make sure that the suet is fresh and clean or use commercially shredded suet. I find Atora very good. If you are a vegetarian, you can substitute hard white vegetarian fat and you will find it easiest if you first freeze it and then grate on a coarse grater. This way no rubbing in is involved. Suet is extremely hard and large lumps of fat would not melt completely when the heat from the oven or steamer was applied, so that uneven texture could result.

Use one-third to one-half suet to the weight of flour and add four to five level teaspoonfuls of baking powder to every 450 g (1 lb) of plain flour. It is not necessary to add baking powder to good-quality self-raising flour. Sometimes breadcrumbs are added to suet pastry to give it a more open texture, in which case the baking powder may be halved.

The most important factor in making suet pastry is the way in which the liquid is added. This must be done all at once, because if the water is added too slowly, the lumps of fat will join together and prevent the moisture from being distributed evenly, giving a very uneven texture. The amount of water depends upon how you are going to cook the pastry. Generally speaking, a wetter, slacker mixture is required for pastries which are either steamed, or boiled, wrapped in a cloth. The filling has also to be taken into account, since if the filling is wet, less water is required in the pastry itself, as it will absorb moisture during cooking.

When mixing, handle the pastry as little as possible and mix to a light elastic consistency. Although raising agents do not normally start to work until heat is applied to them, they may start to puff up as soon as they feel the moisture around them. If you want to be sure of a light pastry, try to cook as quickly as possible after mixing. Baked suet pastry tends to be on the hard side and you may find some of the suet has escaped during baking, leaving the tin rather greasy. Steaming is the best of the moist methods, since the water does not come into contact with the pastry. When suet crust pastry is boiled, wrapped in a cloth, the texture is closer, due to the fact that the cloth prevents the pastry from rising. Moisture nearly always seeps in somewhere, however well you have wrapped up the pudding, and the water will cause the outside of the pastry to be sticky. The only time that suet pastry may be cooked in water without protection is in dumplings, where the well-risen spongy inside and the soft sticky outside are bonus points. When steaming or boiling dishes made with suet pastry the water in the saucepan must be at boiling point so that the starch in the flour can cook quickly and absorb the fat as it melts. After a few minutes reduce to simmering. Steamed puddings must be cooked for at least 1 hour as it takes this length of time for the suet to melt. Further cooking will improve the texture of the pastry making it more spongy. Suet pastry is best eaten hot. If you like a shorter, less spongy texture replace a quarter of the flour with fresh fine breadcrumbs. The quantity given is sufficient for one 1–1.2 litre (1½–2 pint) basin.

Ingredients for Basic Recipe

225 g (8 oz) self-raising flour *or* 225 g (8 oz) plain flour plus 2 level teaspoons baking powder

½ teaspoon salt
100 g (3½ oz) shredded suet
Approximately 125 ml (¼ pint) cold water

Sieve the flour, salt and baking powder, if used, into a mixing bowl. Add the suet in three separate lots, stirring in between to ensure that each particle of suet is coated with the flour. Pour in the water all at once and mix with a round-bladed knife to form a soft elastic, but not sticky, dough. Add either flour or water if required. Scoop the dough on to a lightly floured surface, turn over so that there is a little light coating of flour on top and knead the dough as little as possible into a smooth ball. Preferably use immediately, but if it has to be kept waiting while the filling is being prepared, cover it with an upturned bowl. Steamed puddings take a minimum of 1½ hours, dumplings 15–20 minutes. Cook according to the directions in the recipe.

DELAWARE PUDDING

This is a delicious, filling, fattening recipe but lovely on a cold winter's day. Delaware is a layered pudding and the only tricky part is dividing the dough so that the pieces fit the basin. Serve hot.

One recipe (225 g (8 oz) flour etc.) Suet crust pastry (p. 220)
1 medium cooking apple, peeled, cored and chopped
2 rounded tablespoons raisins
Grated rind and flesh of 1 orange
Grated rind of 1 lemon
1 heaped tablespoon brown sugar
3 tablespoons sherry

Grease a 1 litre (1½ pint) pudding basin. Divide the pastry into three unequal parts. Mix together the filling ingredients. Press the smallest piece of pastry into the base of the pudding basin and top with half the fruit mixture. Cover with the medium-sized piece of pastry flattened with the palm of the hand to fit into the basin. Top with the remaining fruit and cover with the third and largest piece of dough, shaped to a lid and ease with the fingers to seal the top. Grease the underside of a double sheet of foil or greaseproof paper. Make a 2.5 cm (1 in) pleat down the centre and tie securely over the top of the pudding. Steam for 2–2½ hours in a lidded pan containing enough boiling water to reach halfway up the basin. Top up with boiling water during cooking if necessary. Serves four to six.

DUMPLINGS WITH A DIFFERENCE

Basic dumplings can be made from the suet pastry recipe and are better if they are of a slightly softer consistency. Allow 12 g (½ oz) flour plus other ingredients per serving. Shape into balls and drop the dumplings into the simmering stock, stew or soup. Cover with the lid and add to the saucepan 15–20 minutes before the end of cooking time until they puff into spongy spheres.

Here are a few variations on the dumplings theme to be used with one recipe (225 g (8 oz) flour etc.) Suet crust pastry (p. 220).

Bran dumplings

Add 50 g (2 oz) bran to the dry ingredients before mixing in the water.

Carrot dumplings

Add 100 g (4 oz) raw grated carrot to the dry ingredients before mixing in the water.

Cheese whirl dumplings

Roll out the pastry into an oblong about 1 cm (¼–½ in) thick. Sprinkle 75 g (3 oz) grated mature Cheddar cheese evenly over the surface. Roll and cut into 1 cm (½ in) slices.

Each variation makes sixteen dumplings.

PINEAPPLE AND PEEL DUMPLINGS

A nice stodgy winter pud for greedy eaters. Serve hot.

One recipe (225 g (8 oz) flour etc.) Suet crust pastry (p. 220)
1 × 225 g (8 oz) can pineapple pieces, juice reserved
4 generous tablespoons mincemeat
50 g (2 oz) chopped mixed peel
4 rounded tablespoons fresh white breadcrumbs
2 tablespoons sherry
50 g (2 oz) demerara sugar

Divide the pastry into sixteen equal pieces. Roll into balls and flatten into circles with the palm. Mix the remaining ingredients and put a spoonful in the centre of each pastry circle. Moisten the edges and gather together above the filling dolly-bag fashion. Press to seal, then reverse on to a floured surface, shaping into little doughnuts. Put the pineapple juice and sugar in a large shallow pan and add water to a depth of 5 cm (2 in). Bring to the boil, drop in the dumplings a few at a time so that the water does not fall below simmering point, then quickly turn them over and simmer for 15–20 minutes. Serve with custard or cream.

STEAK AND KIDNEY PUDDING WITH PORT AND BRANDY

You have two choices when cooking steak 'n' kidney

pud – either parcook the meat and subsequently reduce the steaming time or do it all in one. The total cooking times work out near enough the same. The pastry should be on the soft side for this type of pudding. Serve hot – gorgeous!

One recipe (225 g (8 oz) flour etc.) Suet crust pastry (p. 220)

100 g (4 oz) ox kidney, cores removed

450 g (1 lb) stewing steak, trimmed and cut into 1 cm (½ in) cubes

Approximately 2 tablespoons flour, well seasoned with salt and pepper

1 small onion, chopped very finely

1 tablespoon freshly chopped parsley

Approximately 200 ml (⅓ pint) cold beef stock

1 tablespoon port

1 tablespoon brandy

Grease and flour a 1–1.2 litre (1½–2 pint) pudding basin, grease a sheet of greaseproof paper and have ready a square of 30 cm (12 in) foil. Put the kettle on to boil and get out a heavy-base saucepan large enough to take the basin with a lid that fits tightly. Roll out two-thirds of the pastry to line the pudding basin, taking into account the depth of the sides and measurement of the base. Roll out the remaining dough just a little bigger than the top, so that there is something to tuck in. Cut up the kidney and toss with the meat in the flour. Arrange the meat in layers in the basin with the onion and parsley, the port and brandy and sufficient stock to two-thirds fill the basin. Cover with the pastry lid, folding the edges underneath and press the pastry edges together to seal. Put the greaseproof paper and foil together greased side nearest the pudding and make a pleat down the centre to allow for growing. Put these over the basin and secure with string. Ask your butcher to give you a lesson in knot-tying as their slip knots are very good. Pour a little boiling water into the saucepan. Put in the basin, then add sufficient water to come half-way up. Clamp on the lid and reduce to simmering and cook for 4 hours. You will have to top up with water occasionally and this must of course be boiling. Serve from the basin wrapped in a pretty napkin, as puddings sometimes collapse when turned out. Have ready some extra stock laced with port and brandy to thin the gravy if necessary. Serves five to six.

Vegetable Oil Pastry

For heart watchers use sunflower oil, but other vegetable oils (except olive) can be used. This pastry is quick to mix and, because of the vegetable oil content, is rather soft so that it is better for tarts or open flans than in covered pies. The rolled-out pastry tends to crack and is not easy to lift. This pastry freezes well. It can either be frozen in a ball or rolled out ready for use. Best results are obtained by refrigerating for at least 20 minutes after shaping. The texture of the cooked pastry is crumbly and short and the colour is pale straw. The flavour depends on the oil used – the thinner the oil the less pronounced the flavour – and fresh oil should be used, since if old it may have gone rancid. Oil is better stored in plastic rather than metal containers. The quantity is sufficient to line a 20–23 cm (8–9 in) flan.

Ingredients for Basic Recipe

200 g (8 oz) plain flour
½ level teaspoon salt
8 tablespoons vegetable oil
2½ tablespoons cold water

Sieve the flour and salt into a mixing bowl, make a large well in the centre and pour the oil and water in all together. Then whisk the oil and water together so that they just combine with a fork, gradually drawing in the flour from the sides. Do not attempt to mix in too much flour at a time or the dough will become lumpy. When the dough forms a soft ball, knead it very gently with the fingertips only. After rolling, shaping and resting, bake vegetable oil pastry in a fairly hot oven, 200°C/400°F/Gas 6, unless the recipe states otherwise.

CHOCOLATE MEDALLION FLAN

In specialist shops you can purchase gold or silver food colouring. Paint this round the medallion rims and leave to dry before putting on to the flan. Serve cold.

One recipe (200 g (8 oz) flour etc.) Vegetable oil pastry
  (p. 226)
175 g (6 oz) cooking chocolate
15 g (½ oz) butter
3 size-3 egg yolks
1 tablespoon sweet sherry
4 egg whites
100 g (3½ oz) bar bitter dessert chocolate
120 ml (4 fl oz) double cream, whipped

Roll out the pastry and use to line a 23 cm (9 in) flan ring. Bake blind in a fairly hot oven, 200°C/400°F/Gas 6, for 10 minutes. Remove the weights. Melt the cooking chocolate and butter in a bowl over a pan of hot, but not boiling, water making sure that the water does not touch the base of the bowl. Beat in the egg yolks and the sherry. In another bowl beat the egg whites until stiff but not dry. Stir one spoonful into the chocolate mixture, then fold in the remainder carefully. Pour into the flan case. Reduce the oven temperature to 180°C/350°F/Gas 4 for 15–20 minutes until the filling has set. Remove from the oven and leave until completely cold before removing the metal flan ring. Meanwhile melt the bitter chocolate and spread over a sheet of non-stick paper to a thickness of 3 mm (⅛ in). Lift the paper carefully on to a tray and refrigerate until set but not brittle. Stamp out rounds with a 2.5 cm (1 in) cutter and leave on the tray until hard.

Arrange in an overlapping circle round the edge of the flan and pipe rosettes of cream in the centre. Serves five to six.

CREAM CHEESE SLICE

Rolled thinly the pastry is very fragile and crisp. The filling is bland but you could add more mustard and some Cayenne pepper if you like. Serve hot.

One recipe (200 g (8 oz) flour etc.) Vegetable oil pastry (p. 226)
225 g (8 oz) cream cheese
⅛ teaspoon mustard powder
2 size-3 eggs, separated
150 ml (¼ pint) milk
Salt
Pepper
1 level tablespoon freshly chopped parsley
4–5 medium tomatoes, skinned and thinly sliced
1 tablespoon vegetable oil

Roll out the pastry thinly and use to line a 23–28 cm (9–11 in) Swiss roll tin. Chill, then bake blind in a fairly hot oven, 200°C/400°F/Gas 6, for 10 minutes. Remove the weights. Beat the cheese, mustard, egg yolks (not the whites) and milk together. Season to taste with salt and pepper before mixing in the parsley. In another bowl and with clean beaters whisk the egg whites until stiff but not dry. Stir 1 tablespoon of the beaten whites into the cheese mixture, then gently fold in the remainder hopefully blending in all the whites without knocking the air out of the mixture. Pour evenly into the tin, tilting the tin so that the mixture reaches the corners. This layer will be shallow. Return to the oven and bake at 200°C/400°F/Gas 6 for 15 minutes. Cover the top with a layer of tomatoes, brush with the oil and bake for a further 5 minutes until the filling is firm. Serves eight.

KIDNEY BEAN AND BEEF PASTIES

A high-protein, easily cooked filling of stewed, not fried, mince and colourful red kidney beans. Canned kidney beans are easily available but if you soak and cook raw beans yourself make sure they are thoroughly cooked or you could get a tummy upset. Kidney beans are not suitable 'done' in a slo-cooker, but on the other hand the pressure cooker method is practically fool-proof. Serve hot.

One recipe (200 g (8 oz) flour etc.) Vegetable oil pastry (p. 226)
225 g (8 oz) freshly minced raw beef
1 stock cube, crumbled
Salt
Pepper
2 teaspoons Worcestershire sauce
100 g (4 oz) cooked kidney beans

Roll out the pastry to a thickness of 5 mm (¼ in). Cut out eight 9–10 cm (3½–4 in) circles. Chill. Meanwhile put the mince in a saucepan with the stock cube and about 300 ml (½ pint) water. Bring to the boil and simmer until nearly all the water has evaporated. Season with salt and pepper to taste and mix in the Worcestershire sauce and beans. Divide the mixture between four of the pastry circles, leaving a 1 cm (½ in) border. Damp the edges of the pastry and fit the four 'lids' on top. Seal the edges and finish and decorate as desired. Brush the pastry with milk and bake in a fairly hot oven, 200°C/400°F/Gas 6, for 20–25 minutes until pale golden and crisp. Serves four.

LEMON MERINGUE PIE

Here is a recipe to satisfy the sweet-toothed cholesterol-watcher. You can also use this pastry with the traditional dessert. Serve hot or cold.

Half recipe (100 g (4 oz) flour etc.) Vegetable oil pastry
(p. 226)

Filling
2 level tablespoons cornflour
125 ml (¼ pint) cold water
15 g (½ oz) polyunsaturated margarine
Grated rind and juice of 1 lemon
25 g (1 oz) caster sugar

Meringue
2 size-2 egg whites
100 g (4 oz) caster sugar

Roll out the pastry and use to line a 15 cm (6 in) fluted
flan ring. Chill for at least ½ hour. Bake blind in a fairly
hot oven, 200°C/400°F/Gas 6, for 15 minutes, then remove
the weights and continue baking for a further 5 minutes to
dry out the base of the pastry. Remove from the oven and
take off the flan ring. Reduce the oven temperature to
150°C/300°F/Gas 2. Combine the filling ingredients in a
saucepan and whisk continuously over a moderate heat.
Bring to the boil and cook for 2 minutes until thickened.
Pour the mixture into the pastry case. Whisk the egg
whites until stiff, add less than half the sugar and whisk
until stiff once more. Fold in the remaining sugar, pile
over the lemon filling, making sure that the meringue
reaches the edges of the pastry to completely enclose the
filling. Flick up peaks of meringue with the point of a
knife. Put the flan on a baking tray and bake in the centre
of the oven for 20–30 minutes until browned on top.
Serves four to five.

Wheatgerm Pastry

You can see the small specks of wheatgerm in this lovely nutty-flavoured wholesome pastry with an appetizing golden colour. In addition to being appetizing it is light textured, easy to mix and roll out and it also does you good. Wheatgerm has a good quantity of protein and is rich in vitamins B and E. Frequently the germ is removed from the flour because many people prefer a smoother product. If you eat bread such as Hovis or Bermalene, you will know that they have a much softer texture than wholemeal bread and there is a similar difference between wheatgerm pastry and wholemeal pastry. Wheatgerm pastry has a certain softness about it and it is crisp, while wholemeal is more dense. It includes a quantity of cornflour which is a pure starch and very soft, so it won't hurt if you knead the pastry thoroughly, provided that you are able to give it a rest afterwards. The quantity is sufficient for a 15 cm (6 in) double-crust pie or a 23 cm (9 in) flan.

Ingredients for Basic Recipe

25 g (1 oz) cornflour
50 g (2 oz) self-raising flour
75 g (3 oz) plain flour
Pinch of salt
75 g (3 oz) hard margarine
1 generous tablespoon wheatgerm
½ beaten egg
2½–3 tablespoons ice-cold water

Sieve the flour and salt into a mixing bowl and rub in the margarine until it resembles fine breadcrumbs. Stir in the wheatgerm. Add the beaten egg and the smaller quantity of water and mix with a round-bladed knife until the lumps of mixture just stick together. Add more water at this stage if necessary. Knead the pastry with the fingertips and shape into a ball. Cover and refrigerate for at least ½ hour. Roll out the pastry thinly on a well-floured board, because since it has a raising agent in it, it will puff up slightly and become thicker. Use at once or store and use as required. Bake in a fairly hot oven, 200°C/400°F/Gas 6, and an unfilled flan case will take 20–30 minutes.

APRICOT AND ORANGE PIE

This delicious pie is not only appetizing but a real health booster. With all that iron and vitamins it should keep the cold germs at bay. Serve hot or cold.

> One recipe (150 g (6 oz) flour etc.) Wheatgerm pastry (p. 231)
> 225 g (8 oz) dried apricots
> 300 ml (½ pint) fresh orange juice
> 1 level teaspoon arrowroot
> 1 rounded tablespoon ground almonds
> 1 rounded tablespoon brown sugar
> Milk for glazing
> Caster sugar for dusting

Soak the apricots overnight in the orange juice, adding water if necessary to cover the fruit. Strain into a bowl. Blend the arrowroot with 150 ml (¼ pint) of the liquid and heat gently, stirring constantly until the sauce thickens and clears. Remove from the heat and stir in the ground almonds, sugar and apricots. Roll out half the pastry and use to line a 15 cm (6 in) shallow pie dish. Spread the fruit over the centre and moisten the pastry edges. Roll out the remaining pastry to form a lid, then seal, finish and decorate as desired. Brush with milk and sprinkle with sugar. Bake in a fairly hot oven, 200°C/400°F/Gas 6, for 25–30 minutes until the pastry is gold and crisp and cooked through. Serves four.

CAULIFLOWER CHEDDAR FLAN

Pastry stretches this dish to serve four and it can be made with fresh or frozen cauliflower (which certainly can do with some camouflaging). Serve hot.

One recipe (150 g (6 oz) flour etc.) Wheatgerm pastry (p. 231)
25 g (1 oz) butter
25 g (1 oz) flour
300 ml (½ pint) milk
Pepper
Salt
1 egg yolk
225 g (8 oz) cauliflower florettes, part cooked
50 g (2 oz) shelled peas, cooked
100 g (4 oz) mature Cheddar cheese grated
Milk for glazing

Roll out two-thirds of the pastry and use to line a 20 cm (8 in) flan dish. Bake blind in a fairly hot oven, 200°C/400°F/Gas 6, for 10 minutes, then remove the weights. While the pastry is baking prepare a sauce. Melt the butter in a saucepan, stir in the flour and cook gently for 1 minute, then gradually add the milk, stirring vigorously until the sauce boils and thickens. Season with pepper and sparingly with salt. Remove from the heat and leave to cool for a few moments. Blend one tablespoon of the sauce with the egg yolk and stir back into the sauce. Arrange the cauliflower and peas in the pastry case, pour the sauce over the top, then cover with the cheese, but do not press this down too hard. Roll out the remaining pastry thinly and cut out strips to form a lattice design. It is easier to dip these in a plate of milk before arranging, rather than glaze them afterwards. Return to the oven and bake at 200°C/400°F/Gas 6 for a further 25–30 minutes until the pastry is golden and crisp. Serves four.

COUNTRY APPLE PIE

Carrots are sweet, have a strong colour and are much underestimated in dessert cookery. You may have to keep the secret until after the eaters have pronounced the pie to be delicious. Serve hot.

One recipe (150 g (6 oz) flour etc.) Wheatgerm pastry (p. 231)
225 g (½ lb) (1 large) cooking apple, peeled and cored
100 g (¼ lb) (2 large) carrots, scraped and grated
½ teaspoon mixed spice
1 generous tablespoon brown sugar
Milk for glazing

Roll out half the pastry and use to line a 15 cm (6 in) ovenproof plate. Chop the apples and mix with the carrot, spice and sugar and place in the centre of the pastry. Moisten the edge. Roll out the remaining pastry to form a lid. Seal, finish and decorate as desired. Milk is a good choice for glazing. Place the pie on a baking tray to ensure the base cooks through. Bake in the centre of a fairly hot oven, 200°C/400°F/Gas 6, for 20–30 minutes until golden brown. Serves four to five.

SMOKED SALMON QUICHE

Nobody can deny that smoked salmon is expensive and few will say that it is not delicious. In this recipe you are using an economical 25 g (1 oz) per person and you could cut costs by buying cocktail pieces which are small slivers or end pieces. Serve hot or cold.

One recipe (150 g (6 oz) flour etc.) Wheatgerm pastry (p. 231)
3 size-2 eggs
300 ml (½ pint) single cream
150 g (6 oz) smoked salmon, cut into strips
¼ teaspoon freshly ground black pepper
1 level tablespoon freshly chopped parsley
Salt
2 lemons

Roll out the pastry and use to line a 23 cm (9 in) greased flan ring. Bake blind in a fairly hot oven, 200°C/400°F/Gas 6, for 15 minutes. Remove the weights and reduce the oven temperature to 180°C/350°F/Gas 4. Beat the eggs and cream together, then mix in the salmon, pepper and parsley, omitting the salt if the salmon is salty. Turn into the flan case and bake for 25–30 minutes until the filling has set. With a sharp knife pare away the peel and pith, slice the lemons wafer thin and arrange in overlapping circles round the edges of the flan. Serves six.

Wholemeal Pastry

Wholemeal pastry is on the solid side, but it tastes so wholesome and farmhousey that you can become quite addicted to it. Wholemeal pastry has a dense, firm, cakey crust and is not difficult to roll out, because it has a higher than usual proportion of fat. In this recipe I use the 100% wholemeal flour. The baked pastry is a brown oaty colour and you may find that the edges of the pastry are more rugged than smooth, but I think that this adds to its appeal. If you prefer a lighter crustier pastry, use three-quarters wholemeal and one-quarter white flour. Because wholemeal pastry is not rolled out thinner than 5 mm (¼ in) thick, it is unsuitable for very small patties. You can buy 8 cm (3 in) tartlet moulds with straight sides which are placed individually on baking trays and are preferable to those with sloping sides. The quantity is sufficient for a 20 cm (8 in) double-crust pie.

Ingredients for Basic Recipe

125 g (5 oz) hard margarine
200 g (8 oz) wholemeal plain flour
1 size-3 egg
3 tablespoons water
2 tablespoons milk
¼ teaspoon salt

Rub the margarine into the flour, beat the egg and blend with the water, milk and salt and sprinkle evenly over the mixture. Stir with a fork until a soft manageable dough is formed, adding a little extra liquid if required. This will depend on the flour you have used. Knead lightly and roll out on a floured surface to a thickness of 5 mm (¼ in). Shape, then rest in the refrigerator before baking at 200°C/400°F/Gas 6 for 20–25 minutes for a flan case or reduce the temperature after 10 minutes to 190°C/375°F/Gas 5 if you are baking a double-crust pie.

CHEESE AND LENTIL PIE

The lentils and cheese are a perfect match providing a satisfying but not too rich filling. This is another savoury pie also suitable for vegetarians. Serve hot.

One recipe (200 g (8 oz) flour etc.) Wholemeal pastry
   (p. 236)
175 g (6 oz) lentils
1 medium onion, chopped
15 g (½ oz) butter
100 g (4 oz) mature Cheddar cheese, grated
1 level tablespoon freshly chopped parsley
1 size-4 egg, beaten
Salt
Pepper

Rinse the lentils, cover in hot water and leave to soak in the saucepan for 1 hour. Bring to the boil, then simmer for 20–30 minutes until soft. Drain. Fry the onion in the butter until soft, then stir in the lentils, cheese, parsley, egg and salt and pepper to taste. Roll out half the pastry and use to line a 20 cm (8 in) shallow pie dish. Fill with the lentil mixture. Roll the remaining pastry to form a lid. Moisten the touching edges of the pastry and seal, finish and decorate as desired. Bake in a fairly hot oven, 200°C/400°F/Gas 6, for 20 minutes, then reduce to 190°C/375°F/Gas 5 for a further 20 minutes to enable the pastry underneath to cook through. Serves four to five.

PLOUGHMAN'S PIE

Serve a well-dressed mixed salad with this pie, which is filling and the sort of thing you would enjoy after a day in the fields or even your garden. Serve hot preferably.

One recipe (200 g (8 oz) flour etc.) Wholemeal pastry (p. 236)
3 large onions
150 g (6 oz) mature Cheddar cheese, grated
½ teaspoon freshly grated nutmeg
2 teaspoons Worcestershire sauce
Level teaspoon salt
Freshly ground black pepper
Beaten egg to glaze

Peel and boil the onions whole until tender, then chop up roughly and leave to cool. Mix in the cheese, nutmeg, Worcestershire sauce, salt and pepper. Roll out half the pastry and use to line a 20 cm (8 in) pie plate, spread the filling over the top and brush the edges with water. Roll out the remaining pastry to form a lid. Press the edges well to seal using the top of a fork. Brush with beaten egg and make a small hole in the centre of the pastry lid. Bake in a fairly hot oven, 200°C/400°F/Gas 6, for 20 minutes, then reduce the heat to 190°C/375°F/Gas 5 for a further 15 minutes or until the pastry is golden brown. Serves four to six.

RHUBARB TART WITH VANILLA SAUCE

Use garden forced or frozen rhubarb but not the canned variety in this recipe and adjust the sugar to suit yourself. Serve hot preferably.

One recipe (200 g (8 oz) flour etc.) Wholemeal pastry (p. 236)

Filling

450 g (1 lb) rhubarb, washed and cut into 2.5 cm (1 in)
  chunks
100 g (4 oz) dark brown sugar
50 g (2 oz) sultanas
50 g (2 oz) currants
50 g (2 oz) raisins
50 g (2 oz) walnuts, chopped
½ teaspoon cinnamon
¼ teaspoon ground ginger

Vanilla sauce

300 ml (½ pint) milk
1 vanilla pod
25 g (1 oz) caster sugar
1 level tablespoon cornflour
1 teaspoon orange flower water
Tiny knob of butter

Roll out three-quarters of the pastry and use to line a
23 cm (9 in) flan dish. Roll out the remaining pastry and
cut eight 23 × 1.5 cm (9 × ½ in) strips. Chill both the flan
case and the strips while making the filling. Cook the
rhubarb without added water over the lowest possible
heat until tender. Add all the remaining filling ingredients
and cook for a further 5 minutes until soft, then leave to
cool. Pour the filling evenly into the pastry case and make
a diagonal lattice on top with the reserved pastry strips,
pressing them into the sides of the flan. Brush the lattice
and edges with beaten egg and bake in a fairly hot oven,
200°C/400°F/Gas 6, for 30–35 minutes until the pastry is
golden. Serves four to six.

To make the vanilla sauce put the milk in a large
saucepan and float the vanilla pod on top. Bring to the
boil, then simmer for 5 minutes, stirring constantly to
prevent the milk from boiling over. Remove the pod and
stir in the sugar. Add the cornflour blended with the

orange flower water plus 2 teaspoons water. Bring back to the boil, stirring all the time until the sauce thickens. Stir in the butter.

YOGURT FRUIT SLICE

Here's another suggestion for the health food devotees. An attractive pâte filling topped with colourful cherries and peaches.

If you are still wondering how to dissolve gelatine this is the best method – sprinkle it on to hot water in a small heatproof bowl then wait for ½ minute before stirring to dissolve. If as the mixture cools it is still cloudy and grainy, stand the bowl or glass in a pan of warm water over low heat. Serve this recipe cold.

One recipe (200 g (8 oz) flour etc.) Wholemeal pastry
    (p. 236)
2 level teaspoons powdered gelatine
275 g (10 oz) cottage cheese
3 as-they-come tablespoons clear honey
350 ml (12 fl oz) natural yogurt
½ teaspoon vanilla essence
3 fresh peaches, skinned and stoned
2 teaspoons fresh lemon juice
300 g (12 oz) cherries, stoned

Roll out the pastry and use to line a 23 × 28 cm (9 × 11 in) Swiss roll tin. Bake blind in a fairly hot oven, 200°C/400°F/Gas 6, for 15 minutes. Remove the weights and continue cooking for a further 10–15 minutes until the pastry is crisp and cooked through. Dissolve the gelatine in 2 tablespoons hot water. Liquidize the cottage cheese or press through a sieve, beat in the honey, yogurt, vanilla essence and gelatine and pour into the baked pastry case, spreading the mixture thinly. Chill until the filling is set. Slice the peaches, dip in the lemon juice and arrange in overlapping lines down either side of the pastry. Fill the centre panel with cherries. Serves six to eight.

Wine Pastry

The high proportion of fat in this pastry makes it soft, while the acid in the wine reduces the richness, resulting in a cross between a short and a flaky pastry. This crisp pastry can be rolled thinly without cracking. Choose a cheap dry wine, as the flavour in the cooked pastry is unobtrusive. Wine pastry needs no rubbing in and you do not have to take special care in folding and rolling, but more wine will be needed when working in a cool atmosphere. In hot conditions the dough may be sticky. The recipe is sufficient for a 20 cm (8 in) double-crust pie.

Ingredients for Basic Recipe

150 g (6 oz) plain flour
Pinch of salt
125 g (5 oz) hard margarine
3½–4½ tablespoons dry white wine

Sieve the flour and salt into a mixing bowl. Cut up the block of margarine into 1 cm (½ in) cubes and stir into the flour until all are equally coated. Add only sufficient wine to mix to a stiff dough with a round-bladed knife. Try to avoid adding extra wine unless there is more than a sprinkling of spare flour. Roll out on a floured surface to an oblong three times as long as it is wide. Fold into three and turn, so that the open end is towards you. Roll out again, fold into three and turn once more, then roll and fold again. Wrap in cling-film and chill until firm for about half an hour. Roll out, fold and then roll out to required shape. Chill pastry before baking. If you wish to freeze the pastry only empty cases or those with a freezable filling are suitable. As a check list – roll, fold, turn, roll, fold, turn, roll, fold, chill, roll, fold, shape, chill. Bake in a hot oven, 220°C/425°F/Gas 7, for about 25–30 minutes until the pastry is golden unless otherwise stated.

BOEUF BOURGUIGNON TOURTE

It is quicker and more fuel-saving to make two batches at one time, but you can prepare and fill both, reserving one to freeze in its unbaked pastry case. Serve hot.

Double recipe (300 g (12 oz) flour etc.) Wine pastry (p. 242)
3–4 tablespoons vegetable cooking oil
½ kg (1 lb) lean braising steak, cut into small cubes
1 large onion, roughly chopped
1 clove garlic, chopped finely
4 rashers back bacon, de-rinded and chopped
2 heaped tablespoons flour
300 ml (½ pint) rich beef stock
250 ml (8 fl oz) medium red wine
1 level teaspoon parsley, freshly chopped ⎤
2 bay leaves   ⎥ or bouquet
1 sprig thyme   ⎦ garni
Salt
Freshly ground black pepper
225 g (8 oz) button mushrooms
Beaten egg or milk for glazing

Heat the oil in a large saucepan and toss in the cubes of meat, a few at a time, stirring briskly to seal the juices in on all sides. Add the onion, garlic and bacon and continue frying until the meat browns. This is important to obtain a rich-coloured sauce. Stir in the flour, cooking until this too starts to brown, then gradually add the stock, wine and herbs and bring to the boil. Season with salt and pepper to taste, then add the mushrooms. Reduce the heat to a mere simmer when only the occasional bubble appears on the surface and put on a tightly fitting lid. Cook until the meat is just tender (about 1½ hours), adding extra water or stock if the gravy becomes too thick. Cool rapidly. When convenient divide the pastry into four, roll out two pieces and use to line two 20 cm (8 in) ovenproof dishes. Remove the bay leaves or bouquet garni and put half the boeuf bourguignone in each dish. Roll the remaining pastry to form lids. Decorate and glaze with beaten egg or milk. Bake in a hot oven, 220°C/425°F/Gas 8, for 20 minutes, then make two off-centre slits in the lids. Continue baking for a further 10–20 minutes, until the pastry is crisp and golden brown. Makes two pies, each serving four.

CHOCOLATE SOUFFLÉED FLAN

This attractive chocolate tart is very rich and you will find that a small slice will be quite sufficient. It looks especially nice cooked in one of those fluted ceramic dishes. Serve warm or cold.

One recipe (150 g (6 oz) flour etc.) Wine pastry (p. 242)
100 g (4 oz) dark chocolate, grated
100 g (4 oz) ground almonds
100 g (4 oz) icing sugar, sieved
100 g (4 oz) butter, softened
Pinch of ground cinnamon
3 size-3 eggs, separated
25 g (1 oz) flour
250 ml (8 fl oz) whipping cream

Roll out the pastry and use to line a 25 cm (10 in) diameter flan dish. Chill. In a bowl mix the chocolate, almonds, icing sugar, butter, cinnamon and the egg yolks.

Add the flour and beat until the mixture becomes smooth and shiny. Whisk the egg whites until only just dry and then gently fold into the chocolate mixture. Tip the mixture into the pastry so that as much air as possible is trapped and bake in a moderate oven, 180°C/350°F/Gas 4, for 40 minutes or until the filling is set but not hard. Whip up the cream. Pile into a bowl and serve separately. Serves six to eight.

TRANCHE FROMAGE

A rich dish for special occasions similar to a fondu spread in a thin pastry crust. Make the pastry case in advance and prepare the filling just before the meal. The dish is best served warm either as a starter or light main course.

One recipe (150 g (6 oz) flour etc.) Wine pastry (p. 242)
150 ml (¼ pint) dry white wine
100 g (4 oz) red Leicester cheese, grated
100 g (4 oz) mature Cheddar cheese, grated
1 level teaspoon granulated sugar
¼ teaspoon grated nutmeg
¼ teaspoon salt
¼ teaspoon white pepper
2 level teaspoons cornflour
1 tablespoon gin
1 bunch watercress, leaves only

Roll out the pastry thinly and use to line a Swiss roll tin no larger 20 × 28 cm (8 × 11 in). If you don't have one this size you can make a very satisfactory shape out of quadruple folded foil. Chill for ½ hour, then bake blind in a hot oven, 220°C/425°F/Gas 7, for 20 minutes. Remove the weights and bake for a further 5 minutes or until crisp and golden. To make the filling heat the wine until hot but not boiling, add the cheese all at once and immediately reduce the heat as low as possible. Stir the cheese with a wooden spoon in a figure-of-eight motion until it is dissolved. This takes a lot longer than you would expect. Add the sugar, nutmeg, salt and pepper. Blend the cornflour with the gin, stir into the saucepan, then stir continuously until the mixture thickens and one or two large bubbles burst through the surface. Pour evenly into the pastry case. Sprinkle with a shower of separated watercress leaves. Serves six to eight.

ZABAGLIONE FLAN

Zabaglione is generally served in tall wine glasses accompanied by a sponge finger biscuit. I hope you will agree that it is much less sickly when served in a pie crust. Serve soon after preparation while it is still fluffy, but not runny. The filling thickens as it cools. Serve cold.

> One recipe (150 g (6 oz) flour etc.) Wine pastry (p. 242)
> 6 size-2 egg yolks
> 50 g (2 oz) caster sugar
> 6 tablespoons Marsala wine *or* sweet sherry
> 2 level teaspoons gelatine

Roll out the pastry and use to line a 23 cm (9 in) fluted flan ring. The pastry left over is for trimmings. In order to maintain the airiness of the pastry, place the trimmings in layers on top of one another and then roll out thinly. Cut strips 23 cm × 5 mm (9 × ¼ in) and twist once or twice. Place on the baking tray beside the flan ring and chill until firm. Chilling is particularly necessary as the strips are delicate. Bake the pastry case blind in a hot oven, 220°C/425°F/Gas 7, at the same time as the twists, which, because they are so small, will bake crisply in 5–10 minutes. The pastry case will take 20–30 minutes in all and should cool before being filled. Put the egg yolks and sugar in a large mixing bowl and whisk over a bowl of hot water until a fork drawn through the mixture leaves a trail. Do not let the water touch the basin or the eggs will scramble. Add the wine and continue whisking until the mixture is thick. Remove the bowl from the pan of water and continue whisking as the zabaglione cools. Sprinkle the gelatine into 2 tablespoons hot water, leave for ½ minute, then stir until dissolved. Add the zabaglione, folding in gently, so that no bulk is lost. Pour the mixture into the flan case and arrange the pastry twists across the top. Serves five to six.

Yeast Pastry

The term yeast pastry conjures up thoughts of bread dough, but if you stop to think, the dough used in pizza, which is bread dough, can be rolled very thinly and therefore turn out very crisp. Yeast pastry or pâte levée is often found in antiquarian cookery books, where it is considered to be a rustic recipe. Even if you are no good at all at bread making, yeast pastry will certainly not disappoint you.

The method of making is slightly different from the usual way of making bread in that two mixtures are produced and later blended together. A greater rise and a much lighter, crisper pastry is obtained, if the blended yeast is mixed with a small amount of flour and then allowed to sponge before being mixed with the remaining ingredients. If you have an electric mixer you could make up a large quantity of the dough and then either freeze before the second rise or after shaping, making a note of which step has been reached. Alternatively store frozen in suitably sized balls, but the dough must be completely thawed before rolling out. The undercrust of the pastry will be crisp with a softer texture on top if the filling has been a moist one. The pastry round the edges is similar to a pastry crust with an open texture when broken. This pastry has proved very popular with my friends and I hope you will like it too. The recipe produces about 450 g (1 lb) pastry and this is enough to line a 28 cm (11 in) flan dish. It is also a most attractive size for pizzas.

Fresh yeast is sold in health food shops and can be stored in the freezer, but you can also use dried yeast. Substitute 2 level teaspoons of yeast granules, which should be whisked into the milk at a slightly higher temperature with a pinch of sugar. Whisk thoroughly with a fork and leave for 10–15 minutes until frothy before mixing with the flour. Dried easy-mix yeast should be blended with the flour.

Ingredients for Basic Recipe

15 g (½ oz) fresh yeast
Just under 125 ml (¼ pint) milk, heated until warm to the touch
250 g (9 oz) plain flour
Pinch of salt
100 g (4 oz) butter at room temperature
1 size-4 egg
40 g (1½ oz) caster sugar, to be added only for use in sweet dishes

To prepare the yeast mixture blend the yeast with half the warm milk. Mix in 50 g (2 oz) of the flour until the mixture is light and well blended. Sprinkle a little of the loose flour over the top and put in a warm place until the mixture has doubled in volume. This will take about half an hour. If you wish you can add a pinch of vitamin C powder to the yeast liquid, which will hasten the rising. To prepare the dough sieve the remaining flour and salt into a mixing bowl and rub in the butter. You will find this easier if you cut the butter into small pieces first. Mix the remaining milk with the egg and the sugar, if being used. When the yeast mixture is well risen and full of holes rather like a sponge, bind the two mixtures. It is easiest to do this with one very clean hand. The dough will be extremely soft and sticky due to the warm conditions melting the butter. Add a little water at this stage only if absolutely necessary. Turn the dough on to a lightly floured surface and knead thoroughly, pulling the mixture towards you between fingers and palms of the hand and lifting up to press back into the centre of the dough, continually turning the dough in a clockwise direction. Some knack is required for this, but when the dough is properly kneaded, it will be quite smooth and no longer sticky. This takes about 10 minutes. Grease the inside of a large polythene bag and put the ball of dough in the bottom, sealing the bag at the very top. This is a better system than rising dough in a mixing bowl covered with a damp cloth, because there is no danger of the outside of the dough drying up which prevents it from rising. Now is a good time to divide the dough and freeze any that you are not going to use immediately. When the dough has doubled in size and the polythene bag is blown up with air, turn the dough out once more on to a well-floured surface, knead lightly and shape as required. Bake yeast pastry in a hot oven, 220°C/425°F/Gas 7, and the cooking times will depend upon the fillings.

FINNEGAN'S FLAN

Serve a wee bunch of glittering grapes with each portion of flan. If you have a large enough serving dish you could transfer the flan using two fish slices and put bunches of grapes at the four corners. Serve warm.

One recipe (250 g (9 oz) flour etc.) Yeast pastry
   (p. 249) including 40 g (1½ oz) caster sugar
3 size-4 eggs
100 g (4 oz) icing sugar
150 ml (¼ pint) sweet white wine
25 g (1 oz) caster sugar
25 g (1 oz) butter
225 g (8 oz) seedless grapes
Beaten egg white ⎱
Granulated sugar ⎰ for frosting

Roll out the pastry thinly and use to line a well-greased 28 × 23 cm (11 × 9 in) Swiss roll tin. Leave to rise for about 20 minutes until puffy. Beat the eggs and icing sugar together until the consistency of thick cream, then stir in the wine. Pour the mixture evenly over the yeast dough and bake in a hot oven, 220°C/425°F/Gas 7, for 10 minutes, then reduce the heat to 180°C/350°F/Gas 4. After baking for a further 15 minutes and while the filling is thickening, sprinkle with caster sugar and dot with the butter. Bake for a further 10–15 minutes until the filling is set. Divide the grapes into small bunches, dip in the beaten egg white and sprinkle with granulated sugar. Leave for a few minutes to set. Serves six to eight.

PIZZA

Pizza house menus list an endless choice of toppings and you can provide the same on your home-made pizza. Use bacon, ham, mushrooms, green or red peppers, anchovy, tuna, salami – but tomato and cheese must always be included. Mine is a very basic recipe using the regular ingredients, but you should change the herbs or add more topping to suit yourself.

One recipe (250 g (9 oz) flour etc.) Yeast pastry (p. 249)
2 large Spanish onions, sliced into rings
25 g (1 oz) butter *or* margarine
2 × 396 g (14 oz) cans tomatoes
2 level teaspoons dried oregano
Salt
Pepper
275 g (10 oz) grated Cheddar cheese
1 tablespoon vegetable cooking oil

Divide the pastry into two and roll out each piece to a circle about 25 cm (10 in). Yeast doughs grow so if you like your pizzas thin and crispy, roll out the pastry to 3 mm (⅛ in) thick. Transfer to greased baking trays. Fry the onions gently in the butter until just soft. Drain the tomatoes and reserve the juice for use in soups. Spread the tomatoes over the pastry leaving a 1 cm (½ in) border. Cover with the onions and sprinkle with the oregano. Season with salt and pepper. Leave for about 20 minutes or until the pastry puffs up. Cover with the cheese. Brush the exposed pastry edges with oil. Bake in a hot oven, 220°C/425°F/Gas 7, for 15 minutes, then reduce to 200°C/400°F/Gas 6 for a further 15–20 minutes until the dough is crispy. Makes two large pizzas.

PLUM AND ORANGE FLAN

Large firm plums are best in this pudding. I include no sugar as there should be plenty of sweetness in the jam base and ice cream, but as it is a matter of personal taste, you can if you like add up to 2 tablespoons sugar in the poaching liquid. Serve cold.

Half recipe (125 g (4½ oz) flour etc.) Yeast pastry (p. 249)
450 g (1 lb) plums
Juice of 2 oranges
¼ teaspoon almond essence
2 generous tablespoons apricot jam
1½ level teaspoons arrowroot
1–2 tablespoons sugar (optional)
Vanilla ice cream

Roll out the dough thinly and use to line a 20 cm (8 in) flan tin. Leave for approximately 20 minutes until the pastry puffs up. Meanwhile parcook the plums in a lidded saucepan in the orange juice and almond essence until tender enough to cut easily without the fruit becoming mushy. Drain, reserving the juice, and remove all the stones. Spoon the apricot jam into the flan and spread to cover the base. Arrange the plums on top. Bake in a hot oven, 220°C/425°F/Gas 7, for 10 minutes, then reduce to 190°C/375°F/Gas 5 for 15–20 minutes until the pastry is brown but not over-crisp. Strain and measure the reserved juice and make up to 150 ml (¼ pint) with water. Blend 1½ level teaspoons arrowroot with 2 tablespoons cold water and the sugar if required and mix into the juice and heat in a small saucepan, stirring continuously until the sauce thickens and clears. Pour over the plums and leave to set. Top with scoops of vanilla ice cream. Serves six.

SMOKY MUSHROOM FLAN

Smoked haddock and mushrooms set in a creamy sauce in a plain yeast pastry case. Serve hot.

One recipe (250 g (9 oz) flour etc.) Yeast pastry (p. 249)
400 g (14 oz) smoked haddock fillet
100 g (4 oz) button mushrooms, sliced
15 g (½ oz) butter
2 size-3 eggs
150 ml (¼ pint) milk
150 ml (¼ pint) single cream
Salt
Pepper

Roll out the pastry thinly and use to line a 25 cm (10 in) round pie dish. Leave for 20 minutes until the pastry puffs up. Meanwhile poach the fish until the flesh is opaque. Drain, then remove the skin and any bones and flake the fish. Lightly sauté the mushrooms in the butter but do not cook thoroughly. Beat the eggs, milk and cream together, season lightly with salt and pepper and fold in the fish and mushrooms. Bake in a hot oven, 220°C/425°F/Gas 7 for 10 minutes, then reduce to 200°C/400°F/Gas 6 for 20–25 minutes until the pastry is cooked and the filling set. Serves four to six.

Yogurt Pastry

Yogurt pastry is a pale, close-textured pastry consisting of crisp tiny flakes. Since yogurt is acid in nature it has a similar effect to lemon juice, softening the gluten to make it more elastic. As such, it is firm and easy to roll out, but should be rested thoroughly before baking. Use the solid live yogurt rather than the soft runny kind, if that is possible, although the other will give reasonably satisfactory results. Yogurt pastry has a strong flavour, blending well with pungent or tangy pie fillings.

The yogurt that you use does not have to be especially fresh. You will find that when you have left some in the refrigerator for a few days a watery liquid appears on top. Pour this away and taste the yogurt and you may find that it tingles on the tongue. This is an indication that it is beginning to ferment and, although still fresh, it is not so pleasant to eat. However this is when it is most suitable for making pastry.

Because of its firm nature yogurt pastry holds up well when baked in flan rings, since when the flan ring is removed, the pastry wall remains undamaged. When making yogurt pastry using a flan ring, remove the ring 10 minutes before the end of cooking, to enable the sides of the pastry to brown. The quantity is sufficient to line an 18 cm (7 in) flan ring or cover a 1 litre (1½ pint) pie dish. A pastry case baked blind will take about 20 minutes in all.

Ingredients for Basic Recipe

125 g (4 oz) plain flour
Pinch of salt

75 g (2½ oz) soft white cooking fat
3 heaped tablespoons yogurt

Sieve the flour and salt into a mixing bowl, add the fat and cut up with a round-bladed knife until the pieces are the size of large peas. Add the yogurt all at once and stir until a soft dough is formed. Turn the dough out on to a floured surface and knead with the fingers. Do not wory too much if you over-knead, as yogurt pastry doesn't seem to care. Roll out and use as required. Being a very tolerant pastry it will not mind if it does not have a rest before baking, but it appreciates a short stay in the refrigerator if that is possible. Bake in a fairly hot oven, 200°C/400°F/Gas 6.

CHICKEN CURRY PIE

There are two categories of curry eaters. The regular 'we can take it as hot as you like' types and the occasionals, who enjoy an English-type curry. This is the mild sort. No Indian would consider eating pastry with curry but someone has to start a trend.

One recipe (125 g (5 oz) flour etc.) Yogurt pastry (p. 255)
25 g (1 oz) butter
1 tablespoon cooking oil
½ kg (1 lb) boned raw chicken
1 medium onion, thinly sliced
1 clove garlic, crushed
1 rounded teaspoon curry powder
1 rounded tablespoon flour
300 ml (½ pint) chicken stock
1 heaped tablespoon sultanas
1 medium cooking apple, peeled, cored and diced
1 tablespoon mango chutney

Heat the butter and oil until the butter sizzles and fry the chicken, onion and garlic until the chicken pieces are opaque and the onions are soft. Stir constantly so that none of the chicken juices escape. Add the curry powder and flour and fry for another minute to develop the flavour of the spices. Add all the remaining ingredients, bring the mixture to the boil, still stirring, then reduce the heat and simmer for 30 minutes. Taste and adjust the seasoning, then transfer the mixture to a greased 1 litre (1½ pint) pie dish. Roll out the pastry and cover the top of the pie. Bake in a fairly hot oven, 200°C/400°F/Gas 6, for 20–25 minutes or until the pastry is pale brown and firm. Serves four.

DUBLIN CHEESE FLAN

Serve this flan hot while the cheese is still sizzling. This is a colourful dish of pink prawns in a thick sauce, speckled with fresh green parsley.

One recipe (125 g (5 oz) flour etc.) Yogurt pastry (p. 255)
175 g (6 oz) cottage cheese
8 tablespoons milk
1 size-2 egg
1 rounded tablespoon freshly chopped parsley
¼ teaspoon freshly ground white pepper
Salt
100 g (4 oz) peeled prawns
50 g (2 oz) red Leicester cheese, grated

Roll out the pastry and use to line an 18 cm (7 in) flan dish. Bake blind in a fairly hot oven, 200°C/400°F/Gas 6, for 15 minutes. Meanwhile sieve the cottage cheese and blend with the milk, egg and parsley. Season with the pepper and a fraction of salt, bearing in mind that there is salt in the red Leicester cheese. Spread the prawns in the bottom of the flan, pour over the egg mixture and sprinkle with the grated cheese. Reduce the oven heat to

180°C/350°F/Gas 4 and bake in the lower half of the oven for 45 minutes or until the top of the flan is golden brown. Serves four.

LEMON FLAN

The pale yogurt pastry gives this flan a cool and refreshing appearance. Only sweetened condensed milk will work in this recipe as lemon juice would curdle fresh milk. There is no need to add sugar as the milk is sufficiently sweet, but extra sugar would not spoil the filling. Serve chilled.

> One recipe (125 g (5 oz) flour etc.) Yogurt pastry (p. 255)
> 1 × 396 g (14 oz) can condensed milk
> 150 ml (¼ pint) single cream
> 150 ml (¼ pint) fresh lemon juice (2–3 lemons)
> Grated rind of 1 lemon
> Thinly sliced lemon ⎫ for
> 120 ml (4 fl oz) double cream, whipped ⎭ decoration

Roll out the pastry and line an 18 cm (7 in) fluted flan ring. Bake blind in a fairly hot oven, 200°C/400°F/Gas 6, for 15 minutes, then remove the weights and the metal ring and bake for a further 5 minutes or until the pastry is crisp. Leave until cool. Thoroughly mix but do not beat the milk, cream, lemon juice and rind together. Pour into the flan case and refrigerate for at least 2 hours. Decorate with lemon slices and piped cream. Serves four.

MANDARIN ORANGE FLAN

Ring the changes with this basic recipe by combining different flavoured yogurts with the mandarin oranges. I like the hazelnut yogurt but this is a matter of taste. Serve the flan chilled.

One recipe (125 g (5 oz) flour etc.) Yogurt pastry
  (p. 255)
2 level teaspoons powdered gelatine
300 ml (½ pint) mandarin flavoured yogurt
1 × 312 g (11 oz) can mandarin oranges
1 level teaspoon arrowroot
150 ml (¼ pint) double cream, whipped
1 rounded teaspoon icing sugar, sieved
Orange food colouring (optional)

Roll out the pastry and line an 18 cm (7 in) fluted flan
ring. Bake blind in a fairly hot oven, 200°C/400°F/Gas 6,
for 15 minutes. Remove the weights and the metal ring
and bake for a further 5 minutes or until the pastry is
crisp. Leave until cool. Sprinkle the gelatine into 2
tablespoons hot but not boiling water. Leave for ½
minute, then stir until dissolved. Pour from a height into
the yogurt thus enabling the gelatine to cool as it falls.
Pour into the pastry case. Refrigerate until set. Drain the
mandarin oranges, reserving the juice, and arrange in a
decorative pattern over the jellied yogurt. Blend the
arrowroot with the juice made up to 150 ml (¼ pint) with
cold water if there is insufficient in the can. Stir over
moderate heat until the sauce thickens and clears. Two
drops of orange food colouring added at this point would
improve the appearance. Leave to cool but not set and
spoon over the fruit – if any air bubbles appear, prick
them with a sterilized needle. Sweeten the cream with the
icing sugar, put into a forcing bag and pipe cream rosettes
around the edge of the flan. Serves four.

Ingredient Chart

Note: The reason for apparent discrepancies in the metric/imperial weights is that since direct conversions are impossible and because it is essential to maintain correct proportions, the measurements have been calculated individually.

S/R = Self-raising flour	Veg = Solid vegetable cooking fat
B = Butter	L = Lemon juice
M = Margarine	W = Water
L = Lard	Van = Vanilla essence
Soft = Soft white cooking fat	

Pastry Type	Flour	Salt	Fat	Liquid	Other
AMERICAN PIE	125 g (5 oz) plain	½ teaspoon	70 g (2¾ oz) M, L or Veg	1½–2 tablespoons ice-cold W	
AMERICAN SELF-RAISING PIE CRUST	100 g (4 oz) S/R		60 g (2½ oz) Soft	1–1½ tablespoons ice-cold W	
BANANA	150 g (6 oz) plain	Pinch	75 g (3 oz) B	1 tablespoon cold W	50 g (2 oz) peeled banana
BISCUIT CRUST	225 g (8 oz) plain	Pinch	100 g (3½ oz) M	1 tablespoon cold W	60 g (2 oz) sugar 1 egg ¼ teaspoon van
BRAN	100 g (4 oz) plain	Pinch	75 g (3 oz) Veg	2 tablespoons cold W	20 g (¾ oz) bran
CHEESE	200 g (6 oz) plain	Pinch	50 g (1½ oz) L 50 g (1½ oz) M	2–3 tablespoons cold W ¼ teaspoon L	70 g (2 oz) cheese Pinch Cayenne
CHOUX	65 g (2½ oz) plain		50 g (2 oz) B	125–150 ml (4½–5 fl oz) W	2 eggs Few drops van

Pastry Type	Flour	Salt	Fat	Liquid	Other
CRUMBLE MIX	150 g (6 oz) plain	Pinch	75 g (3 oz) B or M		
CURD CHEESE	100 g (4 oz) plain		100 g (4 oz) B		100 g (4 oz) curd cheese
EASY PUFFY	225 g (8 oz) plain	Pinch	225 g (8 oz) M	2½ tablespoons W	
EGG WHITE	100 g (4 oz) plain	Generous pinch	75 g (3 oz) Veg	1 tablespoon cold W	1 tablespoon egg white
FLAKY	200 g (8 oz) plain *or* strong plain	Pinch	75 g (3 oz) B 75 g (3 oz) L	125 ml (¼ pint) ice-cold W 2 teaspoons L	
HEART WATCHERS'	75 g (3 oz) plain 125 g (5 oz) S/R		100 g (4 oz) Polyunsaturated M	3 tablespoons cold skimmed milk	
HERB & SPICED	150 g (6 oz) plain	Pinch	50 g (2 oz) L 35 g (1½ oz) M	1½–2 tablepoons cold W	Herbs or spices
HOT WATER CRUST	275 g (10 oz) plain	½ teaspoon	75 g (3 oz) L	150 ml (¼ pint) W	
LOW FAT	100 g (4 oz) plain			6 tablespoons cold W	50 g (2 oz) low fat milk granules 1 teaspoon baking powder
MELTED BUTTER	200 g (8 oz) plain	Pinch	150 g (6 oz) B		1 egg
PÂTE BRISÉE	250 g (9 oz) plain	Pinch	125 g (4½ oz) B	2½–4 tablespoons cold W	1 egg yolk
PÂTE SABLÉE	250 g (9 oz) plain	Pinch	125 g (4½ oz) B		125 g (4½ oz) sugar 1 egg
PÂTE SUCRÉE	100 g (4 oz) plain	Pinch	50 g (2 oz) B		50 g (2 oz) sugar 2 egg yolks
POTATO	100 g (4 oz) plain	Pinch	50 g (2 oz) B or M		100 g (4 oz) potato

Pastry Type	Flour	Salt	Fat	Liquid	Other
PUFF	250 g (8 oz) plain	¼ teaspoon	250 g (8 oz) B	1 teaspoon L 150 ml (¼ pint) ice-cold W	
QUICK FLAKY	350 g (12 oz) strong plain	3 pinches	225 g (8 oz) M	225–275 ml (7½–9 fl oz) ice-cold W	
QUICK-MIX SHORTCRUST	200 g (8 oz) plain	½ teaspoon	100 g (4 oz) Soft	3 tablespoons cold W	
QUICK ROUGH PUFF	200 g (8 oz) plain *or* strong plain	Pinch	150 g (6 oz) B or M	½ teaspoon L 125 ml (¼ pint) ice-cold W	
RICH PIE	150 g (6 oz) plain	Pinch	150 g (6 oz) M	6 tablespoons boiling W	
RICH RAISED	400 g (1 lb) plain	1 level teaspoon	150 g (6 oz) L	125 ml (¼ pint) milk	2 egg yolks
ROUGH PUFF	200 g (8 oz) plain *or* strong plain	Pinch	150 g (6 oz) B or M	½ teaspoon L 125 ml (¼ pint) ice-cold W	
SHORTCRUST	200 g (6 oz) plain	½ teaspoon	50 g (1½ oz) L 50 g (1½ oz) M or B	2–2½ tablespoons ice-cold W	
STRUDEL	200 g (8 oz) strong plain	½ teaspoon	2 tablespoons vegetable oil Melted B	1 teaspoon L 125 ml (¼ pint) warm W	1 egg
SUET CRUST	225 g (8 oz) S/R	½ teaspoon	100 g (3½ oz) suet	125 ml (¼ pint) cold W	
VEGETABLE OIL	200 g (8 oz) plain	½ teaspoon	8 tablespoons vegetable oil	2½ tablespoons cold W	
WHEATGERM	50 g (2 oz) S/R 75 g (3 oz) plain	Pinch	75 g (3 oz) M	2½–3 tablespoons ice-cold W	25 g (1 oz) cornflour 1 tablespoon wheatgerm ½ beaten egg
WHOLEMEAL	200 g (8 oz) wholemeal plain	¼ teaspoon	125 g (5 oz) M	3 tablespoons W 2 tablespoons milk	1 egg

Pastry Type	Flour	Salt	Fat	Liquid	Other
WINE	150 g (6 oz) plain	Pinch	125 g (5 oz) M	3½–4½ tablespoons wine	
YEAST	250 g (9 oz) plain	Pinch	100 g (4 oz) B	125 ml (¼ pint) milk	15 g (½ oz) yeast 1 egg 40 g (1½ oz) sugar
YOGURT	125 g (4 oz) plain	Pinch	75 g (2½ oz) Soft	3 tablespoons yogurt	

Quick Reference Temperature Chart and Average Yield of One Recipe

Pastry	Starting Temperatures	Yield
AMERICAN PIE	220°C/425°F/Gas 7	18 cm (7 in) lidded pie *or* 23 cm (9 in) pastry shell
AMERICAN SELF-RAISING PIE CRUST	200°C/400°F/Gas 6	9–12 tartlets
BANANA	200°C/400°F/Gas 6	20–23 cm (8–9 in) pastry shell
BISCUIT	180°C/350°F/Gas 4	23 cm (9 in) pastry shell
BRAN	200°C/400°F/Gas 6	18–20 cm (7–8 in) pastry shell
CHEESE	200°C/400°F/Gas 6	20 cm (8 in) pastry shell
CHOUX	220°C/425°F/Gas 7	16 small buns, 8 large buns, 7 éclairs
CRUMBLE MIX	190°C/375°F/Gas 5 *or* 200°C/400°F/Gas 6	Average topping 1 litre (1½ pint) pie
CURD CHEESE	180°C/350°F/Gas 4 (small) 190°C/375°F/Gas 5 (large)	18–20 small puffs 20–23 cm (8–9 in) pastry shell
EASY PUFFY	200°C/400°F/Gas 6	2 × 18 cm (7 in) pastry shells
EGG WHITE	200°C/400°F/Gas 6	20 cm (8 in) pastry shell
FLAKY	230°C/450°F/Gas 8	23–25 cm (9–10 in) top-crust pie 20 cm (8 in) double-crust pie
HEART WATCHERS'	200°C/400°F/Gas 6	2 × 15 cm (6 in) or 1 × 20 cm (8 in) pastry shell
HERB & SPICED	200°C/400°F/Gas 6	18 cm (7 in) pastry shell *or* 12–16 tartlets
HOT WATER CRUST	220°C/425°F/Gas 7	1 × 1 lb jam jar mould *or* 4 individual meat pies
LOW FAT	200°C/400°F/Gas 6	18 cm (7 in) pastry shell

Pastry	Starting Temperatures	Yield
MELTED BUTTER	220°C/425°F/Gas 7	23–25 cm (9–10 in) pastry shell *or* 2 × 15–18 cm (6–7 in) pastry shells
PÂTE BRISÉE	220°C/425°F/Gas 7	23–25 cm (9–10 in) pastry shell
PÂTE SABLÉE	180°C/350°F/Gas 4	25 cm (10 in) pastry shell *or* 20 small tartlets
PÂTE SUCRÉE	180°C/350°F/Gas 4	18 cm (7 in) pastry shell *or* 12–15 tartlets
POTATO	190°C/375°F/Gas 5	18–20 cm (7–8 in) pastry shell *or* lids to 6–8 small pies
PUFF	230°C/450°F/Gas 8	As per recipe
QUICK FLAKY	230°C/450°F/Gas 8	2 double-crust pies *or* 4 × 20–23 cm (8–9 in) pastry shells
QUICK-MIX SHORTCRUST	200°C/400°F/Gas 6	20 cm (8 in) double-crust pie *or* 2 × 15–18 cm (6–7 in) pastry shells
QUICK ROUGH PUFF	230°C/450°F/Gas 8	30 cm (12 in) *or* 2 × 20 cm (8 in) pie crusts
RICH PIE	230°C/450°F/Gas 8	20 cm (8 in) double-crust pie
RICH RAISED	230°C/450°F/Gas 8	2 × 13 cm (5 in) deep cake tins *or* 2 × 2 lb jars *or* 1 × 2 lb loaf tin
ROUGH PUFF	230°C/450°F/Gas 8	30 cm (12 in) pastry shell *or* 1 litre (1½ pint) pie crust
SHORTCRUST	200°C/400°F/Gas 6	15 cm (6 in) double-crust *or* 18–20 cm (7–8 in) pastry shell *or* to cover a 1 litre (1½ pint) pie
STRUDEL	230°C/450°F/Gas 8	2 strudels
SUET CRUST	Boiling point	1½–2 pint basin
VEGETABLE OIL	200°C/400°F/Gas 6	20–23 cm (8–9 in) pastry shell
WHEATGERM	200°C/400°F/Gas 6	15 cm (6 in) double-crust *or* 23 cm (9 in) pastry shell
WHOLEMEAL	200°C/400°F/Gas 6	20 cm (8 in) double-crust pie
WINE	220°C/425°F/Gas 7	20 cm (8 in) double-crust pie *or* 25 cm (10 in) pastry shell

Pastry	Starting Temperatures	Yield
YEAST	220°C/425°F/Gas 7	28 cm (11 in) pastry shell *or* 2 × 25 cm (10 in) pizzas
YOGURT	200°C/400°F/Gas 6	18 cm (7 in) pastry shell *or* 1 litre (1½ pint) pie dish

OVEN TEMPERATURES

Gas Mark	Celsius	Fahrenheit	Description
	80	175	
	100	200	VERY COOL
¼	110	225	
½	120	250	
	130	250	
1	140	275	SLOW
2	150	300	
3	160	325	COOL
4	180	350	MODERATE
5	190	375	
6	200	400	FAIRLY HOT
7	220	425	HOT
8	230	450	
9	240	475	VERY HOT
	250	500	
	260	500	
	270	525	
	290	550	

The Celsius temperature has been approximated to the nearest 10°.

Celsius markings are usually at 50° intervals, the lowest being 100°, with markings divided into 10° spaces.

Oven temperatures are never fully accurate, since there can be a variation up to 25° either way on each setting.

Table based on information given by the British Gas and the Electricity Councils.

Index

WINE, BEER AND SPIRIT HANDBOOKS NOW AVAILABLE IN GRANADA PAPERBACKS

Susan Beedell
Pick, Cook and Brew   £1.50 ☐

F Marian McNeil
The Scots Cellar   £1.95 ☐

Ben Turner
The Beermaker's Companion   £1.25 ☐

Jennifer Stone
The Alcoholic Cookbook   £1.25 ☐

HB181

COOKING FOR GOOD HEALTH BOOKS NOW AVAILABLE IN GRANADA PAPERBACKS

Susan Beedell
Pick, Cook and Brew   £1.50 ☐

Ursula Gruniger
Cooking with Fruit   50p ☐

Sheila Howarth
Grow, Freeze and Cook   £1.50 ☐

Kenneth Lo
Cooking and Eating the Chinese Way   £1.50 ☐
The Wok Cookbook   £1.25 ☐

L D Michaels
The Complete Book of Pressure Cooking   £1.25 ☐

Franny Singer
The Slow Crock Cookbook   £1.50 ☐

Janet Walker
Vegetarian Cookery   £1.50 ☐

Beryl Wood
Let's Preserve It   95p ☐

HB381

COOKERY HANDBOOKS NOW AVAILABLE IN GRANADA PAPERBACKS

L D Michaels
The Complete Book of Pressure Cooking   £1.95 ☐

F Marian McNeil
The Scots Kitchen   £1.95 ☐
The Scots Cellar   £1.95 ☐

Cecilia Norman
Pancakes & Pizzas   95p ☐
Micro-Wave Cookery Course   £1.50 ☐

David Scott
The Japanese Cookbook   £1.50 ☐

Franny Singer
The Slow Crock Cookbook   £1.50 ☐

E P Veerasawmy
Indian Cookery   £1.50 ☐

Janet Walker
Vegetarian Cookery   £1.50 ☐

Pamela Westland
Bean Feast   £1.50 ☐
The Everyday Gourmet   75p ☐
Food for Keeps   £1.95 ☐
The Complete Grill Cookbook   £1.50 ☐

Carol Wright
Complete Meat Cookery   £1.25 ☐

Arto Der Haroutunian
Complete Arab Cookery   £1.50 ☐

COOKERY HANDBOOKS NOW AVAILABLE IN GRANADA PAPERBACKS

Elizabeth Cass
Spanish Cooking   £1.25 ☐

Jean Graham
The Poldark Cookbook   £1.50 ☐

Ursula Gruniger
Cooking With Fruit   50p ☐

Marika Hanbury Tenison
Deep-Freeze Cookery   £1.95 ☐
New Fish Cookery   £1.25 ☐
West Country Cooking   £1.25 ☐
The Best of British Cooking   £1.50 ☐
Cooking with Vegetables   £1.95 ☐

Sheila Howarth
Grow, Freeze and Cook   £1.50 ☐

Robin Howe
Greek Cooking   £1.25 ☐
German Cooking   £1.50 ☐

Sheila Hutchins
Grannie's Kitchen
Recipes from the North of England   95p ☐
Recipes from East Anglia   95p ☐
Recipes from the West Country   £1.25 ☐

Kenneth Lo
Cooking and Eating the Chinese Way   £1.50 ☐
The Wok Cookbook   £1.50 ☐

Jennifer Stone
The Alcoholic Cookbook   £1.25 ☐

Arto Der Haroutunian
Complete Arab Cookery   £1.50 ☐

All these books are available at your local bookshop or newsagent, and can be ordered direct from the publisher.

To order direct from the publisher just tick the titles you want and fill in the form below:

Name _____

Address _____

_____

Send to:
Granada Cash Sales
PO Box 11, Falmouth, Cornwall TR10 9EN

Please enclose remittance to the value of the cover price plus:

UK 45p for the first book, 20p for the second book plus 14p per copy for each additional book ordered to a maximum charge of £1.63.

BFPO and Eire 45p for the first book, 20p for the second book plus 14p per copy for the next 7 books, thereafter 8p per book.

Overseas 75p for the first book and 21p for each additional book.

Granada Publishing reserve the right to show new retail prices on covers, which may differ from those previously advertised in the text or elsewhere.